William Betcher, M.D.
A Student-to-Student Guide to Medical School
Intimate Play

Robie Macauley
The Disguises of Love
The End of Pity
A Secret History of Time to Come
Technique in Fiction (with George Lanning)

THE
SEVEN
BASIC
QUARRELS
OF
MARRIAGE

THE SEVEN BASIC QUARRELS OF MARRIAGE

RECOGNIZE, DEFUSE, NEGOTIATE, AND RESOLVE YOUR CONFLICTS

WILLIAM BETCHER, M.D., Ph.D.
ROBIE MACAULEY

VILLARD BOOKS
1990

Library of Congress Cataloging-in-Publication Data

Betcher, William.
The seven basic quarrels of marriage : recognize, defuse,
negotiate, and resolve your conflicts / by William Betcher
and Robie Macauley.
p.   cm.
Includes bibliographical references and index.
ISBN 0-394-57913-5
1. Marriage—Psychological aspects.   2. Interpersonal relations.
I. Macauley, Robie.   II.   Title.
HQ734.B619   1991   306.81–dc20   90-50218

9 8 7 6 5 4 3 2

First Edition

To Martha and Pamela

ACKNOWLEDGMENTS

I would like to express my gratitude to the many people whose work in the field of marriage and marital therapy has contributed to this book. Although I cannot list them all by name, I would especially like to thank my colleagues—Drs. Edward Shapiro, Carolynn Maltas, Judith Jordan, Natalie Low, Irene Stiver, as well as Suki Hanfling and Rosanna Hertz, and all the participants in the seminar of supervisors of couples therapy of the McLean Hospital Couples and Families Institute. I apologize for any omissions from the bibliography of any individuals' work that may have indirectly contributed to the ideas in this book. I would also like to thank my patients and my close friends, who have been my best teachers. Some of their stories appear in this book, but in composite and heavily altered form in order to ensure anonymity.

In addition I would like to thank my agent, Gail Hochman, who has always been a pleasure to work with, and our editor, Diane Reverand, who believed in this book and made many valuable editorial suggestions and revisions.

—William Betcher, M.D.

I want to thank Gerard Van der Leun, who aided and abetted the inspiration for this book over drinks with me at the Cornucopia Restaurant (where Emerson long ago used to read proof on *The Dial*). I want to thank Pamela Painter for invaluable critiques, Roberta Pryor for being such a good agent, and Diane Reverand for being such an understanding editor.

—Robie Macauley

CONTENTS

THE
SEVEN
BASIC
QUARRELS
OF
MARRIAGE

THE
SEVEN
QUARRELS

Falling in love makes a man and woman discover how much they have in common. Living together makes lovers realize how many things there are to divide them. Every couple must learn how to understand their differences, how to work through them, and how to move into a wiser and stronger relationship. Recognizing the basic quarrel is the first step back toward love and sanity.

Most of us are curious about other people's quarrels because our own are so full of unexpected emotions and unforeseen consequences. We are curious because we suppose that other people's clashes will give us a fascinating exposure of their hidden lives and, perhaps, a clue to our own. We assume that the inhibition guards are gone, that these domestic wars should be a true disclosure of emotions and attitudes and that people are then at their most spontaneous and most honest.

The Mortons are having a quarrel. It is their first big blowup in two years of marriage, and it erupted this evening before either of them knew what was happening. Becky Morton perches grimly in the armchair, and Michael paces

3

fiercely up and down. Michael's parents, it seems, are coming for the Thanksgiving holiday weekend.

That doesn't seem serious enough to destroy the customary household peace or to account for the blood in her eye and his urge to break something.

He has just said that he's very sorry that she hates Sarah and Gordon so much, but they do happen to be his parents, and he does happen to love them.

She has replied that she doesn't hate Sarah and Gordon at all. She says they are probably wonderful people, in fact. It's just that they *take over* when they come. "And it's what happens to you, Michael. You turn into a little boy and dutiful son. Sarah marches into the kitchen and tells me how and what to cook for you. Gordon starts inspecting the car to check if we've had an oil change recently and if the brake fluid is okay. He wants to buy us a new hot-water heater because he thinks the shower isn't warm enough. The worst is they say we're using all the wrong psychology with the baby. And you, Michael, just smile and thank them." So, Becky has had it up to here. She says, "They make me itch with guilt every minute they're in the house."

What are the Mortons really quarreling about? Ostensibly, the dispute is over his parents' bossy interference or, depending on how you look at it, caring, concerned behavior. Though Michael and Becky don't know it, the bigger battleground is a complicated basic quarrel that comes from a difference in long-held, deeply ingrained loyalties. The parental visit is only the trigger for the loyalties quarrel, which is one of the most common basic quarrels in any marriage.

About two miles away, on the other side of the city, the Costellos have had a rough Saturday afternoon. Peter has been writing out the monthly checks for the bills and has been trying to balance the joint-account checkbook—without a lot of success. When Pat comes in, she doesn't turn out to be especially helpful, Peter thinks. She's vague about the

American Express charges, and she doesn't seem much interested in the fact that she forgot to record a number of the checks she wrote last month. That's why they can never put a dime into the savings, he says. Pat answers that it isn't monumentally important—and, besides, she contributes almost half of the income. It all ends up with Peter exploding and Pat in tears.

What are they quarreling about? Money—obviously. But it isn't quite so simple as a matter of self-indulgent use of the credit card or congenital stinginess. It's a complex matter that involves two different sets of values about saving and spending, two contrasting attitudes about the family economy now and in the future. In part, the Costellos are differing over dollars, and in part they are fighting over some provocative psychological symbols.

Thus, the Mortons and the Costellos, like millions of American couples, are entangled in one of seven basic quarrels of marriage, without understanding quite where the quarrel comes from or its deep-grained, complicated, and deceptive nature. The reality is that what most couples fight about has a buried meaning. Those causes for conflict make up one of the most obscure zones of everyday life. And what seem to be spontaneous and authentic reactions may be oddly deceptive.

When couples fight, what does it signify? In the best of marriages, it may mean simply that two people can blow off steam, then reconcile their differences and cheerfully go on. In a less secure marriage, it can be a sign of temporary disaffection or change of attitude in one or both partners. In a troubled marriage—one in which two people are out of sync in practical or emotional ways—a quarrel can be a great danger signal. Each may be perfectly successful in friendships or at a job, but irrational and emotionally out of control when trying to deal with his or her marriage partner.

In one sense, all of us who have a one-to-one relationship

behave as two different people: we have a self that deals with other people in the world and we have a self that deals with the person to whom we're married. Unfortunately, the talents that make for good careers, professional success, and popularity are subtly different from the talents that make for mature commitment and mutual understanding, one-to-one.

As a marital therapist, I encounter couples at all different stages of their relationships. I can, of course, help much more quickly and efficiently when a couple is in the early stage of discord, before bitter accusations have destroyed all goodwill between them, before rigid patterns have been set. It takes courage and humility for a couple to admit that their problems are serious enough to need a therapist's help, but those who can recognize a dark cloud on the horizon are the ones most likely to avoid the later gales. This book is directed at people who are alert enough to see the storm signals in their marriages, to the vast majority of couples who have recurring conflicts but also have the will to resolve them and win through.

The longer I talk to people in trouble and the more I research the subject, the more convinced I am that there are certain strong, recurring themes in marital battles. People tend to fight about the same basic things over and over again under different pretexts—without realizing what they are doing. Sometimes the real subject of the quarrel is hidden by a camouflage of deception and self-deception. Sometimes the trivial subject a couple is debating can be a clue to their real conflict. I have learned that once you see through the disguises, there are just a few truly basic subjects for quarrels—and they are remarkably alike in case after case.

WHAT DO COUPLES FIGHT ABOUT?

Mainly, couples fight about the well-known and predictable things—money, sex, power, rivalry, and so on—but the 1980s and 90s have seen some new shifts in emphasis and some contemporary variations. At a time when the whole norm of relationships between men and women has changed so significantly, *how* they disagree has changed somewhat as well.

In 1981, psychologists Dr. Susan Geiss and Dr. Daniel O'Leary made a survey of the problems of marriage. When they questioned marital therapists throughout the country, they found that "communication," "unrealistic expectations," "power struggles," "role conflict," and "lack of loving feelings" ranked high as complaints among couples treated.

Dr. Howard Markman, director of a center for marital and family studies at the University of Denver, concludes that money, sex, and power, the "big three" causes, are still at the top of his own list after fifteen years of study. According to the studies, sources of disagreement are the same as ever, but the emphasis has changed. People now have higher expectations in marriage than they once had. Women look for a much more equal sharing of roles than in the past. Dr. David Olson, a family psychologist and director of the PREPARE/ENRICH marital-counseling program, notes that many marriage quarrels result from the disappointment of those hopes, whatever the apparent subject might be. He would stress "unrealistic expectations" as one of the great offenders. Many young people enter marriage thinking that it is going to be just one long date—warm, sexy, happy, and without any real differences of opinion.

In pursuit not of marital quarrels but marital satisfactions, Olson and his colleague Blaine Fowers took a survey of five thousand couples to find what makes for success. They had a few surprises. Experts in the field have always supposed that two people from quite similar social and economic backgrounds would be most likely to make a successful marriage. Olson and Fowers discovered, however, that as long as both partners wanted the same thing out of the marriage—

especially the same kind of role relationship—where they had come from didn't matter much. What did matter was whether or not they agreed on an "egalitarian" marriage (with equal power-sharing and responsibility-sharing) or a "traditional" marriage in which the husband dominates.

The age of the couple makes a difference, Olson and Fowers also found. Men and women in their twenties largely wanted an egalitarian marriage (although many didn't quite know how to achieve it). Couples in their thirties were more frequently divided over roles. Here, wives were more likely to demand equality and husbands more likely to insist on "love-honor-and-obey." Older couples, as a rule, were both satisfied with the traditional pattern. The survey was a good reflection of the great shift in our attitudes toward marriage— and a good indication of the modern marriage of the future.

There has been an important change in the way we look at marital politics. The methods of discovery have become far more sophisticated and revealing. Once, we simply relied on what couples would say about their marriages or on observations of their behavior under clinic or lab conditions. Now, researchers use videotapes, make visits to homes, take physiologic measures, and employ finely tuned statistical techniques. That means that we now have the tools to analyze interaction between people, which means that our focus has changed from *what* people fight about to *why* and *how* they fight. It is important to know about all three ingredients in this emotional mixture.

MISCONCEPTIONS AND HALF-TRUTHS

At the start of therapy, when people try to explain to me the trouble they're having, they usually blame a "failure in communication." In exploring what they really mean, I usually find that it's their way of saying that they have a lot of frustrating and unproductive arguments, that they tend to avoid touchy issues, or that each feels unable to "get through" to the other person.

To blame all marital troubles on "communication problems" is about as useful as saying that if every nation spoke the same language, there would never be any wars. From my experience in therapy, I find that any couple's problems are both deeper and more specific. After they've progressed in understanding themselves, a couple will abandon the glib generalization of "a breakdown in communication."

The second most common way people have of diagnosing their trouble, according to the therapists in the Geiss-O'Leary survey, is "unrealistic expectations." That bit of conventional wisdom sheds no more light than "communications breakdown." Of course there will be some unrealistic expectations in a romance, and naturally those will have to suffer when the realism of marriage sets in—but most people understand that life has its compromises. When the mismatch between hope and experience seems to be causing a couple's troubles, the therapist wants to know exactly what the expectations are, where they came from, and how they clash. An expectation is simply a vision of the future. Just how two personal visions of the future work together or are at odds with each other can tell the therapist a great deal.

Another common assumption is that "I married the wrong person." Spelled out a little more, that's likely to mean, "I should have known better than to marry somebody so similar to me," or "My big mistake was in falling for somebody so completely different from myself."

There has been a good deal of research on what attracts people to each other—whether it is similarities or differences. The prevailing wisdom among marital researchers seems to be that people tend to choose a partner from a similar background and with a complementary personality; that is, a personality that matches the chooser's needs or deficiencies. The classic personality match is the "hysterical-obsessional" marriage between an emotionally expressive, love-starved wife and a detached, cerebral husband. But this is by no means predictable chemistry; things can go either way. The cerebral husband can learn to participate in emotions, and the emotional wife can discover the virtues of rationality. Or they can reject each other totally.

The marriage of two quite equivalent people can be just as much of a toss-up. Jack and Debby, for instance, are both lawyers in their late twenties. They came to me for therapy, each with an identical complaint about the other: argumentative, stubborn, insensitive. Each comes from an upper-middle-class, Jewish, professional family. Both have busy lives as corporate lawyers. But, oddly enough, all their common values and interests didn't work in the right way to produce a happy marriage. These things had led them to assume they knew each other perfectly. What they hadn't realized was that, in their worst moments, each tended to take a narrow, legalistic view on the opposing side of any question for fear of being dominated by the other.

Their home soon became a courtroom battle between Defense and Prosecution, and their very resemblances drove them apart. This is a case in which "who you are" (similar class, family background, education) is less important than "what you want" in marriage.

The psychologist Jeane Whitehouse says that attractions sometimes prove ambivalent. A, for example, marries B partly because of one seemingly attractive trait, but after a while A begins to find that very trait repellent. People may admire traits but have trouble living with them nearby and integrating them in a long-term relationship.

Another way of explaining severe problems is to say that some people don't understand how to duel skillfully or negotiate diplomatically. This is the approach of behavioral and cognitive therapists, who try to teach couples problem-solving, the way to break off destructive arguments, and similar techniques. That's useful for people who have had little experience in getting along with others in a relationship, but many people who deal smoothly with the world in general lose their skills at the home doorstep. They can maintain poise in an argument with an opponent, treat difficult employees considerately, cooperate well with colleagues in a stressful situation—but they change into brutes at home. Research shows that most people treat their marriage partners far more rudely than they would treat a stranger. In marriage, our codes of conduct and courtesy tend to diminish. When civilized interchange seems no longer possible, we've invited catastrophe.

The blame game is another explanation for marital disagreement that therapists often hear: I'm okay; he/she isn't. Interpreted, that means, "Maybe I *am* a little bit unreasonable at times, but that's a natural reaction to his or her completely pigheaded, outrageous behavior. If only he or she were a little more loving, or more understanding, or smarter, or more attractive, or drank less, or argued less, or were better in bed—then *I* could be nicer myself." Played by both partners, the blame game is a way to avoid any feeling of guilt or responsibility for the marriage troubles.

Blame

I frequently hear a variant of the "communications breakdown" theory when someone says, "We keep the lid on our disagreements too much. We need to get things out in the open." Of course, there are examples of people whose problem lies in avoiding discussion of problems, but the notion that merely getting the hostilities and anxieties into an open debate will solve everything is another fallacy. This can become a truth game that soon turns into a bitter-truth game— and thus is very destructive. Shortly, there are going to be two versions of the "truth," both of them likely to be distortions. The two partners will probably be arguing about their own agenda of grievances without any true comprehension of what their basic quarrel is.

I have noticed a recent trend among couples to blame relationship problems on "codependency," to such a degree that they view even normal interdependence as potential "addiction." Another formula couples frequently offer is that they both grew up in "dysfunctional" families. The trouble is that once they have decided on these labels, they stop thinking. Finding a label has substituted for figuring out the real nature of their problem. Even worse, one partner can use the label as a weapon in the couple's battle of "psychobabble."

Finally, there are the despairing phrases a therapist often hears, "We had it once, but we lost it," and "If we could only get back to the way we were!" This is the "Garden of Eden illusion," and dangerous because it is usually a form of resistance. It is a refusal to face present-day problems on present-day terms, and it relies on nostalgia instead of realism.

WHAT THE BASIC QUARREL IS

There are seven major, significant quarrels in marriage. They are not the only ones, of course, but they are singled out again and again in therapy practice as the most common, the most emotion-filled, and the most deeply rooted of our conflicts. Because they are complex, few people ever come close to understanding why they recur so often and endure so long. They are:

Gender
Loyalties
Money
Power
Sex
Privacy
Children

Everyone knows how bad quarrels can be and how much they can hurt. Most of us realize, in some rational corner of our minds, that what we are screaming at each other about at the moment isn't really all-important. Few of us perceive that the disputes we keep having are full of an unrealized significance. They represent the negative side of our whole relationship pattern, the side we understand least. So, where does this big charge of emotion come from? Why do we feel almost ready to kill over something quite trivial?

What we *seem* to be quarreling about is a pretext. It is little more than a symptom of a deep-running, long-enduring basic quarrel. We are worrying about the nasty-looking red spot when we should be worrying about the sliver deep under the skin. Time will not heal it; we cannot outgrow it; no ordinary compromises or adjustments are going to cure it. Beneath the "communications problem," the daily tiffs, the alienation, hides the primeval feud that is the source of all the surface problems. Sooner or later, it can destroy even the best of marriages.

To look back at the examples at the beginning of this chapter, we said that the Mortons' quarrel came under the heading of "Loyalties." The big provocations for immediate disagreement were his mother's invasion of Becky's home turf and the possessiveness shown by both parents. The real basic quarrel, however, is between two complexes of "invisible" loyalties—the allegiances Becky and Michael each acquired while they were growing up. If we explored their quarrel more fully, we would find that, far from being just a matter of the parents' behavior on the annual visit, it could include differing attitudes about friends, interests outside the home, job commitments versus family commitments, beliefs about child-rearing, concepts of right and wrong, ideas about society, or other things. Before Michael and Becky could resolve their quarrel, they would have to understand its ramifications.

As for the Costellos, their basic quarrel over money is more likely a quarrel over the values they place on certain things in their lives. It begins with the fact that she is a habitual spender and he is a chronic saver—but what does one spend to obtain? Or what eventual goal does one save toward? What freedom does each person allow the other in making decisions about saving or spending? What old debts or past bargains still linger in the mind? Does gift-giving have price tags? Does money become an instrument of reward and punishment in the family? How much does love cost, and is it worth the price? These might be some of the issues the Costellos will have to resolve.

Marriage is a system improvised between two people. Very little of it is logically thought out, and thus it's largely organic. Every couple understands the way their relationship works day by day, but few have a very clear idea of the invisible system that guides it. To deal with basic conflicts of interest, people must comprehend something about the whole relationship pattern.

Why the Basic Quarrel Is Invisible

Some marriages operate as a kind of collusion, an unspoken agreement not to touch on certain matters or, at least, to handle them with kid gloves. For example, Harold has lately progressed to three scotches before dinner instead of one. And Claudia has put on about twenty pounds in the past year. Neither of them is going to allude to these shortcomings—unless they eventually get into a fight. Otherwise, they operate under the rule of "I won't needle you about fat if you leave me alone about drinking too much." That unspoken agreement doesn't stop each from being silently resentful of the other's failing.

In some ways, spouses at odds know each other better than anyone else can. Alternatively, they may be oblivious to things that don't fit into their prejudiced portrait of the other—things that a stranger might pick up at once. Steve, for instance, had a perfectly generous motive for giving Catherine an expensive birthday present. But she, convinced that he had nothing but crass, ulterior motives, thought, He only remembered my birthday because he wants to have sex tonight. And then her next thought was, Or could it be that he's done something that he's feeling very guilty about? This is an example of selective perception. People very often have mixed motives for doing things—a generous motive mingled with a self-serving motive. When a spouse begins to interpret every action in a negative way, that is a reliable sign of an underlying basic quarrel.

It's often hard for couples to distinguish their basic quarrels because they have no sense of the larger pattern of their relationship—they can't see the forest for the trees. Such myopia can cause one to consider another's behavior as originating from character flaws, moral deficiencies, or inborn meanness. The psychologically nearsighted person can't conceive of his or her partner's wrongful actions as just one element of a relationship system that has gone bad. Harry is fed up with Ingrid's irritability, and he now concludes—after seven years of marriage—that she's just a chronically angry person. Ingrid, for her part, has seen Harry withdraw more and more into his work. He sometimes eats three meals a day at his office desk. His true character has come out—he is a hopeless workaholic. This marriage is a vicious circle, or a self-fulfilling prophecy, but neither wife nor husband can discern the pattern.

Our beliefs about how husbands and wives should relate, our expectations of rights and responsibilities, our vision of what a marriage should be, lie in our earliest experiences of growing up. How we were cared for, what we witnessed, heard, felt, or imagined about our parents and their marriage formed our fundamental outlook. We are not aware of much of this. It remains in our unconscious memory partly because we don't have verbal access to many early impressions. It stays hidden partly because all families have some unspoken agreements and selective perceptions that a child may very well sense but never express in words. But what we absorbed about our family and about our parents' marriages will affect us deeply throughout our lives.

Sheer pain is another reason why some people avoid facing their basic quarrel—it is the hot stove touched once and never approached again. Issues that hurt, embarrass, and provoke anxiety are scarcely tolerable to think about—these are things some people try to banish by silence. Wives and husbands retreat; their retreat becomes isolation, and isolation becomes despair. That withdrawal accounts for some of the instances of incest, child molestation, or physical abuse that a family keeps hidden for years. No matter how it may be concealed from sight, the hot stove is always there.

Then there are external forces—public and social—that can foster a basic quarrel. For example, the women's movement, the abortion debate, the question of drug use (especially as it affects the children), religious ideas, environmental concerns, child care, and even more generalized attitudes about politics. Very few marriages or relationships can exist nowadays in the closed shelter of the home, untouched by the world. There are many socioeconomic changes that influence them, though the effects may be subtle and only vaguely recognized by the people concerned.

Just as any relationship undergoes transformation in the course of time, the kinds of disagreement change as well. There can be dramatic events—such as the early death of a child—that instigate a sudden new hostility, but usually changes are much more gradual. During early marriage, the discords spring from passion and inexperience; in middle life, there are economic burdens and family obligations; and finally come the disappointments and physical aches of age. The basic quarrel may shift with a new stage of life, or it may arise out of the change. Since people who have been together for a long time tend to assume that they know each other very well, they are surprised when a new basic quarrel materializes in a new season of life.

Seeing through the Smoke: Symptoms of a Basic Quarrel
When you have a basic quarrel—and not simply some passing disagreements—there are telltale symptoms. Here is a questionnaire that helps to identify them ("you" may mean either or both of you):

1. *Do you get steamed up just thinking about some issue or recent argument?*
2. *Do you tend to overreact in any difference of opinion? Do your feelings run away with you, go to the extreme?*
3. *Does any difference of opinion set off a hair trigger that quickly provokes a hot war?*
4. *Do you find yourself giving a negative interpretation to anything the other person does or says—whether in an argument or not?*
5. *Do you get rigid about the stands you take—you want nothing but unconditional surrender?*
6. *Is there a pattern that seems to repeat itself in your arguments? A broken record you can't seem to turn off?*
7. *Do you know exactly how a fight is going to play before it happens, but you can't seem to stop it from happening?*
8. *Do you find yourselves escalating with exaggerations such as, "I can't stand it when you . . ." "You're driving me crazy. . . ." Do you use such words as* impossible, ridiculous, never, always?
9. *Do you find you can't keep the debate reasonable—it keeps getting nastier and more personal?*
10. *Do you suddenly catch yourself thinking or acting in petty, childish ways you thought you'd outgrown?*
11. *Do you never admit to yourself that you are to blame for anything that goes wrong? Or do you accept the blame for everything?*

12. *Is it fixed in your mind that he/she has to change before things get any better?*
13. *Have both people stopped listening to what each is trying to tell the other?*
14. *But if you're still listening, do you think the other's ideas are useless?*
15. *Are you hopeless about things ever changing for the better?*
16. *Or, have you come to the point where you no longer discuss things at all—both of you wrapped in silent anger?*

If you found that you must give a "yes" answer to any one of these questions, you have recognized a danger signal. If the answer is "yes" on a consistent basis to any one of the questions, you should begin—with the aid of this book—a serious revaluation of your relationship.

Is Change Possible?

Couples entangled in a long-running basic quarrel may despair about ever making things change for the better—I am painfully aware how hard that change can be because I know how resistant marriage systems are once they've been established. Many times when one partner makes a real effort for progress, the other will either ignore it or criticize it. The reasons may be that the second person feels threatened by the altered behavior or because *any* alteration makes him or her uncomfortable. Nine times out of ten, people opt for the devil they know.

There are, certainly, quarrels that come from the inherent differences in two people who don't match in certain ways. One of them might be called cultural in a broad sense. I think of a couple I know who have similar backgrounds—both are middle class, both had a midwestern rearing and an education at the same university. Yet he is unabashedly lowbrow, and she has cultured tastes. She loves opera and he loves boxing; she's a Francophile and he thinks the French are silly; he loves steak and hot dogs and she enjoys haute cuisine; he doesn't mind living in semisqualor while she wants a showplace house. They are equally intelligent and well-adjusted people, but they always fight over life-style.

A difference in intelligence may be another inherent cause for quarrels. I once knew a very bright man who had, on impulse, married a woman he met when she was drawing portraits at a booth in a county fair. She was older than he—another disparity—and below his intellectual level. The disparity was made even more painful by the fact that he was headed for a successful career as a university professor. Early on, they began to have quarrels that sprang from the IQ gap—and those were quarrels that could never be reconciled.

I also knew of couples divided by a psychological problem—one person relatively well adjusted and the other with an addiction to drinking, gambling, drugs, or with a mental disorder that causes emotional instability. These disparities don't automatically make for a troubled marriage, but they are likely to because the handicaps of one partner will probably produce constant bitterness, shame, or contempt in the other. There will never be an improvement in the relationship unless the individual problem can be acknowledged and relieved.

Real differences of nature between people cannot be changed. My experience as a therapist has shown me, however, that the greatest problem between married people is rigid thinking—one's conviction either that the spouse is a hopeless case or that one can't help reacting intolerantly. People tend to blame their own flawed behavior on circumstances beyond their control and their partners' sins on defects of character.

A couple's recurring arguments—no matter how trivial or profound—are *necessary* quarrels. The need to repeat the same battle over and over and the powerful feelings evoked each time are signs that each person has a great deal at stake. These quarrels are necessary because they are rooted in profound differences the man and woman understand only dimly. Only by having the quarrel in a *new* way—without destructive tactics and with a willingness to learn what lies beneath the surface—can it ever be resolved.

One of the most powerful aids that a therapist can bring to any couple who have lost faith in themselves is a new conviction. That conviction says that wounds can be healed, pleasure can return, the marriage can be restored to life. The seven basic quarrels can be overcome.

CHAPTER TWO

GENDER

One basic quarrel more fundamental than any other is the quarrel that arises from the simple fact that he is male and she is female. Although the fact is simple, it has a background of two intricate life stories sharply different in their biological, social, and psychological plots. Nature assigns us physically, and our parents assign us psychologically, to the general roles of either Man or Woman, and thus to our parts in the larger plot of love and conflict.

Gender differences and their misunderstandings form a fault line in every marriage—sometimes the source of minor rifts and tensions, sometimes the cause of a major schism, or basic quarrel. Gender differences, realities to some extent and prejudices to some extent, are just as fiercely clung to in either case. Whenever a man exclaims, "Just like a woman!" and a woman says, "Men!" in the heat of an argument, they are blaming gender.

As the most fundamental of the seven, the gender quarrel is the most difficult to resolve. It is based on a seemingly immutable difference. Anatomy is not necessarily destiny, but gender—the complex aspect of identity that combines our body image, earliest sexual identifications, the roles we take on, and our choice of lovers—is the greatest shaper of our destiny.

Men and women are intelligent in quite different ways. Between them, there is a cognitive distinction, or a difference in the angles from which they perceive and reason about the world; each sex may have its own version of any significant human truth. People have long recognized—although not very precisely—the disparity between these two outlooks, and thus we have the stereotype that man's approach to the world comes through logic and reason and woman's through feeling and intuition. Like many great rules of folk wisdom, those stereotypes combine a general truth with a general misinterpretation. The work of this chapter will be to offer better insights into this and other gender differences as they affect our marital behavior and conflicts.

One of the compelling allegiances we feel but seldom analyze is a loyalty—often even a kind of chauvinism—to our gender. This is because masculinity or femininity is a basic part of our identity. In any issue between male and female, we first tend to sympathize—consciously or unconsciously—with our own side. Are some dear friends getting a divorce? Wife tends to sympathize with wife and husband with husband. Is a man accused of rape by a woman? The male policemen are likely to accept his plea that "she led me on; she asked for it."

The antagonism hidden in gender loyalty comes out when men and women want to belittle or to wound the opposite sex. She says, "That little man in the grocery store infuriates me, he's so stupid." He says, "I told my girl to look in the files for that correspondence, but she must have forgotten, as usual." Escalated into insult, this kind of remark attacks a woman's femininity—when she's called a bitch, a slut, or a cunt—or a man's masculinity—when he's called a wimp, a prick, or a fag.

The classic pair of opposites in a marriage are the reserved, distant, coolly critical husband and the dependent, sensitive, love-starved wife. It is a polarity of cold and warm, or in terms of cognition, logic versus emotion. The most extreme form of this—and one I treat frequently—is what therapists term the "obsessional-hysteric" marriage.

In his book *Neurotic Styles*, the psychologist David Shapiro describes the obsessionals, who are usually men, and the hysterics, who are usually women. He believes that an obsessional tends to be a rigid, aloof type who focuses on factual details in a situation and thus misses the tone, the trend, or the implicit meaning. Work is both his fixation and his painkiller; he is uneasy unless he has an ongoing project. Whim, intuition, mystery, or fantasy baffle and upset him. He worships method and directives. At his best, he is stable, responsible, clearheaded, and competent; at his worst, he is dull, unimaginative, hidebound, and oblivious to other people's feelings.

The hysteric, in contrast, is a swarm of impressions and emotions. Facts are dispensable. She can overlook shortcomings or negative realities in the hope that all's well that ends well. She follows her hunches; she is open to suggestions and distractions; often she doesn't have much factual knowledge about whatever she's involved with. At her best, she is sensitive, creative, enthusiastic, and full of vitality. At her worst, she is shallow, capricious, inconsistent, and theatrical.

The psychiatrist Joseph Barnett describes the way obsessionals and hysterics are often attracted to each other—which makes for very strange bedfellows. In the beginning, each idealizes the other's characteristics—the hysteric sees him as profound, strong, well-organized, successful, and the obsessional sees her as loving, exciting, joyful, imaginative. For the moment, it appears to them a wonderful balance of opposites—until they get to the inevitable reappraisal, and then his strength and organization begin to look like threat and dogmatism to her, and her excitement and imagination seem to reveal themselves as feverish nonsense to him.

Barnett concludes that there is a fatal dynamic in such marriages. Without realizing it, each wounds the other in his or her weakest place when the hysteric comes to demand more show of love and intimacy while the alarmed obsessional withdraws further into his privacy.

With Barnett's polar opposites, there is probably little hope of compromise, but chances are much better for people with no more than moderate obsessional or hysteric traits. Quite often the original illusion—"I love you because you have what I lack"—can be a basis for a successful marriage, especially when the obsessional type can open himself to feelings and play as the hysteric type learns to incorporate reason and self-control.

I think of the hysteric-obsessional marriage as an example of one of the three basic themes of gender quarrels in marriage. It springs from a kind of obtuseness about the character of one's partner, a refusal to understand its complexity, a tendency to define it as a caricature. It is due to an unconscious need to rid oneself of a trait that then becomes exaggerated in the other. This is what psychotherapists call "projective identification," or making the idea of a person fit a preformed image, an image that can become more and more distorted and unflattering.

The second theme of misunderstanding lies in language. As Dr. Carol Gilligan notes in *In a Different Voice*:

> Men and women speak different languages that they assume are the same, using similar words to encode disparate experiences of self and social relationships. Because these languages share an overlapping moral vocabulary, they contain the propensity for systematic mistranslation.

In certain African tribes, women have contrived a language of their own, unintelligible to men. Gilligan has noticed a subtler form of gender noncommunication in our own language. This gap lies not in some special vocabulary or structure, but in loaded words and emotional overtones, in the abstractions that convey larger meanings. It is there that men and women fail to grasp the same sense.

The third thematic misunderstanding comes from our conservatism about traditional gender responsibilities. Once our gender identity is established, we find it very hard to change. In the past two decades, we have seen a social change in women's roles, both in the workplace and at home—but the effects are less radical than we sometimes think. Querying 489 married couples in 1986, sociologist Dana Hiller found that the majority agreed that child care and money management should be shared responsibilities of husband and wife—but many also believed that the husband should produce the family income and the wife do the housekeeping. Their assertions, furthermore, didn't fit their practices. Of the four fifths who said they expected to share child care, less than one half actually did so. Of the more than half who said they expected to share housekeeping chores, only one third of the husbands shared two tasks equally—dishwashing and shopping.

The reason behind this surprisingly traditional finding is not that most men actually hate working around the house or find their children repellent but that any threat to change ingrained gender roles produces anxiety. What we find it natural to do in our daily lives flows from our sense of gender identity. Most people tend to think there is "men's work" and there is "women's work" and feel uncomfortable trying to do something that is supposedly the other sex's function.

In the early 1960s, researchers found that people found their marriages less satisfactory if the wife was employed outside the home, especially if she worked full time. Some of the writers on the subject believed this would change for the better as the working wife became a generally accepted phenomenon. Conditions have changed in the past thirty years, although, according to Lotte Bailyn, the key question is whether the husband of a working wife can divide his own time between work and family by his own choice. This kind of couple, other research shows, collaborate in all their responsibilities better than couples with only one earner in the family—even though that male reluctance to share the domestic burden is still there.

At this time of new male-female social alignment, we all, I think, feel an insecurity about roles and identities. Marriage is one of the stages in life where we seek confirmation as to whether we are making the grade as a man or a woman. Each partner thus has tremendous power to feed or allay the other's self-doubts.

"True" Gender Differences

Again, it is the old question of nature or nurture—how much of our gender comes from immutable biology and how much from the social forces that shape us as we grow up? Although the debate is far from being settled, we can learn a lot about it from both the psychoanalytic theorists and researchers with new clinical information.

Freud's basic premise was, "Anatomy is destiny." He believed that the development of the two sexes is the same until about the age of five. At that point, girls discover that there are two sexes, one with a penis and one without. Freud further theorized that the girl next assumes that she has been castrated, and, blaming her mother for the fact, she turns emotionally to her father in hopes that he will provide her a baby in compensation.

In addition, Freud concluded that the clitoris is a vestigial male organ and that women must develop a capacity for vaginal rather than clitoral orgasm in order to reach mature sexuality.

As for the boy, Freud thought that the discovery that girls lack a penis suggests that he, the boy, could also have his taken away by a father grown angry at his closeness to mother—and the result is castration anxiety. The solution to this fear is to renounce Mother and identify with Father.

Freud thus saw the realization of gender arriving in one traumatic moment—when we first comprehend a single anatomical difference. Femininity, for Freud, was based on a lack, a negative, a deprivation.

The psychoanalysts Ernest Jones and Karen Horney later disagreed. They pointed out that boys and girls show significant differences even before they can be aware of anatomy, and they suggested that femininity is innate and positive. They reasoned that the sense of femaleness is based on awareness of the vagina. To the extent that Freud's penis-envy idea had any truth, it was metaphorical: phallic power is merely the power society denies women and gives men.

Carl Jung, one of Freud's original followers, developed the interesting theory that each person carries within himself/herself the essence of both sexes—or, as he put it, the unconscious archetypes of masculinity and femininity. To become mature, we must have some integration of the two.

Today, Freud's theory is considered disproved, Jones's and Horney's too narrow, and Jung's fascinating speculation. Research observation has now shown that gender identity is firmly established by the age of two or two and a half. Contrary to Freud, Jones, and Horney, anatomy is not the key, according to recent theorists. The true key may be identification, the desire to imitate a close-by adult. If one sex is primary, it is the female, because fetal development begins as female and remains that way unless there is a surge of androgens.

Dr. John Money and his associates come down on the side of nurture as the determinant of gender. They believe that a child becomes male or female less through anatomy, sex chromosomes, or hormonal status than through assignment to one sex by its parents. While Freud saw the discovery of gender as traumatic, the new analysts and researchers believe that consciousness of a particular gender comes slowly and without conflict. It is a learning process, not a frightening shock.

Harry Stack Sullivan insisted on the importance of the "chum group"—the peer group where a child learns intimacy before lust is a factor.

A further blow to Freud's theory came from Masters and Johnson, who showed that there is no meaningful difference between a clitoral and vaginal orgasm, thus demolishing Freud's theory about what is "mature sexuality" for women.

Nancy Chodorow and Robert Stoller stress the importance of models. They suggest that gender is determined because boys must rebel and girls must identify. In the critical period of gender development, they observe, a child's primary caretaker is the mother. Girls identify with the mother, and this attachment is formative. Boys have to break the attachment and identify with the father in order to strengthen their sense of gender. Males, then, learn to reject emotional connection and to take on a certain autonomy as part of the gender-finding experience.

The one generally accepted principle in all of these variant theories would appear to be that learning is more important than anatomy or biology—nurture over nature. And yet it would be foolish to banish nature so readily. Real physiological sex differences do appear at a very early age. For example, one study shows that newborn boys startle more easily than newborn girls. The girls, for their part, smile more than the boys—which might suggest a very early sense of sociability that males lack. Another study found that infant girls are more responsive to the cry of a six-month-old.

Androgens—the steroid hormones that develop and maintain masculinity—do seem to be involved with aggressiveness. Along with that, it is obvious that having breasts and a vagina and experiencing menstruation and pregnancy as opposed to having a penis must shape the process of nurture in significantly different ways.

As sociologist Alice Rossi says, "It makes no sense to view biology and social experience as 'primary causes.' Biological processes unfold in a cultural context, and are themselves malleable, not stable and inevitable. So, too, cultural processes take place within and through the biological organism; they do not take place in a biological vacuum."

Parents are not merely static figures that the child identifies with or reacts against—they are an active force in the whole gender process. One psychological researcher found that middle-class mothers handle infants of different sex in quite different ways, even at the age of three weeks. Mothers will hold boys farther away from their bodies and stimulate and arouse them more than they do girls.

It seems clear that nature and nurture both play a part in gender development, that gender is established in the first two or three years of life, and that it will develop thereafter but without any radical shifts. In our maturity, gender is largely a matter of identity (how we think and feel about ourselves), role (what typically masculine or feminine actions we join in), and partner choice (what sort of person we choose for love, sex, and/or marriage).

Recent controversies and social changes affect the ways couples deal with gender issues within their marriages. The gender identity and role each person brings to marriage will affect, and be affected by, that relationship. So, just as in our early years, both inner and outer forces influence how we interact within the smallest and most intimate circle of our life.

SPECIFIC MALE/FEMALE DIFFERENCES

Research and Survey Findings

Basic quarrels very often have their origins in disappointments, or the failure of expectations. It is thus important to know what gender differences men and women assume they will find in each other and to what extent these differences are real or imaginary.

In 1976, the psychologist Inge Broverman asked professional mental-health workers to give descriptions of a healthy man, a healthy woman, and a healthy person.

Their pictures of the man and the person were much the same—one with a capacity for autonomous thinking, responsible action, and clear decision making. As for the healthy woman, she would be passive, dependent, tactful, and, in fact, would resemble the typical hysteric in many other ways. The invocation of these stereotypes is all the more striking in that they reflected the thinking of presumably psychologically sophisticated people.

Other surveys show generally held beliefs that women are passive, irrational, weak, overly emotional, dependent, submissive, intuitive, changeable, tender, coquettish, manipulative, inscrutable, and indirect in expressing anger. Male stereotypes portray men as aggressive, strong, objective, logical, independent, achievement-oriented, and inexpressive of emotion—except for anger.

How much of this derives from conventional wisdom and how much from observation is hard to determine, but there are examples that suggest much of the former and little of the latter. In one study, fathers of newborn babies were asked to describe the infants before they had actually seen them. Sons were described as "strong" and daughters as "delicate." In another study, some mothers were given infants unknown to them and observed as they played with the children. If they were told that a child was called "Adam," they treated it in quite a different way from a child introduced as "Beth."

Scientific observation does show certain verified gender differences in behavior and aptitude. In 1974, Eleanor Maccoby and Carol Jacklin summarized the established findings:

1. *Males are more aggressive as early as age two.*
2. *Girls have greater verbal ability, on average, after age eleven.*
3. *Boys, on average, have greater mathematical and visual-spatial abilities after ages twelve or thirteen; the disparity widens in high school.*

The Maccoby and Jacklin findings are most notable for what they excluded—assumptions that they considered unsupported by reliable research.

In 1983, sociologist Alice Rossi surveyed the considerable research that had been conducted since the Maccoby and Jacklin publication. The newer results made a number of different and more specific male-female distinctions:

If you were born female:

You are more sensitive to touch, sound, and smell.

You register any sound twice as loud as it would be to a male.

You are also better attuned to nuances of sound, and you are six times more likely to sing in tune than your brother.

Because you were four to six weeks more fully developed neurologically than your brother at birth, you learned to speak sooner and more fluently and you remembered things better.

You pick up peripheral information faster and understand it more quickly.

You are more interested in human facial expression, and you perceive its changes better; thus, you read emotions more easily.

If you were born male:

You have a superior visual and graphic sense.

You are more sensitive to light and the changes in light.

You can manipulate objects and visualize objects in space better.

That is, you can rotate objects mentally, read maps, find your way through a maze, or know directions better than your sister.

You are also several times more likely to suffer from dyslexia or stuttering than she.

You are more likely to act according to the rules and less likely to perceive the undertones of any situation.

In the same year, Dr. Leslie Brody, a developmental psychologist at Boston University, reviewed the research on gender differences in emotional development with a warning that none of it can yet be considered conclusive. Psychologists have theorized and tried to prove or disprove that women are:

More expressive of emotions

Less angry and less bothered by guilt feelings

More likely to feel shame

Likely to keep their feelings internal rather than giving them external expression

Prone to masochism, anxiety, envy, vulnerability, and helplessness

Brody concluded that some research seems to support certain of the above hypotheses, but there are no truths ready to be chiseled in stone as yet. For instance, she found considerable research endorsing the idea that women recognize nonverbal signs better and more often use "internally oriented defenses." Results of one study tend to show that women are generally stereotyped as more scared, sadder, more emotionally expressive, and abler at discussing emotions than men. The interesting thing about these revelations was that a majority of women who were questioned about the stereotypes agreed that they are true.

Brody believes that we tend to condition boys or girls according to what seem to be innate gender differences in temperament. For example, one study indicates that as boys grow up, they suppress the outward show of any emotions, while girls suppress just the show of socially "unacceptable" emotions such as anger. A tentative explanation for this is that infant boys express their emotions more intensely than infant girls do, and therefore, parents believe, must be urged more strongly to control them. Boys are taught to think analytically about their feelings and so rely on the left side of the brain to deal with emotion, while girls are influenced to think intuitively, using the brain's right hemisphere. One study of married couples even suggests that men get more agitated physiologically during a fight and usually try to avoid a showdown.

Going a step beyond the growing-up process, Brody cites some of the theories about the way adult men and women adapt to different roles as dictated by society. Women have to accommodate their emotional dispositions to low status, low power, male aggressiveness, and child-rearing assignments. Brody believes that this explains why women would be inclined to blame themselves, to set up internal defenses, to express sadness in place of anger, and to be especially sensitive to nonverbal meanings.

Males, on their part, adapt to the masculine world and its goals of achievement by setting up external defenses, learning to hide all emotions except anger, and relying on expressed statements rather than nonverbal meanings.

A Therapist's View
In my own professional reading and practice, I have found four rough common denominators of gender differences. I

make no claim that they appear in all people or in all couple relationships, but they are common enough to be significant. They are:

1. Doing and Making in Contrast to Giving and Enabling

Two large-scale and comprehensive studies of adult male development, one by George Vaillant and another by Daniel Levinson, conclude that men's self-worth results from goal-seeking. That means fulfillment of their inner-directed aspirations rather than satisfaction in relationships. The goal, or "dream," Levinson says, is a sense of one's part in the adult world and a sense of one's possibilities. This generates the chief excitement of life.

According to Levinson, men also need mentor figures and a "special woman," but these are little more than supports and supplements to the pursuit of the dream. No woman is of lasting importance; a woman is someone who enables him in the effort of "becoming one's own man."

Dr. Jean Baker Miller, in *Toward a New Psychology of Women*, comments on the way women have been assigned to a helper role and what this does to their sense of self-worth. She says that women are deeply concerned as to whether they are "giving" or can give enough, and they are upset if they feel they fall short of some standard of providing for others. The idea of having to stop giving frightens them.

She feels that, on the other hand, few men think of giving as a necessary part of their identity. Men are concerned with "doing." It is only after men feel that they have earned manhood and success that they can turn their interests to giving.

For most women, sheer achievement for achievement's sake belongs to a second and lesser role; it is something that comes after the primary role of giving and enabling for others. Irene Stiver, a psychologist at McLean Hospital, has pointed out that many women are bewildered in the workplace (unless it happens to be a service enterprise like a charity, school, or hospital) because none of its objectives requires values of nurturance and empathy. Women feel that when they go to work, they must leave their femininity at home, and this is a cause for internal conflict.

Men thrive in the workplace, and the more successful they are, the more manly they feel. When a job has heavy requirements for sensitivity about people and close relationships, however, they are far less capable. A number of businesses have come to realize that a Personnel Department run and staffed by men almost always produces morale problems among workers while those managed by women are much more effective. Perhaps one of the reasons that women have recently entered the American workplace in such numbers is the great shift from a manufacturing and industrial business world to service enterprises. Service businesses, on the whole, require helpfulness, congeniality, tact, and an understanding of customer or client.

The deep divergence of achievement/fulfillment attitudes between the sexes may be due in large part to cultural conditioning. Matina Horner's work on women's "fear of success" demonstrates how women associate achievement with disconnection and abandonment—a fear closely linked with women's apprehension that if they compete seriously, men will disapprove.

2. Aggression and Strength in Contrast to Receptivity and Vulnerability

Men's greater aggressiveness goes along with their readiness to display anger; women's submissiveness goes along with their tendency to direct their anger inward. Jean Baker Miller and other feminist psychologists have pointed out that women, as an underclass, have developed such behavior as a way of accommodating to the more powerful sex. When men see a woman step out of her passive role and show real anger, they interpret it as a rebellion and a power threat rather than what it most often is—an assertion of individuality. Men are likely to become anxious and perplexed when women turn angrily assertive.

In one case of a couple with problems, the husband said to the therapist, "Meg's usually a very quiet woman, and she's always wanted to be just a housewife, as far as I know. But lately she's had some real fits of bad temper about how she feels stifled and frustrated. I gather what she's really saying is that she's mad at me—but I can't figure out what I've done wrong. I've always treated her well, and I sure as hell don't have any guilty secrets."

This man had committed three major blunders in trying to read his wife's feelings: first, he had taken her former passivity as a sign of acceptance of an inferior role. Second, he had misinterpreted her recent outbursts as pathologic and, third, had taken the defensive attitude that he had no part in causing her anger. A woman, very likely, would have been able to interpret the outburst correctly.

This is an almost archetypal example of how gender-based misreadings can escalate a quarrel. Meg's husband had little ability to shed his gender viewpoint and put himself in her emotional place.

The gender quarrel is also fueled by some profound misunderstandings about the nature of strength and weakness. What seems to be male strength is often no more than a man's desperate attempt to reassure himself of his superiority—as so many small lads have been told, "Cowboys don't cry." Consequently, men who abuse women are usually people with fragile egos. They have to define their sense of self and power by anger and acts of hostility against women. Anger puts aside all other feelings in a great show of strength—and often it is no more than a show.

Women's emotionality under stress is usually taken as a sign of weakness—and sometimes it is but often it is not.

Unlike the man's angry, protective, false front, a woman's show of emotions represents her propensity for being at one with her feelings; by being able to express feelings and talk about them, women have an enormous personal authority. Here, too, one must be wary of misinterpreting the obvious. A woman's tears can as easily be a sign of anger—serious and directed anger—as a man's shouting and pounding his fist.

3. Thinking in Contrast to Feeling

The classic obsessional-hysteric union can become a gender caricature, but most men and women have something of the same cognitive differences in subtler form. Head versus heart, logic versus emotion are the common ways of describing them. We must be careful not to be too categorical or too sweeping in drawing the distinction because, as the Brody survey shows, much of the research in this field is contradictory or indecisive.

The psychoanalyst Michael Stone is properly cautious in warning that if there is any validity in these stereotypes, it comes from left-brain/right-brain differences between men and women. Males do seem to have superiority in logical and mathematical functions and to have a better capacity for visual-spatial tasks as well—all right-brain qualities. Females are likely to be better at language learning and oral expression and at "tasks requiring an intuitive, holistic grasp of complex (particularly, nonverbal) patterns and stimuli"—all these accomplishments associated with the left brain.

What interests me about this question is not so much the attempts to measure cognitive differences scientifically but the fact that experience has taught me to recognize certain recurrent patterns of logic and thought in each sex. The very fact that two honest versions of the "truth" exist is a good starting point to examine the basic quarrel.

4. Autonomy and Independence in Contrast to Interdependence and Connection

Men put a high value on autonomy and independence—whether or not most achieve them is another matter. One of the well-known studies in this field—Dr. George Vaillant's Grant Study of former Harvard undergraduates—is a remarkable example of the self-fulfilling prophecy. The study began in 1937, with Harvard deans choosing the men to be included, and as one dean said, they picked "the ones who could paddle their own canoe." Thus, from one elite group of success-oriented men an even more elite group was selected. This was like trying to discover the average male physique by examining players on a National Football League all-star team. It was also, on the part of those running the experiment, an instance of the male's assumptions about the value of his own autonomy.

Feminist psychologists, commenting on this preoccupation, have pointed out that the traditional definitions of maturity have a heavy bias in favor of autonomy as important to a "mature" personality.

In a study of sex differences, Susan Pollak and Carol Gilligan employed the Thematic Apperception Test—a test requiring people to invent stories to go with a series of pictures that could be interpreted in many different ways. When a picture showed two people close together ("affiliation"), most of the men wrote stories full of violence and danger about it. When the pictures showed people in some "impersonal achievement situation"—a man alone at his office desk or two women workers in a laboratory, the women in the test group found them threatening or dangerous. One picture showed two trapeze artists, a man and a woman, in midair. In many of the male stories, one or both fell to death. For the female authors, there were no disasters, and many of them thoughtfully provided a net not shown in the picture.

From the results, Gilligan deduces that men see connections as dangers but women do not, while women see in separation a danger that men do not feel. She believes that a woman imagines life as a web of relationships while a man's vision of life success is being alone at the summit.

Jean Baker Miller, agreeing with this, notes that society penalizes women for their belief in affiliations as all-important and accepts the male ideal of autonomy. This is one somewhat abstract way of defining the basic gender quarrel. Recall that in the Gilligan-Pollak experiment, the most threatening picture for women was a man sitting alone at his desk in a high-rise office building. He is powerful; he is alone, without evident connection to a woman or a family; he is autonomous. Men found the picture of the trapeze performers touching in midair the most threatening. Here, one's life depended entirely on the goodwill of the other. A momentary impulse to treachery or even an inadvertent mishap would cause death. Thus, don't trust connections; don't bet your life on the cooperation of another.

These gender-connected, deep-lying fears are so different that they can produce a basic marital quarrel simply out of the clash of anxieties. This is equally true of long-term aims and satisfactions.

In this connection, the feminist psychologists' observation that the men of their profession have been the ones to define adult maturity, and have defined it in male terms, is apropos. In the old definition, men were independent and women had "dependency needs." A more accurate way of describing it, the feminists point out, is to say that women thrive on interdependence and connection. They seek responses in life and respond in turn. Their instincts are participatory. Men's responses and participation are much narrower and more pragmatic; their urge for independence is goaded by anxiety—and so they are likely to depreciate the instinctive feminine values. When women's desire for emotional reciprocity is frustrated, it can indeed turn into unsound or neurotic "dependency needs."

There remain some interesting questions about that nebulous thing called "maturity": when are the female wish for interdependence and the male urge for independence not really aspects of maturity, but defenses against their opposites? Do women require connection because they are fearful of standing alone? And do men want to feel autonomous because they dread intimacy?

When a relationship is in trouble, people do seem to retreat to such extreme gender positions and therefore move farther and farther apart.

Common Problems that Come from Gender Issues
Gender quarrels are by no means predestined or inevitable. It is only when the differences get misunderstood, devalued, and exaggerated in a marriage that the trouble begins.

The "Adam's rib" version of gender psychology—the male-oriented version— has been criticized and discredited. To take its place, we now have a feminist version that seeks to reclaim women's identity. This new version is thoughtful, cogent, and well-intended, but it is prone to a kind of gendercentricity similar to that we have seen in Freud and his descendants. We are now in an era when male psychology is being defined by women—a kind of "Eve's rib" version.

For example, I suspect that most women have difficulty appreciating male-to-male bonding or the combination of competitiveness and devotion to a team both spectator and player feel. It is hard for a woman to value the idea of aggression as a healthy part of male intimacy, particularly in a time when we've come to understand men's aggression toward women as often abusive and damaging.

Whenever one sex tries to define the other, there are going to be mistranslations. I believe that this problem among the gender theorists is quite the same as it is in ordinary life, among married couples. The wife or husband deduces the opposite partner's psychology just by extrapolating from her or his own. Some of this can be overcome; most of it is inevitable.

Struggles Over Autonomy and Interdependence

The classic battle of autonomy versus interdependence is usually expressed in many smaller skirmishes. The dispute over commitment is one of the most common. Two people meet and decide they're in love; then she looks forward to marriage, while he thinks they ought to live together for a time first. Another dispute develops over decision making. He wants to make his own decisions about his life, and she thinks that because they are a pair, important decisions should be mutual. She wants to be consulted and to consult. Still another argument arises over confiding. She thinks it's important to share emotions and opinions, and he thinks there are certain feelings or problems that everybody has to work out for himself, without gratuitous advice from the outside.

How does a couple define love? Very often, the woman defines it as intimate dialogue and exchange of feelings. This leaves out something that is a main factor for the man— providing for the family and safeguarding the household, which is to say creating the environment in which a marriage can live. Her first value is intimate caring and his is caretaking from a distance.

In my work, I've often observed a couple come to therapy with the wife in the lead, figuratively dragging her husband along. Her first observation is usually about his being "closed in" or "too distant." She, on the other hand, speaks openly, is reflective, and displays feeling—in short, she's the kind of patient therapists prefer to work with.

The husband is true to his wife's description. When he

tries to explain what he feels, he seems lost, out of touch, and defensive.

One of my first questions to myself is—How much of the disparity is due to immanent character and how much to defensive reactions? Along with that, I wonder how much of his difficulty in handling and expressing feelings is a reaction to his wife's obvious competence at it. My task then is to get them both to articulate their sense of values in their relationship and then each to understand the other's. I try to help each to express his or her worst fears—usually fear of abandonment on her part and of suffocating closeness on his.

Misinterpretation of Anger and Sadness

Earlier in this chapter, I mentioned that men tend to feel comfortable in expressing anger and women in expressing sadness. I believe that these two affects are also channels for a variety of other feelings. Paradoxically, men may actually be sad when displaying anger and women may be angry when they appear sad—and thus they systematically mislead each other. The true feelings are camouflaged by the ostensible ones because in this culture a woman is not expected to be furious—except in melodrama—and a sad man is merely pathetic, while an angry man gains an automatic respect.

Different Approaches to Sexuality

Women expect a combination of sensuality and tenderness in sex, while men can be physically aroused but emotionally distant. Dr. Irene Stiver describes why this gender-based discrepancy is so disruptive to marriage:

> Our culture allows men to be more explicit about their sexual needs since they appear as rights divorced from emotional neediness. As long as men experience sexual needs as simply for physical release, they feel this does not betray weakness

and their search for intimacy may be primarily through the sexual experience.

As long as a woman's needs are not being met, she will at least unconsciously be resentful and hostile toward any expression of man's neediness; this may be why women sometimes resist men's sexual needs since they recognize underlying yearning for nurturance and resent it. Also as long as women experience their own neediness as shameful, they will have difficulty tolerating dependency in men. Their wish for the man to give them the strength they feel they lack is part of their propensity to idealize the man, attribute great power to him, and feel disappointment when he deviates from this ideal.

It is also said that many men need sex in order to get close to their feelings while many women need to feel emotionally close before they can respond sexually.

These are useful, broad generalizations that seem to be true in the main but with many individual exceptions. Because most people accept them as a universal rule of gender relationships, that very acceptance can be harmful in particular cases. When a woman has an ingrained belief that *all* men automatically divorce sex from emotion—and therefore her own needs will never be met—she may be wrong about her husband and may be damaging her own marriage relationship. When a man accepts the conventional male wisdom that women agree to sex as a mere corollary of intimacy, he may be misjudging his wife and distorting their relationship in a similar way.

Stiver's points, nevertheless, help explain why men and women express sexuality in such different ways. Couples often lose sight of the way their basic gender difference affects their sexual attitudes. As a result, each may misinterpret the other's motives as hostile and frustrating. "*I* feel frustrated" gradually becomes "*You* are frustrating me," then "You *don't want* to give to me."

As couples mature, they may become more aware of these gender-based sexual differences, but aging brings new room for misinterpretations. While women's sexual desires may increase, men's may decline. For example, a man may come to depend on a woman's genital stimulation before he can attain erection. This dependence suggests to the man that he is no longer able to be potent without her help and suggests to the woman that she is no longer attractive enough to arouse her husband without special efforts.

Rigid Gender Roles and Projective Identification

People often have within themselves a certain quality or qualities with which they're uncomfortable. They realize vaguely that these qualities don't fit the image they have of themselves as masculine or feminine, and they itch to be rid of the anomaly. For example, a man who has always presented a stalwart image to himself and the world also happens to have a sentimental side. When sad or affecting things move him, he is ashamed. Unconsciously, he begins, figuratively speaking, to unload that set of feelings onto his wife. Gradually, she becomes tagged as the hypersensitive one, the bleeding heart of the family. She, on her side, has a certain combative streak that doesn't seem to fit with her generally staid and gentle nature—she unconsciously tries to transfer that streak to him. This process is called "projective identification." The result is that she accepts his unconscious donation and he accepts hers. She weeps in sad movies, and he blows up at the delivery boy.

Without their realizing it, both have grown more tightly locked in their stereotypes of gender. They have colluded in further limiting each other's personalities and have narrowed the scope of behavior. This event is not necessarily dysfunctional, but it can become so as the two roles grow more and more rigid. Natalie Low points out such couples don't realize that they both want to maintain these stereotypes, each in order to support his or her own fragile gender identity.

The Struggle Against the Enemy Within

Like the sentimental man just mentioned, many men feel it obligatory to show that they are in no way feminine, and so they take care to suppress anything about themselves that seems emotional, vulnerable, dependent, or needful. Young men in particular struggle hard to attain manliness, Daniel Levinson notes, and therefore fear a danger from any more "feminine" impulse. They reject all that does not fit in with toughness, athleticism, and achievement.

Males, according to Dr. Teresa Bernardez, bury all the affective richness of feminine character when they are compelled to separate from their mothers. Having been instilled with a shame about any "feminine" feelings in himself, and having been "abandoned" by the female closest to him, the young male is determined to dominate any femaleness within himself and any females close to him.

The psychoanalytic term for a defensive attempt to repudiate aspects of the self and to emphasize their opposites is "reaction formation." In a marriage, this may be combined with the projective identification I mentioned above—the process of unloading unwanted traits onto one's partner. The sentimental man and the scrappy woman made their emotional trade without undue harm, but in other cases the act of projecting one's troublesome emotions on another can result in envy or disdain. If, for instance, the sentimental man not only shifted his feelings onto his wife but then criticized her constantly for her soft-heartedness, this could mean stormy weather for the marriage.

In one of the stranger paradoxes of gender, women have found their refuge and their support in weakness. It has become so much their home ground that they believe in it and hate to give it up, Jean Baker Miller says. Women are on the right path, she observes, when they begin to perceive their own life experiences as sources of strength rather than accepting the male definition of what it is.

Deviating from Expected Role

One of the great shocks in marriage is when one partner trades a long-maintained gender role for a new one. Nowadays, this comes about most often when a wife steps out of the home by undertaking a marketplace career of her own, or resuming her education, or involving herself in some creative enterprise. I have seen husbands whose confidence is so fragile that after such an assertion of independence they feel devastated and angry. It isn't just that they are faced with a coequal breadwinner—if that is the case—but they also face a rival for success. Even a relatively secure man will have difficulty seeing his wife win a measure of prestige and achievement close to or higher than his own. The quarrel that results is fired by envy and insecurity on the male side and guilt and fear of abandonment on the female. The therapist always finds this problem hard to address because the husband usually thinks that to admit any insecurity on his part is unmanly.

I believe that Dana Hiller's research, cited earlier in this chapter, is illuminating. There are increasing numbers of men, mostly young, urban professional men, who know that it is wrong to resent a wife's independent activities and know it is wrong to refuse to share the housework—but who aren't prepared emotionally for such shifts in gender roles. The American solution for the housework problem is usually to buy more sophisticated appliances and, for those who can afford it, to hire help. This works as a kind of expedient, but it doesn't solve the fundamental gender issues that new generations of couples will continue to confront.

The Problems of Dominance and Inauthenticity

The major feminist accusation has been that men have made women into an underclass. Until recently, women, like any subject population dependent on its masters, have adopted the tactics of servitude: indirect aggression, ingratiating behavior, passive resistance, and an overt acceptance of inferior status.

A generation of women writers and activists have delineated how much women have suffered from this system, yet men, too, have paid a price for their own dominance. First, they have received a deceptive view of the true nature and feelings of women, and, second, they have lost the chance of learning some important truths about themselves. Basic quarrels are so destructive because their true causes are only vaguely recognized and because people never seem capable of ending them. Quarrels that do not escalate out of control and lead to a new understanding are a healthy and instructive part of marriage.

We still suffer to an extent from this inauthenticity of the male-female relationship. Simone de Beauvoir thought that women have accepted a submissive role because they do not dare to take a stand or to live authentically. Karen Horney remarked on women's tendency to live vicariously through the lives of men. When women consciously rid themselves of "the tactics of servitude," and men accept a new equation based on that change, both can live authentic lives and have authentic marriages.

The Lack of Models

As we have seen, a child looks to a gender model, usually a parent of the same sex, and gender identity is closely associated with identity formation in general. When the child growing up has a bad or ambivalent relationship with his or her parent of the same sex, that child will have gender problems in adulthood. The same is true when one parent disparages or abuses the other parent. That is, a girl who was always at odds with her mother and a girl whose father would depreciate her mother are likely to be vulnerable about their gender identity as adults.

The psychologist Samuel Osherson, in his book, *Finding Our Fathers*, points out that many men have had a troubled relationship with their fathers because they have regarded them as remote figures, rather scary and hard to understand. Boys who grow up with a sense of internalizing a "wounded father"—that is, an image of a father who was inadequate, rejecting, or absent, later have trouble grasping what it is to be a husband and father on their own part. Their scanty past experience offers so little to draw on that, as Osherson puts it, they have to invent themselves.

In my clinical work, I have found that this void in experience can have—for both women and men—the peculiar effect of making the person invest too much emotion in his or her love relationship. As a way of obtaining the love that the gender-model parent never gave, the husband or wife entrusts all devotion to the partner. Such women do not have female friendships, and such men have no male friends. They are entirely cast on each other—which is especially troublesome when both lack a secure gender identity. Neither can then affirm the other's.

The Denial of Need

Many people have trouble understanding their own needs. As Irene Stiver observes, when a man denies any need to be cared for, he's asserting his independence. When a woman denies it, she does it from a guilty feeling that the needs of others ought to come first. Stiver goes on to say that a man is unaware of how much he depends on his wife to supply his emotional needs until children arrive and he is no longer the focus of attention. Men have an urge to hide their needs.

Jean Baker Miller elaborates on this when she says that women seldom examine their own needs and desires—they simply accept the notion that serving others will provide all necessary satisfaction. Men, for their part, may conceive a hate for any woman on whom they are dependent because they feel trapped by that dependency.

Dealing with Gender Differences

That bizarre barter of characteristics between the obsessional and the hysteric might be taken as a metaphor—an extreme one—for many marriages. Marital therapists are used to seeing projective identification, or a disclaiming of parts of the self, in one degree or another, but they also know that a "reclaiming" process in marriage is possible. Reclaiming is not easy, and it involves stretching one's own self-concept while refusing to let husband or wife narrow it with their projections.

One couple I treated illustrated this clearly. They had maintained their traditional gender roles for years, but their financial circumstances had then changed, and the wife had gone to work. She was successful in business. After a while, she held an executive position in her company.

When they began couple therapy with me, he would subtly belittle her vocation or suggest that their two teenage children needed more of her attention, and she would be furious.

In the course of time and therapy, she began to point out to him what he was doing. She also realized how vulnerable she was to his negative comments because she had been brought up to ignore any of her own needs that might distress someone she loved. In turn, he was able to acknowledge—grudgingly at first—how betrayed he felt by her departure from home. It was not just her physical absence but her withdrawal from the marital role in which he'd cherished her. Each had to face the loss of their old ways of relating to each other.

49

Natalie Low astutely makes the point that the recipient—or victim—of such projection first reacts as this woman did, angrily. She had a double pressure, from her husband and an inner pressure that told her to resume the role she had played in the past. As she became more secure in the therapy, she learned to deflect his projections with a simple refusal.

For a man to reclaim parts of himself he had disowned as "too feminine" and a woman to reclaim what she had rejected as "too masculine" is a gradual and contentious process that may take shape as a basic quarrel. If both people can tolerate the anxiety, the process has enormous healing potential. Each married person must cope with the polar opposites of male and female within himself or herself. If people can be aware of this double presence and value both sides, the struggle for integration need not become a basic quarrel.

"Naming" One's Gender Identity

Anyone can probably name his or her gender model (or models)—usually parents, sometimes grandparents or other adults who were close in childhood. As time goes on, however, the outline of that figure grows indistinct, and we recall the feelings of our formative years without the substance. Samuel Osherson has described a man's search for that vague and shadowy personage as "naming" one's father, giving specific shape and texture to the relationship, filling in the memory outline of the father.

I think that one must come to terms with such internalized parent figures before one can be truly mature, which means being able to embrace and affirm some aspects of what they have passed on to us while being able to reject unwanted aspects. No one can have a grown-up intimacy with wife or husband without understanding, affirmation, and separation from one's childhood models.

At one remove from the parent figure, there is another influential person called the mentor. Daniel Levinson has studied the magnetism that older, wiser, and usually more powerful men possess as role models for younger men—as has Samuel Osherson with rather more skepticism. Equivalent relationships are no doubt significant for women. Most women college or university graduates, for example, can name a woman teacher who exerted a strong guiding influence on them. Such mentors frequently help to sponsor the careers of young men or women. More often as figures of respect rather than of great intimacy, they serve the important function of fixing the gender identity of the younger person. They also make a place for him or her in the club, or, as it were, open the door to the world.

Those people who enter marriage with a strong gender identity rooted in the past, and—at the same time—a discerning sense of the negatives and positives received, have a much better chance of preventing the marriage from ever becoming a battleground for unresolved gender hostilities.

The "I-Self" and the "We-Self"

We all carry within ourselves a masculine principle and a feminine one. George Klein makes that more specific by using the term "I-self" to describe the masculine notion of self-worth—the function of the self as an independent agent, achieving and competing in the world—and the "We-self" to describe the feminine impulse toward establishing connections, enabling, and interdependence. A complete and successful self requires that both of these half-selves exist in harmony. Carol Gilligan thinks that some of our worst problems ensue when this does not happen, when the man follows the traditional masculine drive and the woman concentrates on traditional feminine concerns. The media and other powerful forces tend to reinforce gender stereotypes, and many people, by assuming the roles expected in the workplace or the home, take on these clichés as their entire identity. One of the most useful services a wife or husband can perform is to help her or his partner keep in touch with both I and We, both principles of selfhood.

Valuing Differences

Early in this chapter, I observed that we often have fierce gender antagonisms—men stereotyping women with contempt and vice versa. The theme of this chapter is that we all have two different sets of traits, some by convenience called "masculine" because they predominate in men and some called "feminine," but both of them, actually, human traits shared in different degrees by everybody. Any violent rejection of the other gender—as in the contemptuous dismissals I spoke of—is a rejection of part of oneself and therefore devalues both partners.

Some theorists suppose that males must thoroughly reject their attachment to the mother in order to become men. This idea seems extreme to me. I believe in divergence and then convergence as the pattern of life. We establish our gender identities early, in all the ways I have described. Once those identities are stable and secure, the two sides of the self— whether one calls them yang and yin, I-self and We-self, or masculine and feminine—can converge within the mature person without disturbing the hard-earned primary identity.

Marriage itself is a convergence of genders—and therefore it is an outer event that should parallel and support the inner convergence. For any person to accept two types of humanness while maintaining predominantly his or her own—that is the challenge.

Gender is the substratum of the other six basic quarrels. In this era when gender politics and gender rivalry have become more pronounced, loyalties to one's own sex often take on an adversarial tone. That tone can easily flow from strictly gender issues to any one of the others.

Quarrels over money take on overtones of gender when one partner—usually the man—demands control over finances by eminent right of gender. The social and economic gender politics of the marketplace dictate what each member of a working couple contributes financially to the marriage.

How each sex defines power and wields it in a marriage is shaped significantly by gender beliefs.

Gender and sexuality are, of course, inseparably linked. As we will describe in Chapter Six, there are basic differences in male and female attitudes toward sexuality and aggression.

Men and women also differ in their sentiments about privacy, with women characteristically seeking emotional connection, a shared privacy, and men preferring solitude.

Finally, gender differences figure prominently in couples' quarrels over children—what the roles of mothers and fathers should be, who is best suited to nurture, who is responsible for the everyday details of rearing the children.

Gender is not the only basic quarrel that overlaps with others. Each of the seven quarrels reflects a basic aspect of married life, and any one may include some elements from the other six. Recognizing that no major quarrel has one exclusive theme, we should try to discern the difference between predominant causes and minor tributaries in our conflicts.

CHAPTER THREE

LOYALTIES

The first promise people make in the marriage ceremony is a promise of loyalty and love—a call on two profound sentiments, one almost as mysterious as the other. We seldom realize what an accumulation of loyalties we bring with us to a marriage, and how much of a gamble it is trying to unite them under the arch of the new commitment.

There are the obvious loyalties—fidelity to someone we're in love with, devotion to kin, to a religion, to a moral code, to a profession. But their meaning is less self-evident than it might seem. In the real world of relationships, there are conflicting claims on us; some of our loyalties are ambiguous; and we feel a powerful pull of obligations we're only dimly aware of. When two people make that first promise, they may *think* they are pledging the same thing, but they are not. Each has a loyalty concept acquired and shaped by two different experiences of family and growing up. It will be much later before they discover all that their promise actually signifies.

A marriage is a merger of many things, and one of the most important hidden clauses in the contract calls for reconciling those two sets of loyalties. Each person has to come to terms with his attachments to the past and to the facts of his own ethical character: what do the ideas of loyalty, duty, fairness, mean to me? The partners have to understand how their private and public loyalties match or don't match. There are those just dues we quietly owe each other and there are those dues we owe to our society, as part of a culture. At best, two sets of loyalties will never quite duplicate each other; at worst, they will disagree so drastically as to foster a basic quarrel. The loyalty stakes are high. Wives and husbands will excuse each other for many sins, but the unforgivable sin is disloyalty.

THE MEANING OF LOYALTY

There is a difference in the way women and men learn to know loyalty. This is not simply a matter of roles in marriage, because, as we know, those have altered. Many women now share in the male-originated values of business or professional worlds. Many men, of course, have strong friendship and family loyalties.

Still, there are deep patterns of culture that go back to the beginnings of humankind, and the ways in which men and women form loyalty bonds are two different figures in those patterns. The male hunting party, anthropologists believe, was the origin of one kind of loyalty and the female work group in the camp or the cave the origin of another. These very old habits of thought and emotion condition our loyalties in ways we are unaware of—even to the woman business executive or the husband who shares equally in baby-sitting and housework.

Women view human relationships as—to use a metaphor —a kind of great cooperative association. One person helps another and can call on others for help when she needs it.

The group can be relied on to rescue or defend its members in good standing. None of this is codified or set down in any rulebook—it is all a matter of goodwill, custom, and sensitivity to need. The concerns of the cooperative society are largely directed inward, to support and animate the lives of its own.

Traditionally, women live in a world of personality and individuals; they seek a rewarding network of relationships and emotional interaction. For them, affection, trust, love, and liking are the positive side, and envy, anxiety, or enmity the negative. Women's egos extend out among the people closest to them by a process of identification. Women tend to become alienated or depressed when they must loosen or break the connections that are central to their lives. Goodbyes and rejections are among their worst moments.

The metaphor for male society is, predictably, the team, and its view of life is embodied in a code. Part of the code says that there must be strong competition for place in the hierarchy of the team, but on the field there must be disciplined cooperation. The ambitions of the team are directed outward and are ultimately aggressive. They range all the way from building a successful business, or army, or political party, to solving an abstruse scientific problem.

So it is that men's loyalties focus more on the career, the profession, the achievement, the service, the company, the organization, or the team. In the male zone, human connections are somewhat different, with such values as cooperativeness, esprit de corps, fair play, assertiveness, and efficiency as the good modes, and sheer egotism, overreaching ambition, ruthlessness, and betrayal as the bad (although men often have a sneaking admiration for antiheroes with those dark traits).

This, of course, is an outline of general patterns, but the general patterns persist, and they are cause for conflict in many marriages.

Different Definitions of Loyalty

Some of the diverse definitions of loyalty show up in these case-history examples:

Last week, he left his office to go to a party with two old college friends but didn't think to invite her along. The next day, they had a bitter fight in which both accused the other of being disloyal.

Their basic difference? He perceives loyalty as a negative thing, an *avoidance* of doing harm. She, of course, sees it as a caring, positive effort to demonstrate that the other is the most important person in one's life.

Not long ago, another man went to a business convention and, in the course of four days, had dinner and went out dancing with his attractive blond office manager. He told his wife about this—and was surprised when she furiously accused him of betrayal. His idea of loyalty is total emotional honesty. He thinks that you shouldn't be inhibited from doing whatever appeals to you strongly, and you shouldn't conceal it. She thinks that loyalty is a matter of absolute emotional and sexual fidelity.

For a third husband, loyalty means providing well for the family, being always faithful to his wife, and giving their children all the advantages. His wife regards him as a good man, but no more loyal than a stranger. She thinks that he has been emotionally distant from her and has ignored her need for intimacy, understanding, and friendship—which is what she believes loyalty is. He defines loyalty in terms of virtues; she defines it in terms of empathy.

Another wife has a four-year-old who is becoming something of a problem child. The wife's mother is critical of the way her daughter is trying to handle the situation and suggests some different methods. Husband and wife then discussed this, and the husband suggested that her mother is probably right. The wife was infuriated, and the discussion quickly turned into a loyalty quarrel.

She feels that his first loyalty should be to her; he feels that, in this case, he owes first loyalty to the child's welfare.

As these small scenarios show, loyalty has many different faces. Some people think of it as commitment to the marriage, others as sexual faithfulness, practical responsibilities, or as emotional support, total unity of viewpoints, or demonstrations of devotion.

Dr. Caryl Rusbult and her associates at the University of Kentucky tested people's perceptions of loyalty with a list of statements that required yes or no answers (in which "him" stands for "him or her"):

When my partner hurts me, I forgive him.

When there are things I don't like about my partner, I accept his faults and weaknesses and don't try to change him.

When my partner is inconsiderate, I give him the benefit of the doubt.

No matter how bad things get, I am loyal to my partner.

This is an example of defining loyalty as a personal commitment to the partner. According to Rusbult's yardstick, the real test of loyalty is keeping faith even when the other person behaves badly. My own experience in working with couples tells me that they usually do prize that quality of forgiving and standing firmly united, no matter how bad things may get. And yet, taken all together, yes answers to all these questions would give us a profile of a submissive, dependent personality. The point here is that people have to know how to tolerate and forgive and yet stay reasonably and firmly detached at the same time. Keeping faith and still remaining independent—that is a delicate balance.

THE ETHICS OF LOYALTY

Loyalty involves ethics, and when couples argue about issues of loyalty, they are talking about the "right" and "good" ways of behaving. This helps to explain the intense feelings loyalty quarrels generate and the difficulties in resolving them. All the built-in "Thou shalt" and "Thou shalt not" commands seem to be a part of what we are and what we believe. When we try to compromise in a loyalty quarrel, some deep interior voice tells us that we are abandoning our moral principles.

There never has been a clear agreement among people as to loyalty to abstractions versus loyalty to people or between absolute versus situational loyalty—and we shall see that the three loyalties of marriage are mixtures of all these.

SOME COMMON LOYALTY PROBLEMS

The Dangers of Visible Versus Invisible Loyalties

Not all of our loyalties are conscious ones. Some have become second nature to us or, internalized. Dr. Ivan Boszormenyi-Nagy, a leading authority in this area of study, describes them as invisible loyalties, which are "like invisible but strong fibers which hold together complex . . . relationships in families as well as in larger society." He describes these as reliable commitments, shared loyalty to the principles and symbolic definitions of the group, bonds of consanguinity and marriage, and commitment to the maintenance of the group itself.

Some of these ties are unconscious because they are so much a part of our culture or early family life that we've never thought to question them. Others are invisible because they are suppressed. That is, we feel conflicts about certain obligations toward parents and their view of life. We are duty-bound and yet duty-burdened at the same time. Others are loyalties that we have never been able to articulate because they are real to us alone—and unknown to the other person or the group.

The Dangers of Ambiguous Loyalties

Often, our terms are unclear. When two loyalties pull in different directions and we can't decide how to choose between them, we face a moral dilemma, particularly when partners have to make a choice between one of the old, ingrained loyalties and new allegiances of marriage.

There was a good example of this in the case of Maria, a devoutly Catholic mother with three children of close to the same ages. Through family precepts and religious teaching as she grew up, she was opposed to birth control. Yet she and her husband—a middle-level state employee—both had a fervent desire to send all their children to college. Having more children meant a lower standard of living for the family and no college education for one or more of them. Loyalty to her origins was therefore in sharp conflict with loyalty to her present family. Maria sensed a further complication in that she wasn't sure whether her use of birth control was solely for the benefit of her children or whether it was for a more selfish reason—because she and her husband were tired of raising babies.

Marian and Andrew faced another facet of the same loyalties conflict when Marian's father had a stroke and was semiparalyzed. Her old loyalties told her that she should bring him home and take care of him herself with the help of a part-time practical nurse. Andrew argued that she owed her first loyalty to herself, the children, and him. Being on call twenty-four hours a day made her a slave to the sick-room. Better, he thought, to put Dad in a good nursing home where he would have medical attention and professional care.

Such questions of the "right" choice are hard to resolve because we think of loyalty as absolute, and yet we are always discovering that it is ambiguous. To decide how much loyalty we owe to a parent as opposed to a child as opposed to a spouse can demand almost-impossible distinctions.

The Dangers of Loyalties in Concord, Loyalties in Discord
As demonstrated in some of the case histories above, the discovery that her definition of loyalty is quite different from his can come as a shock. Another kind of unpleasant discovery can come even when partners look at loyalty in essentially the same way, and that is the shock of finding one of the pair less committed than the other. (He couldn't resist that one-night stand with another woman, but because he knows it was disloyal, he lies about it to his wife.)

The Dangers of Difficult Choices
Impartial logic usually doesn't work very well on such deeply rooted attitudes as loyalties. We rarely solve loyalty disputes in a perfectly fair and judicious way—one person usually ends up the loser. The chief consideration is to limit the emotional damage, to avoid real violation of the loser's sense of loyalty obligations. Our relationships get onto treacherous ground when a wife or husband feels that she or he has been forced to betray important commitments.

The Dangers of Chosen Loyalties Versus Coerced
We can be more or less compelled into certain loyalties. A wife takes on her husband's belief in something because she is afraid that he will love her less if she doesn't, or he'll consider her disloyal. A husband subscribes to one of his wife's causes not because it appeals to him very strongly but

because he thinks married people should put up a common front. Clinician Jay Haley believes that good marriages have a balance between compulsory and voluntary loyalties. Certain loyalties have been dictated to us by the fact of the relationship itself, and these are anchors. Others we have taken on voluntarily, and these are pledges. Each person then feels that the other cannot depart on a moment's whim because of anchor loyalties accepted and pledge loyalties freely given.

THE DANGERS OF THE ABSOLUTE OR THE RELATIVE

When two people see loyalty as a black-or-white issue—either you're loyal or you aren't—they are probably going to face quite a few crises in their marriage. If any deviation is wrong and any shortcoming disloyal, there is no room for negotiation.

At the other extreme, when people think of loyalties as purely relative matters—less important than other values in marriage—they invite just as much trouble. The "open marriages" of the 1970s, with their penchant for self-fulfillment at the expense of fidelity, proved that.

The Dangers of Love or Sex Alone

Many people assume that loyalty is no more than a matter of love. Others, just as innocently, assume that loyalty is no more than sexual faithfulness. Both of these simplifications are wrong.

The psychiatrist Henry Grunebaum has noted that there are individual thresholds of comfort in each of these things—love, sex, and commitment. Many people find one or another of them hard to sustain, and thus we can never assume that the measure of relationship loyalties is going to have equal proportions for everyone.

In my practice as a therapist, I've seen couples who have sex infrequently and unenthusiastically yet are thoroughly loyal and committed. I have also talked with couples who have a good and rewarding sex life but a faltering love. And, finally, I have seen the paradox of those who love each other genuinely but can't seem to avoid straying.

THE THREE KINDS OF LOYALTY: TO ROOTS, PARTNER, AND COVENANT

In every marriage, there are three kinds of loyalty. There is that system we inherit or absorb from our family, learn in school, or acquire from the world around us as we grow up. It may range from abstractions such as patriotism for our country to the more tangible ties of family solidarity or loyalties we feel toward a group of best friends. This rich set of allegiances is part emotional and part cerebral, with some strands apparent and some invisible. Through them, we define ourselves, create our own personal myth, and through them we are bound to our parental culture. These can also be called loyalties to one's roots.

Next are the one-to-one loyalties a man and woman have for each other in marriage—sexual faithfulness; agreement of ideas and attitudes; loyalty to a common approach to problems; loyalties to certain elements of the adult life such as particular people, undertakings, institutions. When a married couple, quite naturally, presents a united front to the world, it is because they combine love and this one-to-one, or partner, loyalty.

The third set of loyalties is a little more abstract—it is the obligation both should have to the common interest, to the union, to the family. It is a loyalty to the contract and to the terms of that contract, with its understood division of responsibilities and its concerns of the children of the marriage. It is the marriage as distinct from the married partners, the pair bond as distinct from the pair.

Perhaps it might seem strange to speak of this as independent of the one-to-one loyalties, but it is demonstrably so in many marriages. It was so in the case of John and Cindy, who, after ten years together, parted with bitter feelings. In spite of that, they managed to accept the spirit of "no fault" and work out terms of the divorce that were fair to both and to agree on joint custody for the children. No longer loyal to each other, they still felt bound to honor the covenant they had created.

We refer to these as "covenant loyalties," and, just as with the other two kinds, there are visible and invisible aspects to them.

THE VISIBLE LOYALTIES TO THE FAMILY OF ORIGIN

One ancient piece of wisdom tells us that if we are true to ourselves, it follows that we will be true to others. Most people accept this proposition and hope to marry someone who is true to himself/herself and who therefore has consistent values and standards of conduct. That would seem to be the best guarantee of loyalty. The only trouble is that this good man (or woman) is hard to find.

Making a resolution to be true to oneself is easily done, but it is much more difficult to know how to put into practice because each self is a synthesis of all the many influences and relationships we have encountered in life. And no one has grown up in a completely consistent world.

First among these shaping influences are, of course, the family where we were bred (called "the family of origin" by psychologists) and its basic values. Next come the bodies or institutions most Americans belong to in early life: the class in school; Boy Scouts or Girl Scouts; club; church, temple, or synagogue; college or university; fraternity or sorority; and— of prime importance in America—the team. Along with our individual friendships, they teach us the three great social lessons: cohesiveness, cooperativeness, and altruism. These are of major importance because success or failure in group loyalties almost directly foreshadows how well a person eventually succeeds in the adult world of work and organizations. Successful or unsuccessful relationships with parent, sibling, or friend are omens of future rapport or conflict between wife and husband.

Attachment to Mother

The first loyalty in life is the natural, biological one from mother to infant, and the child's response is the first stirring of what will eventually grow into loyalty to mother, parent, protector. When there happens to be some failure in this earliest relationship, the child will carry the mark of it through the years and into adulthood. The woman or man who has never gained a secure sense of maternal loyalty will seek it with intensity, almost desperation, in marriage. He or she will demand constant and monolithic devotion—but will constantly suspect that devotion is on the point of disappearing. Some of the most bitter loyalty quarrels spring from this.

When, on the other hand, the child begins life with a secure sense of love and loyalty, in later life he or she will probably have a stable, even temperament and will be able to handle the usual small loyalty troubles of marriage with composure. Even better, he or she won't have to cling to the marriage partner with a stranglehold of love.

The Oedipal Triangle

The original love/loyalty triangle is having to share Mom— her time and affection—with Dad. We first learn that no loyalty is absolute when she occasionally chooses that large interloper over us. As the father comes to be familiar and then important, the child has to manage conflicting loyalties with both parents. The child learns, in time, to play one parent off against the other, but if the parents are engaged in their own marital struggles, the child will be faced with constant loyalty dilemmas: which one of them is right? Whom should I believe in?

The loyalty triangle will become a pattern that repeats itself, and throughout life we will find ourselves confronted with three-sided relationships in which loyalties to one person must be reconciled with those to another. An employee might find himself/herself torn between loyalty to a colleague who has done something wrong and loyalty to a respected boss. In a family, a sister might be divided in allegiance between a quarreling brother and sister.

Siblings

Siblings produce some of the early loyalty triangles we have to contend with, but they also help to enlarge our sense of loyalty to include the idea of family loyalties. No matter how much siblings fight among themselves, they usually side with each other against strangers. An adult who was an only child enters marriage with quite different habits of loyalty from the adult who was raised with five siblings.

Friends

As we grow up, our area of loyalty grows beyond family to friends. The "best friend" a child acquires will change frequently, but in time there will be more lasting friendships, and through them the child learns a peer loyalty that isn't based simply on nurturing and blood kinship. Realizing what we owe a friend and what we expect in return is our first, small entrance into general society. As we increase the network of friendships, we find out that there are different standards of loyalty—and different kinds of betrayal. A person who has not had those close, formative friendships in early life will have missed out on a significant experience that may well affect his or her loyalty—or lack of it—in marriage.

Dating and Sex

Our loyalty system gets even more complicated when we begin to be interested in the opposite sex. Then we run into the ancient paradoxes of lust and all the ways it can reinforce loyalty or double-cross it. We have just built up a reliable kind of peer loyalty with children of our own sex when we are seized by this fickle imperative that seems so incompatible with friendship.

Institutional Loyalty

In time, we encounter two kinds of institutions that demand a new sort of loyalty from us—loyalty to the formal group. The first of these has a social aim; in Boy Scouts, Girl Scouts, school clubs, and so on, we learn some skills, develop some talents, and, most important, discover how to behave as members of a society. The other institution is the team, which teaches a kind of cooperative aggression. In the drama club or sorority, we find out how to get along with many others. In that fiercely exclusive unit called the team, we learn how to defeat others. One imparts a sense of social loyalty, and the other, all too often, reinforces the sense of group chauvinism.

Loyalties to Kin

The living embodiments of the old family loyalties are, of course, parents and in-laws. Many of the old versus new loyalty issues will come out in our transactions with them. Every couple has to find a day-to-day manner of dealing with its close kin and a style of diplomacy to go with it. (There are always such questions as, "We spent Christmas with my folks, but does that really mean we have to visit yours for Easter?" Or, "I think you ought to take that transfer to the San Diego office; living just down the street from Mother is driving me a little crazy." Or, "I don't care if your parents want to put up the money, Bobby is *not* going off to the General George S. Patton Military Academy.")

Relations with in-laws ought to be friendly but tempered with neutrality, but often they can run to an extreme. One wife I knew developed the warmest of relationships with her mother-in-law and father-in-law because they seemed to have the charm and responsiveness her own parents lacked. A husband I knew rejected his in-laws coldly even though they were interesting and attractive people. To show any liking for them would have betrayed his loyalty to his own parents. Both of these reactions produced an upset—though not a true basic quarrel—in the marriages. The husband of the woman who loved her in-laws felt emotionally snubbed by the three people closest to him; the wife of the man who rebuffed his in-laws felt somehow depreciated along with her parents.

Loyalty to Ideas

We usually begin by accepting our parents' attitudes and ideas. We may add some new thinking from what we learn in school. Until adolescence, we seldom question our body of received ideas. At that point, many of us begin to dispute our passively accepted intellectual loyalties; it is a way of declaring independence from our parents, of asserting our individuality. This is the time in life when ideas take on emotional power. Many people carry the emotion of ideas into marriage—both the emotions of family-derived ideas and the emotions of dissent. The two different sets, reacting differently in husband and wife, can cause a serious clash.

Class Loyalty

One of the more generalized allegiances that form us—and this is intimately connected with the family—is the matter of class. Many of our invisible loyalties come from our family's identification with a certain social status. This is something we Americans find hard to admit, but however much we deny it, we do have class lines and differentiations in this country. When we deny that class exists—contrary to evidence around us—we are really saying that we think no one class is inherently better than another and that we believe in upward mobility. Class in America is not, of course, based solely on lineage, as in Europe, but on such things as ethnic origin, money, education, and accomplishment.

A working class Italo-American Catholic with a high school education, brought up in Chicago, has a body of ingrained loyalties that are quite different from, say, those of a Virginian raised in an Episcopalian, upper-middle-class, small-town family and educated at William and Mary. That's obvious. What is not quite so obvious is how these loyalties will affect their behavior as adults—especially in marriage.

In my clinical experience, the marital quarrel over class usually has to do with in-laws. ("Your parents have never accepted me," or "You've always looked down on my family.") The nub of the quarrel is a feeling of having mistakenly married down or married up, and so become a displaced person.

In such a quarrel, the wife, let us say, will defend her family against her husband's criticism ("Maybe my parents are Polish working class, but they're just as good people as your folks!"). This will become a conflict between family-of-origin loyalty and one-to-one loyalty.

Religious Loyalties
Religious loyalties are, of course, vital for many people. America has gone through several different changes of attitude about this. The Puritans looked on loyalty to their own brand of reformist Protestantism as all-important. Immigrant groups that followed—German Anabaptists, Irish and Italian Catholics, Central European Jews, and others—all carried with them a vigorous loyalty to their creeds. During the as-

similation and melting-pot era, devotion declined and tolerance increased. Interfaith marriages were common. Religious education had less and less emphasis. The country grew more and more secular. But now, in the 1980–1990s era, there is a reverse trend. Evangelism has produced many born-again Christians, and many Jews have sought their cultural roots in a renewal of faith. There is a dispute between liberal Catholics who favor such things as birth control and conservatives who defend the Vatican's teachings. Thus, some marriages are prone to discord through a clash of religious loyalties.

As with the issue of class, loyalty quarrels over religion are often played out as a drama of parents versus in-laws. I remember a Jewish friend who married a Catholic woman. His parents—however tempted—did not pretend that he had died and sit *shiva* (a mourning rite), but they were continually critical of the wife.

Although the young couple themselves had no strong religious concerns, the husband always had to choose sides between his wife and his parents. By marrying her, he had, in effect, chosen her over them. His guilt from having betrayed a family loyalty compelled him to accept his father's mediocre business advice and to listen to endless berating over the telephone from his mother. That, of course, threw a shadow across the marriage. When the couple quarreled about the telephone calls and the bad results of the business advice, they were actually having a quarrel over loyalties.

The second crisis time in interfaith marriages often comes when the children arrive and there must be a decision about what religious teaching they will have, if any. By that time, it may be too late. For many such couples, the right decision time is when the original marriage compact is made.

Even couples who marry in the same faith and same sect can have differences. I knew, for example, the case of a Catholic couple, well suited to each other except for the fact that she was far more observant than he. He had a dim sense that she had chosen the church over him for reasons he couldn't pin down. He felt that her priest, whom she revered, had somehow diverted her from her proper marriage loyalty. On her part, she felt that her religion offered the support and emotional rewards that her marriage lacked.

In another case, a man had grown up in a nominally Protestant but nonchurchgoing family that had a good deal of parental and sibling strife. As an adolescent, he longed for security and spiritual serenity. He met and married a Christian woman with strong fundamentalist ideals, hoping that this would offer him the kind of stability his family never had. As it turned out, she was a literal and intolerant true believer—and they quarreled. From his viewpoint, her loyalties had made her narrow; from her viewpoint, his background had made him incapable of taking on real loyalties.

These are just a few examples of the great complex of early loyalties we accept or acquire. In the best-case scenario, husband and wife can find the necessary compromises between the two sets of their early loyalties. In the worst case, they can have a collision of two personal cultures—a feeling on one side or both that loyalties from the past are threatened by alien ideas and behavior. Out of this comes a basic quarrel. Here is one of that kind.

Curt and Valerie

Shortly after the wedding, Curt was offered a transfer to Sacramento by his company, and he was excited about the idea of moving to California, where he'd always wanted to live. Beside that, he felt he owed it to his company, where he had a good career ahead of him. Curt's father had been an air-force officer and, when Curt was growing up, the family moved from base to base without much ado about it. His family ties weren't close, he wasn't dependent on friends, and he didn't mind pulling up stakes and going on to some more interesting place—"I travel light," he always said.

Valerie couldn't bear the thought. Sacramento seemed like a million miles away, and probably out in the desert. She had grown up in North Carolina and had graduated from Chapel Hill. She was a Tarheel, born and bred. Her parents lived in Raleigh, and that's where her brothers and sisters had settled. The idea of having to deal with strange Californians every day filled her with dread. Most important, she was very close to Mom and Dad, brother Walter, and sister Susan. Couldn't Curt understand all that?

Curt won. It took some emotional bribes, a lot of persuasion, and an expensive vacation in Hilton Head before they were finally settled in Sacramento—but well worth it. The job was even more challenging and interesting than he'd imagined. And the growth opportunities for the company were tremendous. Not only that, but the boss and three or four of Curt's colleagues were among the most effective people with whom he'd ever worked. Naturally, Curt wanted Valerie to feel involved in his career, and so he used to describe the daily details every night at dinner.

Valerie tried to listen, but her worries got in the way. Some weeks, she would call Mom every night, not because there was anything new to report—there never was in this town—but just for the sound of Mom's voice. When she hung up, she was even more homesick than before. She called Susan; she called Walter; she would call one of her ten or twelve closest friends in Raleigh or Chapel Hill whenever she had the impulse.

Valerie flew home to North Carolina for Thanksgiving, Christmas, Mother's Day, the Fourth of July, Mom's birthday, the family reunion, and her class reunion at UNC. Curt went along on Christmas and the Fourth, but the rest of the time he was too busy. He seemed to think all this flying back was a little foolish—he hadn't seen his own parents for three years, he pointed out.

After the two children were born, Valerie's life changed for the better—they needed all her love and attention. She made far fewer trips back home. When they were old enough to go to school, there were new worries, and her greatest cause for concern was that they would grow up to be "California kids," traditionless, mannerless, self-indulgent, undisciplined. Curt thought that California kids were okay—independent and straightforward with you, he said. Valerie, disagreeing, took the children back to Raleigh for every summer vacation and lived for the day when they would enter Duke or UNC.

In their eleventh year of marriage, Valerie and Curt began to quarrel more and more openly. When they finally decided on a divorce, they said it was because they had such drastic differences about where they should live—Valerie hated Sacramento and Curt loved it. The real quarrel was, in fact, between the two sets of those early loyalties that people carry like a second skin through life.

What were Curt's? First, he was brought up in a service family that moved a lot. Thus, all of his friends were temporary; he was wary of getting too close to anyone because he knew that the family might move on at any time. As a regular officer, his father had a prime loyalty to the air force, a place where the male values of hierarchy, discipline, esprit de corps, and groupthink are necessary. Curt developed very similar loyalties toward his company and his colleagues. Although he did love his wife, almost all of his early experience had taught him team loyalty and profession loyalty.

As a result, he couldn't deal with Valerie's strong personal loyalties to parents, friends, and a family culture. His own family had had a military regimen and little room for warmth or emotion. The frequent moves had left Curt a friendless boy and then a friendless man. His substitutes for friends were colleagues united in working toward the same goal—in that relationship he could feel warmth and shared emotions.

In the early years of marriage, Valerie filled the role of a dear colleague. The common goal was a combination of stable home, sexual enjoyment, companionship, social respectability. As time went on, it became clear that their "early" allegiances were in conflict, their one-to-one loyalty doomed to be temporary, and their loyalty to the contract all that was left.

Valerie, for her part, had been so intimately tied to her own family by invisible loyalty commitments that she had a hard time trying to accept the idea that loyalty to Curt was now supposed to be uppermost. She felt that she had somehow abandoned her parents and brother and sister—and she felt guilty.

When the children were born, a great deal of her guilt was lifted. She could now give them the care and devotion her parents had given her. As Ivan Boszormenyi-Nagy says, "Parenthood is a unique chance to pay reparation for internally sensed guilt over imputed disloyalty." Later, Valerie made determined attempts to reproduce her own happy North Carolina childhood in the lives of her children.

In the meantime, the one-to-one loyalty between Curt and Valerie diminished. Curt began to realize—mostly subconsciously—that Valerie had rejected his version of early loyalties, which probably included Sacramento Little League, Boy Scouts, and ROTC for his son, in favor of her own. And, by implication, she had rejected him as well. He did not quite comprehend that he had been the first to loosen the one-to-one loyalty because of his devotion to company and career.

According to Boszormenyi-Nagy, a couple's healthy first move would be to redefine their family-of-origin loyalties. In other words, they should emancipate themselves from the most dominating of the old emotional ties. If Valerie had decided to bite the bullet and learn to create a life for herself in California, it would have been an emancipating decision. If Curt had been able to appreciate and respond to her family devotion, they might have been able to refashion old loyalties into a new working relationship.

INVISIBLE LOYALTIES TO THE FAMILY OF ORIGIN

Those deep-lying, invisible loyalties can be fundamental features of our value system—such as class or religion—or can be as trivial as a minor habit. I recall one couple's argument over his habit of drinking a glass of orange juice with snacks. In his boyhood home, this had been routine, but in her large family, where everything had been strictly rationed, it would have been against the rules. Although she could not explain why, she would get very upset over this—not because the orange juice had any significance in her present situation but because it was a psychological tie to her parents' frugal way of life and to her old loyalties.

Such loyalties are invisible because we have lost the actual context while retaining the old, often irrational family roots from whence those loyalties came. "We do things this way" becomes, in the child's mind, "This is the right way to do things." Many loyalties are invisible as well because they are nonverbal. They are simply repeated actions or details of a way of life that the child has observed and absorbed.

Invisible Loyalties and Basic Quarrels

"The more rigidly the maturing child is tied to his parents with invisible loyalty commitments, the more difficult will it be for him to replace the original loyalty with a new relational commitment," writes Ivan Boszormenyi-Nagy.

Couples are very likely to develop a basic quarrel when the old allegiances compete with the new ones of marriage. The wedding over, each partner suddenly finds herself or himself sharing the house with a stranger. That stranger has very odd ideas and prejudices about how to do things, big things or small. Whether these things make for minor irritations or swell into major quarrels depends, Boszormenyi-Nagy notes, on how inflexible the family of origin was.

Some families are nearly closed systems with ill-concealed distrust of outsiders. In one family I knew, the children were discouraged from bringing friends home to play, sleepovers with other children were forbidden, and "undesirable" playmates were weeded out by the parents. Naturally, the parents chose playmates who conformed to their own image —which tended to make the family even more ingrown. Such a family loses its children to marriage with great reluctance, and its invisible loyalty ties on the young are like steel cables. The young woman or man from the closed-system family who tries to rewrite his or her old loyalty code to fit the needs of a new marriage may fall into a basic loyalty quarrel.

There is an even more extreme version of this kind of family, the family fraught with destructive behavior and yet fiercely defensive against any interference. A typical case is the family that denies and hides the problem of its alcoholic or its abuser.

The offspring of families with highly charged secrets and denials will have loyalty bonds of anxiety, guilt, and fear so strong that such people are likely to recreate the same patterns in their own marriages, even if there is no violence, addiction, or incest to hide.

Prolonging the old family-of-origin struggles, guarding its old rituals, protecting its old wounds, and righting the wrongs one suffered from it can be a catastrophic affair. Even when a child of the closed family has an urge to reform and correct the familial errors, there is danger. His wife or her husband hasn't signed on to play a supporting role in this psychodrama and may sense that there is no exorcism for all the spouse's parental ghosts.

Another situation has one person complaining to his or her parents about the partner. Ostensibly, this is just a way of asking for support or sympathy. More subtly, it is a way of saying, "I guess I made a mistake when I traded our family for this unsatisfactory marriage." The rebellion against the spouse may simply take the form of sharing a secret with Mother or Dad while keeping it from wife or husband—as if assuring the parent, "*You* are the only one I can really trust."

Even worse is the case when the need to show loyalty to the past transforms itself into sexual failure (sexual inhibition, impotence, or anorgasmia). In the logic of the subconscious, to take full joy in sex would be a disloyalty to parental love. In a milder form, this rejection of the spouse could be simply a matter of preserving an emotional distance from him or her in order to keep faith with the old loyalties.

There may be still another script when the child of a family rebels against its loyalties as an adult. He or she has felt suppressed and dominated by the laws of the family culture. That defiance may translate into a buried wish to defy any family loyalties—even the new ones of marriage. And that, in turn, often translates into an extramarital affair.

ONE-TO-ONE LOYALTIES, OR PARTNER LOYALTIES

First comes the question of why any two people fall in love. We cannot understand their loyalty commitment until we first understand the principal reasons that brought them together. The first psychologists who considered the matter produced two theories. One said that people with many similarities ("homogamy") were strongly attracted to each other. The other theory said that people who were quite different fell in love when they complemented each other, strengths on one side making up for weaknesses on the other.

Later psychologists made a neat synthesis of the two opinions by postulating that people fall in love because they are similar and because they are different. That is, one attraction lies in similar personalities, similar cultural and socioeconomic backgrounds. Another attraction lies in complementary needs—the insecure person marries the self-confident one; the introspective person marries the extrovert; and so on.

Bernard Murstein then arrived at a more sophisticated theory, "stimulus-value-role." He argues that people are first of all attracted to each other by certain stimuli: looks, sexual signals, charm. They next try to match their values: attitudes, serious interests, beliefs. Finally, the crucial measure is whether they can correlate their two roles: complementary aims, cooperation, life-style harmony. Others in the field, such as Charles Bolton, have developed even more elaborate psychological studies of the attraction and courtship process.

During the course of my work as a couples therapist, I often ask couples who have been together for many years why they were originally attracted. The answers—usually on the order of "good looks," or "I was ready to get married"— almost never offer a clue as to why the two have stayed together so long. When I question a little further, I frequently find that "ready to get married" means either that a handicap had just been removed or marriage would be a compensation for some loss. One of the most frequent instances was the death of a parent.

Though we seldom look at it this way, many marriages are problem-solving moves for one or both partners. The test that comes a little later is whether marriage is a lasting solution. If marriage is simply a ticket to get out of a bad situation and nothing more, marriage loses its meaning when the bad situation is left behind. If, on the other hand, it is both a solution to a problem and a desired move in itself, chances for success are good.

Naomi Quinn of Duke University, has analyzed the meaning of the word *commitment* in marriage, and has found three basic meanings: first a promise (or pledge) that is either kept and lived by or forgotten; second, dedication, or devotion; third, an attachment based on physical connection, exclusivity, and enduringness.

She goes on to say that in some marriages commitment means that a couple has identified certain goals to be reached; in other marriages, commitment is simply the success of the union or partnership.

Development of One-to-One Loyalties

If there were a credo for one-to-one loyalty, it might be Boszormenyi-Nagy's: "Have you proven to me that you can hear me, consider me, and care for me? If your actions prove that you do, it is natural for me to feel and act loyal to you, i.e., to consider you and your needs. You oblige me through your openness."

Listening, having consideration, caring, being open: These are the elements of loyalty. They are not quite the same thing as love, but they are its closest allies. We never take on loyalties by learning a pledge of allegiance; they are accumulations of time and experience. In marriage, loyalties are built up though sexual fidelity and the rhythms of intimacy and the weathering of crises together.

In the 1970s, the one-to-one loyalty in marriage was sharply questioned and much debated. That was the era when swinging marriages and open marriages were the fashion, although more of them may have occurred in the popular press than in real life.

Francine Klagsbrun, in *Married People,* has a wise comment on the notion that sexual fidelity is not very important in marriage. She says, "One of the reasons the open marriage movement of the 1970's came and went within the flick of an eye, I believe, is because it disregarded the need partners have for exclusivity in marriage, for being the most important person in the other's life. Once others are brought in, the trust is diluted and the old fears of revealing oneself take hold."

Klagsbrun makes another worthwhile point when she notes that couple loyalty depends on awareness. She asserts that couples who exchange their emotional readings in a free, full, and candid way create the firmest loyalties.

This exchange would not be very meaningful if it were limited only to couples who possess the rather rare talent to put obscure or undefined feelings into words. For some thirty years, anthropologists and psychologists have been studying what they call "the silent language." This wordless communication expresses thought or feeling through such things as body language and symbolic actions. The silent message is sent without the sender being aware of the transmittal, and it is received and understood in just the same way.

The anthropologist Edward T. Hall, the man who first defined the silent language, believes—on the basis of certain studies—that each of us has a personal rhythm and that "[p]eople in general don't sync well with people they don't like and they do with those they love." In his book *The Dance of Life*, he gives the example that "when a mate becomes involved with someone else, there is a shift in his or her rhythm. It's as though a third person were in the house, and in a way they are, because their rhythm is there."

The woman who sensed that her husband was moving to a slightly new and different tempo probably would be unable to articulate the feeling, but she would intuit an evidence of changed loyalty. And so it is with many other unspoken messages about the state of loyalty to each other.

When a couple tells a therapist, "Our communication has broken down—we just don't communicate anymore," they think they are talking about speech, which, according to anthropologists' estimates, carries only about 35 percent of the meanings humans transmit. What the couple really mean and can't quite explain is the fact that they are sending just as many messages as ever—but the messages are all negative.

Those messages are, of course, in the silent language, in which subconscious intent or attitude comes across stripped of hypocrisy—although, just as with spoken language, one can misread the signals at times.

There are a number of actions that specialists in nonverbal communication call "intimacy signals." Two people who are fond of each other will, literally, be very close. They like to stand or sit together within "intimate distance," which ranges from a space of about eighteen inches to actual contact. And they like to touch frequently. When they talk, they tend to face each other squarely and keep up a good deal of eye contact. They share, or emulate, movements and postures, too—that is, for instance, if one lounges in the chair, the other will probably do the same. If they are deeply involved in an exchange, they will unconsciously take positions that exclude other people around them. Researchers have discovered these and many other telltale signs through observation and photographic evidence.

Negative Signs in One-to-One Loyalty

All of the above are signs of positive emotional response. When such signals begin to alter decidedly or diminish, there's a good chance that the emotional message is turning negative. In addition, there are subconscious signals that distinctly transmit the new chill. A kind of selective forgetfulness is one of the most significant.

A relatively common example is that of a man who has promised to meet his wife at a certain place but is very late. He explains by saying, "It just slipped my mind."

Answering intuitively, she says, "It's really because you don't love me any longer. A year ago, you wouldn't have forgotten."

He says, "No, it was because I was on the phone to Paris talking over an important business deal."

She counters that with, "But you had just as important deals going on a year ago."

Americans put a high value on time, and to make someone wait longer than a few minutes is something we consider an aggressively negative act. If this incident happened in the context of other negative messages, the wife is probably right: something has gone wrong between them.

There are many everyday instances of selective forgetting in a strained marriage—the man who forgets his wife's request to mail her letters, or to do some shopping for her, or to pay her department-store bill. Or a wife who keeps losing her wedding ring, or (seemingly) by accident breaks something her husband sets great store by, or forgets to pass on an important message to him.

People who say, "We can't communicate," are probably angry or frightened by the kind of communication they are receiving through the sixth sense. Since these are messages they don't want, they deny that there are really any messages at all. They are, in effect, saying to the therapist, "We know we're in trouble, but only God knows why."

One-to-one loyalty is a great defense against a basic quarrel ever developing. Loyalty is based on trust. A long-running fight between two people who have implicit trust in each other is nearly impossible. When the silent language begins to convey the fact that one-to-one loyalty is disintegrating, that's very likely to be the portent of a basic quarrel.

The sociologist Nina S. Fields reported an interesting survey of couples who had been married for at least two decades. Each person was first requested to try describing himself/herself in terms of appearance, interests, personality, emotional temperament, and social needs. They were asked, What subjects do you feel most strongly about? What are your strengths and weaknesses? Then each person was requested to write the same kind of description of his/her wife or husband.

In the successful marriages, a husband's description of his wife was very close to her description of herself, and vice-versa. In the less successful marriages, the portraits were at odds. Those results suggest that in good marriages both the spoken language and the silent language carry the same messages and the same pictures.

Specific One-to-One Problems

Many people marry without thinking much about it, and for quite superficial reasons. I hear such reasons as, "I was on the rebound from an affair with a bad ending." Or, "I was thirty-two and I wanted to do it before it was too late." Or, "We had such a good time in Bermuda. We laughed a lot. I thought it was going to last." Or, "She was really good in bed—in those days."

In most cases, the marriage outlives the impulse, and the couple is left without any loyalties but with a basic quarrel over the old mistake of a hasty marriage for the wrong reasons.

There are the couple who violate the privacy of the marriage. They exhibit their secrets and parade their grievances in front of their friends. It's a sure sign of a marriage heading for the cliff when this kind of torture replaces one-to-one loyalty. The deliberate testing of loyalty by outrageous behavior is another aspect of this game of marital "chicken." He tries to embarrass her in front of friends with semifictional tales of her foul-ups. Or, she plays an obvious come-on act to an attractive man at a party, with her husband present. These actions are really suspicious questions: "Are you really loyal to me? Or can a little provocation bring out the truth?"

Another type of loyalty violation is the long-kept guilty secret. I hear about many of them, such as: He hated to mention his one afternoon a week at the racetrack until the equity loan on the house got out of control. Another case: He's rather straitlaced, and so she didn't mention the pot-smoking habit she picked up in college and still indulges on the sly. Another case: She didn't know he'd been picked up for drunk driving several times, and even had his license suspended, until the night he ran into the bridge abutment. All these were strong signals of mistrust and breaches of loyalty.

Sexual disloyalty is, certainly, the most flamboyant offense against the one-to-one pact. Infidelity can have many contributing causes and complications apart from the act of breaking the loyalty bond. It will be discussed at length in Chapter Five.

COVENANT LOYALTY

The third kind of loyalty is a bit more complicated in that it accumulates more and more meanings as the years go by. In early marriage, it applies to all the implications of the compact between the couple. A little later, it grows to include the community of interests, understandings, and possessions most marriages build up—in both a figurative and real sense, the "common wealth." Children, as they come along, are of course the most vital part of this mutuality.

In what ways do we show this loyalty? In most families, there are certain accepted ways of behaving and certain unspoken policies that make up a code of conduct, or an *ethos*. When a wife says, "It's not fair of you to do that"—instead of "You hurt my feelings when you did that"—she's appealing to covenant loyalty and its spirit of justice rather than to one-to-one loyalty.

I have seen couples who have managed to stay together for many years in spite of the fact that they disagreed about almost everything. It wasn't that they were creatures of habit or that they couldn't find escape hatches from the marriage, or were bound together in a pathological trade-off of needs. It was simply that they had an overriding loyalty to the principle they had agreed to. In a very personal sense, they were people of the law.

Thus, covenant loyalty includes a code of fairness, a recognition of rights, and an allocation of responsibilities in the family. As the family grows, this small scheme of governance includes the children as well—what loyalty is owed them and what they owe.

Most "nuclear" families differ in loyalties according to their different moral codes and life-styles. That is, a Mormon farm family in Utah might have a traditional, paternalistic scheme of things, with the father as the center—and definer—of family loyalties. An upper-middle-class couple in Boston might have a quite egalitarian marriage, with as even a division of rights and duties as possible. Their loyalties would be defined by compromise and common assent. As for the farm owner, he would probably consider his first loyalty obligation that of keeping up a well-managed, productive farm for his children's future. The Boston couple might regard saving money to provide a good college education for their children as first priority.

No matter how far Deseret may be from Beacon Hill, those two and all other American nuclear families have the same terms and obligations in common. They must maintain the value of family ties, the responsibilities to children, the continuity of generations, and the duties to kinship.

A close look at any nuclear family would give an idea of how it defines its covenant loyalty. But in one of the unforeseen social developments of our time, the unity of many nuclear families has been overwhelmed by a new kind of extended family. The old sociological term *extended family* once meant grandmother and grandfather, aunts, uncles, and cousins, children, and grandchildren. In the nineteenth century, most of them were likely to live in the same community and enjoy a clan spirit of cooperation, shared social activities, and a similarity of belief and outlook.

The traditional kind of extended family was a great conveyer of loyalties—almost as important as the nuclear family in that respect. The new extended family is a much different kind of social phenomenon. Parents divorce and remarry, move to different parts of the country, and start second— sometimes even third—families. A child's growing up may be divided among two or three different physical settings and different family cultures whose sets of loyalties may be in conflict. A child no longer acquires loyalties in the time-honored way, and after he or she grows up and marries, those conflicts often cause trouble and disorientation in the marriage.

I work at the Adolescent and Family Treatment Unit at McLean Hospital, an inpatient program treating adolescents who have depression and behavioral problems. At one time, we would have a good idea of the makeup of the family we were dealing with. If we requested that the whole family come in for a therapy session and some members refused, that gave us a good clue as to where resistance to therapy lay. It's no longer so.

In the case of certain families after divorce, there is a biological father who may or may not have specific rights of authority in the family. There are stepparents who may take on any of a number of roles, from one of complete responsibility for the children to almost total disconnection.

Stephen Toulmin of the University of Chicago points out that new, ambiguous circumstances in our society result in ambiguous attitudes about loyalty. The modern version of the extended family is so centerless and diverse that it is no wonder that loyalties will be confused and uncertain.

Quarrels in Covenant Loyalty

A number of quarrels come directly from issues of covenant loyalty. Perhaps the most common—and most significant— ones arise from the three-cornered tension among the two parents and each child. There are complex questions of discipline, authority, different measures of love and attention, and self-interest versus the common interest. A discussion of children and family, however, must be reserved for fuller treatment in Chapter Eight.

DEALING WITH LOYALTY QUARRELS

First of all, it is important to take a close look at our sometimes irrational family-of-origin loyalties and try to see how they relate to the present quarrel.

Each person must ask the question, "Have I made the quick leap from 'This was the way my family always did it' to 'This is the way all families *should* do it'?" If the answer is yes, we have become our parents' agents in perpetuating the behavior patterns we don't like as well as those we approve. If our sense of loyalty to origins makes it hard to rid ourselves of unacceptable patterns, it is even harder to modify those we favor. To bring our loyalty values into accord with the realities of our adult, married lives, we must understand that this isn't a question of condemning parents but of quietly getting rid of the worst parts of the psychological inheritance from them.

One example I recall is the problem Gerald and Connie bumped heads over in the first years of their marriage. She came from a family of enthusiastic do-gooders. Her mother and father had involved themselves in every worthy cause from Bangladesh relief to Save the Whales. In addition, Connie's mother would invite lonely strangers to the house for dinner, make endless visits to the sick, and volunteer for work in centers for the homeless. Her father was equally involved in charity and community-improvement projects. As a lawyer, he took an unpaid job as a public defender.

Gerald's family would help a relative in need, but that was the extent of their charity. His parents were not so much stingy and unfeeling as believers in self-sufficiency and the work ethic.

The crisis came when both of them began acting true to family form and a quarrel developed. "Look," Gerald said, "charity begins at home. Your mother and father spent so much time bailing other people out of trouble that they didn't know what troubles their own kids were having. They didn't realize how heavily into pot your brother Mike was, for instance. And you yourself say that there was never enough money for new clothes, travel, even going to the movies. In *our* family, we've got to put our own kids first."

Connie answered, "Just because you grew up in a family of emotional tightwads, you don't have to be that way yourself. We're very lucky because we have a good income, we live in a nice place, and we don't have any real problems. But what good are we if we don't try to share some of that luck with people who've had a rough time in life?"

Old loyalties like these that chafe against each other and cause the basic quarrel must be in some large part replaced by the new one-to-one loyalties, which means a new sharing and acceptance. To make this happen, the partners must first discover what each means by loyalty and what it means in practice. In short, this can become a renegotiation session of immense value.

In spite of the quarrel, Gerald and Connie had a sound marriage based on love and goodwill. They finally got together in a negotiation and outlined terms for a compromise. Compromises never satisfy either side completely, nor did this one—but it worked. Gerald gave up some of his extra time to work together with Connie in some of her service activities. On her side, she agreed not to take on any more of them and to limit her effort to a few she thought most important.

These two people could come to an agreement on loyalties when they were able to realize that they had been attracted to each other partly because each of them represented something the other longed for—Gerald saw Connie's socially conscious, generous upbringing as counterpart to his own Spartan background. Connie saw Gerald's heritage of putting the family's children first as a welcome contrast to the neglect she sometimes resented in her own childhood. Each needed the other to modify the embrace of the past.

Most married people feel an inner struggle much like this—an appreciation of the other's loyalty model along with a reluctance to give up their own family-of-origin loyalties. The friction between them acts as a way of dodging the conflict within. Once they recognize this, each is freer to concede something to the other.

Happily, the arrival of children can be a natural support for the attempt to revaluate the personal loyalties. A mother and father develop a primary devotion to their child, and the needs of the helpless infant are a counterbalance to both parents' guilt over loosening their lifelong obligations to their families of origin. Fulfilling the new obligation frees them from their guilt over disloyalty.

Absolving themselves from the most onerous of the old loyalties and declaring a new one-to-one loyalty relieves a couple of the dead hand of the past and creates a code for the present—but there is also the future to take into account. Children will grow out of infancy, the parents will arrive at middle age, and there will be a different set of problems. The mainstay of that time of life is going to be covenant loyalty.

One form covenant loyalty can take is a romantic idealization of what the other person represents. It is a fragile image and one that can, if it lasts long enough, be a sign of immaturity. In contrast, "mature idealization" is an idea of the marriage that combines all its best aspects. It is a kind of realistic optimism. Otto Kernberg calls it a commitment to an ideal represented by what the loved person is or stands for and what the couple united might become. In the face of apparently irreconcilable personal loyalties, having a clear sense of and maintaining one's commitment to this shared task can provide a star by which to navigate.

Finally, there is the supreme factor of equality. A full and open moral relationship is only possible when two people are on an approximately equal level. That is the whole basis of loyalty freely given and freely returned. Real loyalty cannot exist in a marriage in which one partner dominates the other by psychological or physical force, or where one partner clings to the other out of desperation.

CHAPTER FOUR

MONEY

Sigmund Freud thought he detected a symbolic connection between money and excrement—that is, one of the things we value most equated with the thing we value least, an idea that was long ago summed up in the biblical phrase "filthy lucre." Later theorists, such as Otto Fenichel, had a much broader concept of the matter, seeing money as a many-sided symbol associated with a variety of different psychological comforts or ills.

Those rectangles of printed paper we carry with us are daily life's most ordinary and ever present symbol. Worthless in itself, this arbitrary unit of exchange can be a bearer of almost any symbolical value we choose to put on it: success, power, ability, worth, freedom, status, love, or security. Equations like this are the commonplaces of our commercial society, and they imply that, as the humorist William Hamilton says sardonically, "Money is life's report card." Money can also denote negative qualities, such as aggression, ostentation, manipulation of others, extravagance, rivalry, avarice, hoarding, or guilt.

In marriage, money can symbolize undeclared needs or expectations in conflict with each other. According to the psychiatrist Ann Ruth Turkel, couples often explain away their quarrels about money by citing a difference in family backgrounds or in personalities. She adds, "Their money transactions reflect accurately the state of—and can be called a mirror of—their marriage."

Take the case of Rick and Jennie. Both come from blue-collar Pennsylvania backgrounds. Jennie, already pregnant, married her high school boyfriend two weeks after she graduated. After a rocky six months and the birth of the baby, her husband disappeared, leaving Jennie to exist on welfare and a little support from her mother. Jennie got a divorce and, not long after, met Rick.

Rick is a tile-layer—his father's trade—and he made a good-enough wage to support himself comfortably. After he'd met Jennie and they'd fallen in love, a lot of new charges went onto his MasterCard. One of the things they never talked about over dinners at a restaurant or on their trip to Disney World was money.

A year after the wedding, they talk—bitterly—about little else. Jennie now has a job as a waitress, and she works hard. She is amazed that Rick can go to the ball game in the afternoon or pass up a tile-laying job in order to take a hunting trip with his buddies while the bills pile up. She reminds him frequently that this isn't "the good life" they'd promised each other in marriage.

On his part, Rick is a little shell-shocked by all the angry scenes and accusations. The man is supposed to be the provider—he knows that from his own upbringing—but with today's prices, they just can't make it from month to month without Jennie's paycheck. Not that he is happy to have her working. She would be a lot better occupied, he feels, staying home to run the house and tend to her child. Somehow, the more pressure she puts on him and the less love she shows, the harder it is for him to produce.

Carol and Sy, who come from middle-class families, have a different kind of money quarrel. Sy is an assistant curator at a museum of natural history. They met and married in graduate school, but found that their two teaching assistant-ships just weren't enough to pay the rent and the grocery bill. Carol, whose mother was a high school teacher who always criticized her work, was having trouble finishing her papers. As a result, they decided that Carol would drop out and Sy would go on for his doctorate. They are now in their early thirties and have no children.

After dropping out, Carol worked as a secretary but found that job routine and boring—she was always "overqualified." She'd like to feel more independent financially, but she can't face another menial job and the thought of finishing the requirements for her graduate degree terrifies her. She has bouts of depression and gradually has lost most of her friends.

Sy makes thirty-five thousand dollars, enough income for them to live modestly well—but he always has the nagging thought that Carol isn't really contributing. She won't get a job, and yet she can't cope with running the house. For instance, when he needs a freshly ironed shirt before going off to his office in the morning, he's likely as not to find all of his shirts still in the wash.

Carol hates ironing and every other household chore. The only times she feels useful are when she's helping Sy with museum paperwork or going with him to a professional function. The trouble is, she says, that Sy seems to take all that for granted.

Their fights are frequent and mean. They do have a trade-off in their marriage, but it is a miserable one. Carol surrenders her individuality in return for protection from the working world. Sy collects his emotional IOUs, likes to be in control, feels superior because she is so inept at managing her life, but at the same time feels martyred at having to shoulder the whole burden.

*　　*　　*

In contrast, Ray and Janice would seem to have it made. They aren't rich, but they are well-rewarded young professionals with a combined income over $150,000. She is a stockbroker at one of the big Wall Street firms, and he runs his own retail computer business. In a year when the bonus is good, Janice earns almost as much as Ray. With each of them making enough to support a family, they ought to have few anxieties over money.

When they were living together before they were married, they kept their finances separate except for a fifty–fifty split on the household expenses. Afterward, they found that things were no longer so simple—they were spending every Sunday afternoon allocating the items on bills or checkbook stubs. There were some hurt feelings over exchanges like: "I really think you ought to pay about eighty percent of the price tag on this one, since I doubt if I'll ever use it much at all," answered by, "But you were the one who was all gung-ho for buying it in the first place."

They finally agreed on a trial run to pool the greater part of their incomes and treat all expenses—except for a few strictly personal ones—as common obligations. Any big or extraordinary expenditure would require a mutual consent.

It didn't work. For many couples in the same situation, that would have been a reasonable solution, but for Janice and Ray it wasn't. The partial loss of control over a large part of his money made Ray nervous and faultfinding. Their decision-making sessions turned into battles, and many of the things one or the other really wanted to do or to acquire had to be sacrificed to rancor. They then went back to the separate-but-equal system.

As for Janice, she had something of a guilt feeling about not doing the things a woman is traditionally supposed to do. She almost never made a meal because they ate in restaurants. A professional decorator had furnished their apartment. She lived most of her life outside the home. All of this made her sense that Ray, in reaction, was losing interest in the marriage.

The big problems came from the fact that Janice and Ray, having equal functions, had split authority so evenly that neither had real authority. In her book *More Equal than Others: Men and Women in Dual-Career Marriages*, Rosanna Hertz describes this as a couple made up of two husbands and no wife.

These three case histories demonstrate that financial transactions or dissensions mirror the state of the marriage, even though money symbolizes quite different things in each. For Rick and Jennie, it equates with gender roles and the dream of financial security. For Sy and Carol, it represents self-esteem, control, or dependence. For Janice and Ray, it denotes an impasse in authority, a marriage that is more a standoff than a partnership.

ATTITUDES TOWARD MONEY AND WHERE THEY COME FROM

As a couples therapist, I've come to learn that money quarrels yield a valuable set of clues to some of the deeper complications of marriages like those described above. Interestingly enough, psychiatric literature on the subject is small and sketchy—which suggests that the privacy taboo about money affects even psychotherapists, who seem to avoid exploring the subject with their patients. Although we have no hesitation over inquiring about many shadowy matters from whips and chains in the bedroom to murderous fantasies toward one's mother, we hold back from asking a patient how much money he makes because "that's too personal."

The therapist knows, of course, that people bring to marriage many of their family-of-origin attitudes about money.

And these usually stem from that family's ethnic, cultural, class, and economic background. Traditionally, working-class and middle-class families in America cherished the Protestant work ethic, but it has been much diluted by post–World War II affluence and the habits of our throwaway society.

The rich, as we've been told, are different—and thus less predictable as a social group. "Shirtsleeves to shirtsleeves in three generations" is a common American dictum about the rich, but vigilant protection of their wealth is probably even more characteristic. Brought to a marriage between one rich and one nonrich partner, that disposition can easily make for a basic money quarrel.

Children absorb parental feelings about money. Even if the subject is never discussed openly, children do learn to associate money values with material things and certain abstractions. If there is a sudden adverse change in the family fortunes, children are soon aware that money and security are closely linked. If working parents spend so much time on the job that they have little energy or time left for their children, the children learn to relate money-poverty to love-poverty. If there are quarrels between parents over how family money is spent, a child will associate money with tension or strife.

Family attitudes toward money can come from differing ethnic and cultural backgrounds. A family that has suffered rampant inflation in its country of origin (Mexico or Brazil, for instance), will regard money in a different light from that of a family always used to hard currency. One that has enjoyed prosperity from the manipulation of money through stock investments will have ideas about wealth quite different from the family that has saved its assets penny by penny.

The formative times in our lives also affect our ideas and feelings about money. Those Americans who grew up during the Great Depression, for instance, learned how fragile economic security could be. Banks failed; the stock market crashed; factories closed; unemployment grew to almost 10 percent. All this had some broad effects on the generation just coming of age. It soon called for and supported unprecedented social "safety-net" legislation to protect most people from future catastrophes. In a reaction against its deprived childhood, it bestowed on its own children the permissiveness of the 1950s. Today, the college freshman who has his own Porsche will find it hard to understand his grandfather who, in the 1930s, had to walk to work on those mornings when he didn't have a dime for the trolley car.

These are some of the broad patterns of different family attitudes toward money. Although they are subject to individual variations within these general sociological formulas, family-of-origin outlook and received class perceptions about money govern much of our marital behavior. The nuclear family as an emotional entity can't be separated from the nuclear family as a small economic system.

WHAT RESEARCH SHOWS

As many as one quarter to one third of all married couples consider money their chief source of discord. When Daniel P. Sternberg and Ernst G. Beier did a study of conflict in fifty marriages in 1977, they found that newlywed husbands and wives ranked money third in their list of serious interpersonal problems. A year later, both husbands and wives ranked money first. Nineteen seventy-eight was a year in which per capita personal income rose about 10 percent but still did not keep pace with double-digit inflation and high interest rates.

Paradoxically, though, few couples have drastic disagreements over the ranking of basic needs. David J. Rolfe, in 1974, made a survey of 134 engaged couples and found that men and women agreed on the three highest-priority items—

rent, food, and medical insurance—and showed little disagreement in ranking the next seven. This survey, however, took little account of the problems of affluence; it assumed that the couples would be "living on a very low income when . . . first married." This suggests that money quarrels have less to do with disagreements about necessities than about options, not about the mortgage payments and the doctor's bill but about disposable income.

Still, prosperity seems to enhance the success of a marriage—and vice versa. In 1986, Charles M. Schaninger and W. Christian Buss analyzed a number of surveys and concluded that the better the family income, the higher the husband's occupational status, and the greater his employment stability, the more successful the marriage will be. On the other hand, the higher the wife's occupational status and the greater her income is in comparison with her husband's, the more likely that trouble is ahead. More recent studies suggest that husbands are growing somewhat more positive about a wife's career success.

Happily married couples are more likely to buy goods and property than the unhappy. In 1951, Harvey J. Locke reported that people in successful marriages owned more expensive homes and more major appliances of all kinds than those who were later divorced. Subsequent studies indicate that the more stable a marriage is, the more savings and assets a couple will acquire.

The old American adage would seem to be wrong—money can buy happiness. Or at least the two go hand in hand: these surveys seem to tell us that if you are prosperous, you have a good chance for a thriving marriage; if you are poor, you have a good chance to end up divorced. This is not necessarily so. Satisfaction doesn't come from your relative place in the income statistics, it comes from your perception of how adequate your income is to meet your needs. That's an individual judgment based on many things.

Satisfaction also comes from such things as an absence of rivalry in income contribution, a satisfactory sharing of money management, and a sensible way of settling any disputes over money.

The amount of money you have is less relevant to marital happiness than how you manage that money. There are four main systems of family money management according to the British sociologist Jan Pahl: the "whole wage" system in which one partner (usually the wife) manages all household finances; the "allowance" system in which the husband divides responsibility by giving the wife a certain amount for household expenses but keeps control over the rest; the "shared management" system in which partners have equal access to and responsibility for all family money; and the "independent management" system in which each partner manages a separate income exclusively.

In her study of American dual-career couples, Rosanna Hertz found two basic systems of accounting most prevalent: separate and pooled. In her definition, separate accounting means that each of the pair is financially independent but that both share household expenses. When a wife earned as much or more than a husband, they were likely to use separate accounting; when she earned less, they usually pooled resources. Hertz concluded that the adoption of separate accounting often reflects a step toward equalizing marital power.

COUPLES TEND TO AVOID DISCUSSING MONEY ISSUES

One common bit of folk wisdom is that you shouldn't do business with a friend—unless you want to endanger your friendship. As one couple lamented to me, "We thought they were such nice people until we sold them our house—and they probably feel the same way about us."

In marriage, we can't help mixing money with friendship. Sensing what an explosive mixture that can be, most couples are too full of anxiety to talk about it very much. When it does come up, it usually appears at last in the form of an argument full of long-suppressed resentments. My experiences in therapy make me realize that most of us have little skill at mixing money and friendship—and even less ability to confer about it with a spouse.

The inhibition begins in courtship—our idea of romantic love makes us separate it from the subject of money, and we usually go into marriage with only general ideas of what to expect in the way of financial arrangements. That squeamishness is fairly recent. Under the old system of arranged marriages, parents carefully investigated the monetary worth of the bride or bridegroom. And the dowry was fixed by mutual agreement.

For that practical system, we have substituted one of heedlessness during courtship, money battles during a marriage, and bitter and destructive money wars in the divorce court.

WHY MONEY IS SO HARD TO DISCUSS

It is "the last taboo." In 1913, Freud wrote, "Money questions will be treated by cultured people in the same manner as sexual matters, with the same inconsistency, prudishness, and hypocrisy."

One night, the Robinsons took the Atwells out to dinner. The two Robinson children—eight and ten—were included, having been heavily indoctrinated to be on their best behavior. And they were—until the check came. When the waiter laid it down, Billy Robinson turned it over and said in a loud voice, "Wow! Eighty-five dollars!"

The Robinsons were embarrassed because the price tag on their gift, the dinner, had been held up to view. When something becomes a gift, it is no longer supposed to have a market value—it has been transformed into a token of friendship or affection. Revealing the price of a gift is, in most cultures, an injurious mingling of money with friendship.

Billy Robinson, the dinner-party spoiler, was a little too young to have absorbed his parents' constraint about mentioning money openly. Most children, as they grow up, begin to realize that their parents are anxious, defensive, or embarrassed by the subject. The children, in fact, rarely find out how much a parent earns or how large the family income is. Money often becomes, in the child's mind, one of those dark and sensitive secrets that adults keep to themselves.

The psychiatrist David W. Krueger says:

> Parents may establish secrecy as a model for matters associated with money. When income, expenses, and other financial matters are not discussed in the family, there is no opportunity for children to integrate a realistic sense of money. The alternative can be fantasies of desperate poverty or, more commonly, of tremendous, hidden wealth.
>
> The child sees, hears, and senses the parents' attitude towards money: their comfort in dealing with it, the importance, regard, and symbolism they bestow upon it, their ease in talking about it, how obtainable and sufficient it seems to be, and the regard in which parents hold those who have more or less money than themselves. The child fashions attitudes and conclusions from these observations.

The internal taboo is handed down from one generation to another. In a curious way, it may prevent us from thinking clearly and rationally about money problems. We worry about money, of course, and from time to time we have to confront it seriously. We seldom look at the worries behind the worries.

Even though the dark, parental secret has conditioned us not to think about it unless absolutely necessary and not to make it an evident factor in marriage, it is still bound closely to our basic needs and our capacity to love—and therefore we must learn to understand its meanings.

MONEY'S VARIOUS MEANINGS

As we've said, money can be made to represent many abstractions, but we are usually unaware, or only half-aware, of what it signifies to each of us personally. Something of this variety comes to the surface in our common folk sayings. "Time is money," for instance, equates one esteemed American value with another. "The love of money is the root of all evil" goes back to fundamental Christianity, our guilt feelings about acquisitiveness, and our age-old association of poverty with purity of spirit. "If you're so smart, why ain't you rich?" makes the common American assumption (statistically quite true) that intelligent people acquire more money than others.

"Money can't buy happiness" suggests that other values beside wealth are the real satisfactions in life. In typical American fashion, this is answered by, "Maybe money can't buy happiness, but it sure does lessen the pain." Then there is the mortality reminder to the proud and prosperous: "You can't take it with you," which is a note on the ultimate egalitarianism. Finally, we have the conclusive American view: "The lack of money is the root of all evil."

THE MEANINGS CHANGE WITH TIME

As the years go by, couples face new and different financial situations and new interpersonal problems along with them. The first major one is usually buying and furnishing a home or an apartment. Because that means large costs, and since she usually has the greater responsibility for both expenditures and results, the wife takes on most of the emotional burden, but it can be a trying time for both husband and wife. The second crisis of finances, and of nerves, usually comes with the birth of children, and the third about the time children get to be very expensive—that is, in their college years. Finally, there are new problems and conflicts at retirement time, when it is usually the husband who is more troubled by change-of-status and money neuroses.

In these life changes, money can become the scapegoat for many other problems. We externalize our internal conflicts and tie them to money. A man turns down a promising business opportunity because it would "involve too much expense," when he is actually afraid of leaving his safe and familiar job. A woman whose cherished daughter wants to go away to the university protests that it will be too expensive—and the local community college will serve almost as well. In such ways, the lack of money is a wonderful excuse to avoid the decisions we want to avoid and to allay deep worries. That lack can be held up as the workings of Fate—something ordained and irrevocable. And it can give false comfort.

The idea of money is full of ambiguity for many people. It may represent deeply contradictory feelings—a surface current and a deep countercurrent. For example, the Big Spender suddenly feels as if he's overdrawn his account. The wife who has kept within a tight budget for months suddenly splurges on an expensive purchase just to reward herself. A congressional committee considering an appropriations bill amounting to billions spends three days wrangling about cutting back on small, specific items that involve a few thousands. In a marriage, the wife plays the role of a frivolous, impulsive spender and the husband the role of tightfisted guardian of the purse strings. But the truth is they need each other. Without her, he would have nothing to curb. Without him, she would have nothing to transgress. Their quarrel is the balance wheel of their marriage.

Whatever equivocal feelings we may have about money, it still has one or another quite definite equation in most people's minds. If we understand the equals sign—the powerful correlation between money and what it variously means to people—we are beginning to get at the root of money quarrels.

THE MEANINGS OF MONEY

Money = Power

To have all sorts of desirable things, to influence people and events, to control one's destiny—these are the dynamic powers of money. The very rich are fascinating to the rest of the world not because many are exceptional people and not because their life-styles are endlessly interesting. They are fascinating because, as Henry Kissinger is supposed to have said, "Power is an aphrodisiac." Perfectly commonplace beings such as Imelda Marcos, the shah of Iran, and J. Paul Getty excite enormous interest because they seem to be able to do anything they wish—except live forever.

In the small world of a marriage, control over the money—and thus the general weight of authority—has been shifting in recent years. The women's movement and the increasing number of two-income families have made a difference, but not so much as one might suppose. Phillip Blumstein and Pepper Schwartz (in *American Couples*, 1983) found that "the amount of money a person earns—in comparison with a partner's income—establishes relative power." At another point, they say, "In our study, fewer than a quarter of the wives felt it was not important for their husbands to furnish them financial security." Department of Commerce statistics quantify that by showing that, in 1986, over 42 percent of male workers earned more than twenty-five thousand dollars a year and under 18 percent of employed women were in the same income bracket. In the subsequent years, women workers' income has risen faster than men's. Though the money/power relationship between the sexes is shifting toward more equality, the change is slow. One factor that might make it even a little slower is the depressing note from psychiatrist Adriane Berg who says, "Women for whom financial care equals love will see their own financial competence as a disastrous loss of femininity."

All the old, familiar uses of money control appear in marriage just as they do in the larger world—as a stick, as a bribe, as a reward, as a rebuke.

Money = Love

In one sense, money is the adult version of mother's milk—life-sustaining, gratifying, love-bearing. In this way, it carries the meaning of altruism and support. Our currency displays the pictures of men who devoted their lives to their country. In an ironic reversal, the oldest money fable tells the story of King Midas, who, given the power to transform anything to gold with a touch, found that he was choking on his golden food and wine. He was, of course, choking on his self-love and his refusal to share his gift.

In many families, money becomes more than a symbol of love—it is a direct substitute. A parent who can't express the emotion in any other way gives money, or something costly, to show love. The same parent might withhold the same kind of rewards to show anger or rejection. In this way, money acquires the false valence of love. Children of the marriage eventually—often years later—learn that the substitution is a sham, and after that realization comes emptiness, depression, and resentment.

Money cannot buy love, but the longer I work with couples who have money problems, the more I realize that the capacity to manage both money and the emotions surrounding it is closely related to the capacity for love. This includes mature giving and receiving, the balancing of needs, and the ability to look at matters from another's viewpoint. A financially balanced budget and an emotionally balanced budget are great supports for each other.

Money = Self-Esteem

From money as power, it follows that money is also identified with competence, success, self-esteem. *New York* magazine and others are fond of giving us articles that list incomes of real people, from the left fielder who makes a million dollars a year to the cleaning woman who makes seventy-two hundred. From it, we can discover where we fit in as true Americans.

Successful acquisitors are often people driven by narcissism, which is responsible for the spectacle of the multimillionaire who is still striving to get more millions. He is constantly trying to reassure himself of his own personal value by accumulating the world's valuables. Seeing his yacht, his stretch limousine, his rating in Dun and Bradstreet, others will realize how important he is and will pay him the honor he most wants—envy. This type includes more than the very rich, of course, and his cousin on Main Street or at Shady Hill Mall will be doing the same thing for smaller stakes.

A more destructive variant of this is the compulsive spender, who tries to banish his anxiety by spending, in the way many people eat or drink compulsively. His self-indulgence is a way of nurturing his shaky self-esteem. Often, he gets no real pleasure from what he buys—the pleasure lies in the public display. It is the psychic equivalent of lighting a cigar with a twenty-dollar bill.

Money = Independence

To have enough money is to be one's own man or one's own woman, a free agent. On the other hand, if one has that kind of money and yet surrenders control of the purse strings, it can be the sign of an undesirable dependency. If, for example, a wife leaves all the financial decisions to her husband, that may be her way of prolonging the dependency she once had on her father—in effect, she is renouncing money responsibility and asking someone "older and wiser" to tell her what to do.

For many people, a sense of financial independence translates into a freedom from having to make friends or allies— "Because I have money, I don't have to pretend to like you. I can get what I want without that." Money allows one to be impersonal, and being impersonal keeps one free, they assume.

Donald Regan, chief executive officer of the largest brokerage firm on Wall Street, became President Reagan's White House chief of staff. When the appointment was about to be announced, he told the president, "I've got something these other guys (James Baker, Meese, and Deaver) haven't got. I've got fuck-you money. Anytime I want, I'm gone."

A more extreme example of this—in the words of Dr. David Krueger—is the person who "avoids responsibility, schedules, and demands—anything that restricts independence. He may see money as the currency of freedom, its acquisition ensuring future autonomy." While he is obsessed by the idea of autonomy, he is actually afraid of it.

The passion for independence can operate in less arrogant and more beneficial ways as well. As Rosanna Hertz points out in *More Equal than Others*, in dual-career marriages, a woman with a good income of her own—or even marketable skills—doesn't have to tolerate a failed relationship. The new earning power of women gives them independence and freedom of choice as never before.

Money = Time
Especially in America, we endorse the idea that "time is money." We say that we can't "spend the time" or "can't

afford the time," or ask, "Don't you realize my time is valuable?"

Most of us are paid according to the amount of time spent on the job—not according to the profit-producing or societal value of the work accomplished.

In many marriages, there is a money = time = love equation that can be quite negative. The husband—or, in dual-career marriages, both husband and wife—is working hard to make money. Thus, he can't afford the time to be the friend/companion/lover his wife wishes for. In effect, he is withholding time and therefore denying love.

A variation on this is the rich or prosperous man who has given up on his marriage and prefers to spend much of his time away from home. To compensate, he furnishes her with a generous allowance, gives her an expensive house, and pays her large bills without complaint. He is, of course, paying her off in dollars because he cannot give time or love.

There is another equation of money with time—in a peculiar way—in the case of people who amass money with the wish to perpetuate their names and their presences through time to come. Inheritances to children and grandchildren, endowed chairs in universities with the name attached, buildings with the name carved in stone above the doorway, are attempts to buy immortality.

Money = Masculinity
Significantly, there are no women's faces on American coins or banknotes. Miss Liberty is gone, and the Susan B. Anthony silver dollar was disastrously unpopular. In this country, the man has always earned the paycheck, paid the rent and the food bill, owned the house, dealt with the bank, invested in the stock market, or made fiscal policy in Congress. On a date, the man usually pays the restaurant check, although the custom is less rigid than it used to be. If the woman pays, she may slip him the money under the table.

Now, even with women well established in the work and business world, the husband's income is still perceived as the mainstay of the family. This comes from a deeply in-grained psychological bias that money is somehow a masculine possession. It can be delegated to, loaned to, given to, bequeathed to, a woman, but it is never truly hers.

Money = Corruption

Ever since the Bible gave it a bad name, money has had the taint of worldliness, base motives, shady behavior, and compromised ideals. Most people enjoy the downfall of characters like Ivan Boesky just as their ancestors enjoyed medieval morality plays.

The opposite stereotype is the idealist/ascetic, whom Americans admire, rarely choose as a role-model, and usually find somewhat awkward to deal with. Nuns and monks, relief workers, Peace Corps volunteers, missionaries, and public defenders are anomalies in a materialistic society. Along with these sincere people, there is a type that Edward M. Hallowell calls "pseudo-ascetics" in his book *What Are You Worth?* He says, "Money (for this kind of person) may be a forbidden fruit. His desire for it is so wrapped up in guilt and shame that he has to pretend that he doesn't want it at all. He is so ashamed of the part of him that wants money that he hides it, showing people only a disdain for money, the attitude that it doesn't matter." The generalized feeling that money is somehow contaminated and demeaning is one of the reasons couples find it so hard to discuss and why money quarrels can turn into silent cold wars.

One explanation for that sense of "contamination" would be that we feel guilt about money and are insecure about our own virtue in regard to money. Then we try to transfer the guilt and put others in the wrong by calling their motives tainted. By washing our hands of any direct connection with money, we are trying to cleanse our souls, as well.

Money = Transformation

In our contradictory selves, we also have the deep-seated feeling that money contains magic. If we won some great lottery, we could transform our situations, our personalities, our lives, into something new and rewarding.

We also tend to feel that such magic is too good to be true. The story of Doctor Faustus—who sold his soul for enormous riches and power and eventually had to pay the price—dramatizes that feeling. There are, as well, the many folktales based on the situation of a man (or a man and his wife) being granted three magic wishes. After they have gained moderate wealth on the first and second wish, they overreach on the third wish and have it all taken away. The meaning is always that wealth *can* appear magically, but always temporarily—and its disappearance leaves people worse off than before.

A marriage can be damaged if one partner—or both—is possessed by the idea that money can transmute a base life into a precious one. It is like staking the rest of your life on the caprice of the roulette ball.

Money can, for some people, become a fetish to replace human relationships, or, like the gold coin gentlemen used to carry on their watch chains, a charm to ward off evil.

Money = "Action"

By constantly walking on the edge, the compulsive gambler believes he transforms a dull life into a vivid one. Regardless of whether he wins or loses, he is only happy when he is at risk. While he keeps the adrenaline pumping, all the things he doesn't want to think about can be pushed out of mind.

Few people are so totally addicted, but this attribute of money as risk-taking is present in many of our transactions. We may not gamble compulsively or for large stakes, but we do it as willfully as the compulsive gambler. People have different levels of risk acceptance, and the marriage of a thrill-seeker with a security-seeker is bound to result in trouble.

Money = Gifts

There is a protocol for giving others gifts of money. Most people (unless they are bribing or paying off somebody) are reluctant to hand over substantial checks or envelopes full of bank notes. Some root-of-all-evil stain is on such a gift. Instead, money passes in the sterilized forms of bequests, trust funds, bank transfers, gift certificates, or objects with price tags carefully removed. Thus, we find a cutout so that money, or value, passes in a more innocent form.

Love, affection, respect, honor—these are the good gift motives. Paying off, buying influence or love, erasing guilt—these are the bad-motive gifts. There are even examples of some gifts intended to embarrass or humiliate. In his book *The Gift*, Lewis Hyde says, "Gift exchange is an erotic commerce, joining self and other," and elsewhere he adds, "When either the donor or the recipient begins to treat a gift in terms of obligation, it ceases to be a gift . . . and the emotional bond, along with the power, evaporates immediately."

DEALING WITH MONEY ISSUES

Acknowledge Your Anxieties

The first step is to examine how each of you usually responds to money problems. Perhaps one or both of you tends to micromanage an obligation or difficulty, dealing with it in laborious and unnecessary detail. One woman I knew received an IRS communication challenging three deductions on a past year's income tax. Instead of furnishing a simple answer by mail, she reviewed the couple's entire tax records for the year, compiled a portfolio of information, and demanded a hearing in the United States tax court.

A money problem, in contrast, may seem so tiresome and confusing that you don't even want to think about it and you'll accept the first means of escape that occurs to you, whether or not it seems to make much sense. Perhaps you never mention the subject of money between you. Or perhaps it seems to keep coming up all the time. These are flashing signals of anxiety. First of all, you must acknowledge them.

Forgive Each Other's Money Hang-ups

Achieving a mature attitude toward money is a major psychological challenge. For instance, you know that you have hang-ups about money—you've made that first step of realization—but, on the other side, he or she always seems irrational about the subject in his/her own way. As you understand it, the problem is learning to deal with money in a nonneurotic manner, viewing money as numbers rather than as a fear or a hope. You want to be as cool as a bank teller. The trouble is that no one can be dispassionate about his or her own money.

Finding a way to handle money without many neuroses takes some doing, especially in a culture that is driven by it. Our concept of money has a strong element of domination—and thus women and men have a profound psychological resistance to collaborating equally on money concerns. Establishing mature and unemotional teamwork on finances is quite as delicate a matter as establishing an emotionally mature sexual relationship. It doesn't come naturally. It is the result of communication, hard work, mutual problem-solving, and a capacity to change one's mind. The first step is one of attitude—the couple who can decide to be forgiving toward each other and to feel less shame about admitting to money apprehension are on the right road.

Don't Let Issues Go Long Without Discussion

Usually, by the time a couple has been able to summon up resolve to talk about a troublesome money issue, one or both is so angry that it's hard to have a productive discussion. Don't let hostility build up; talk about the problem as soon as possible.

Define Personal Money Styles

Psychiatrist Edward M. Hallowell, in *What Are You Worth?*, describes four different kinds of "money styles":

The spenders, who seek action and freedom in money
The skeptics, who want security and control
The enthusiasts, who look for power, freedom, and self-esteem
The underinvolved, who derive only anxiety and dependency from money.

These categories are useful for distinguishing your own association with money. For example, if you had a windfall, would your first thought be to buy security in the form of insurance, savings, or investment with it? What sort of money risks are you likely to take, and how high are the stakes you can live with? Having considerable money brings with it what sort of social responsibilities? What would you consider reasonable perks and what mere conspicuous consumption? What ethical compromises would you be willing to make in order to get a great deal of money?

Once a couple has a good fix on their "style," or different styles, they can proceed to collaborate on a list of their priorities.

MONEY QUARRELS AND HOW TO HANDLE THEM

Unspoken Contracts and Secret Bargains

Couples frequently make covert bargains—a present sacrifice for future repayment. Barbara and Bob were a good example of that—she worked as a secretary in the office of a lumber-yard in order to keep the family afloat while Bob went to graduate school for his MBA. She hated the job. They never really discussed it, but Barbara thought they had an under-standing that once Bob had his degree, she would quit work and have a child. When that time came, Bob had different ideas. He didn't mind if she quit her job, but as for a baby—he wasn't ready for that development just yet. And so the unspoken bargain had turned out to be no more than Bar-bara's wrong inference or Bob's wrong implication.

Every couple has at least one tacit agreement or trade-off in their lives. It is most often the ones that involve money that are left to implication or only vaguely discussed. This comes partly from that reluctance to speak frankly about money and partly from a fear of committing important sums in ad-vance of some still-hypothetical event. Here are some repre-sentative IOUs of family life:

He agreed to buy a house in the suburbs even though he much prefers an apartment in the city. The decision means a long daily commute for him and two hours less leisure time every day.

She has made sacrifices on behalf of his family. When his mother was bedridden with an illness, his wife took a leave from her job in order to help out. His unemployed brother came to live with them for nearly a year. Part of their joint income goes to his mother.

Although they couldn't really afford a second car, he bought one for her and took a moonlighting job in order to keep up the payments.

Some of these IOUs may never be called in; others may await recompense for years; some may not be consciously recognized as debts by the recipient. In any of these cases, they are potential dangers at some future point. A marriage, like a good set of accounts, has to be reckoned up from time to time so that the partners are clear about what obligations each thinks the other owes.

First, the couple must lay out all the IOUs each holds from the other. That will usually produce some surprises. The list may even seem to indicate that one person holds most of the IOUs and has had little in return. There may be some barely apparent quid pro quos—perhaps masochistic ones—that have to be searched for. Exploring all of the unspoken contracts requires the help of a therapist.

Recognize Different Values
Obviously, we all put different values on the things that money can buy—security, freedom, pleasure, prestige, or love. When couples quarrel about specific expenditures, they seldom realize that they aren't arguing about things but about differing values.

Marcia married John and they live in Connecticut, but she grew up in Oregon and all her friends and family are there. Keeping in close touch is emotionally important to her. Every month, the long-distance charges on the phone bill make John furious.

John has his own weakness. He loves music and has spent years—encouraged by the manufacturers of expensive speaker systems, hi-fi, stereo, tape decks, and CD players—trying to find the perfectly pure sound. Marcia, who doesn't mind hearing a little soft rock now and then and who would be perfectly content with a small radio, can't understand John's outlay for this expensive equipment, especially when it's always being superseded by something new. He accuses her of "telephonitis," and she reproaches him for "gadget frenzy."

They are, of course, arguing about something beyond the

cost of sound systems or the AT&T bill. Marcia trades money for emotional security, warm understanding, a connection with her roots. John buys himself a reward for his hard work at the office. Listening to music is his way of freeing himself from tension and frustrations. Their problem is not a scarcity of money or, as each thinks, a foolish outlay of money, but a failure to understand what it is she uses to sustain herself emotionally and what he uses to soothe himself.

Control the Overtime Compulsion

One of the best-known American types is the workaholic, money-acquisitive husband. Now that more women are in business and the professions, some of them are beginning to acquire the disorder. The moral of the case is that it's impossible to have a real relationship with a workaholic. He or she is constantly gaining symbolic wealth in the form of self-reassurance but is unable to spend it in the form of love and reassurance. The trouble is that this usually seems to be an accelerating process. The more successful a workaholic becomes, the harder he or she works, the less time there is for anything but work. The more criticism the workaholic gets for that, the more withdrawal into his/her work.

Harvey is a market analyst in a Manhattan economics institute, and his wife, Jean, is an editor in the trade department of a New York publishing house. When they first began living together, in 1981, he was in graduate school and she was an editorial assistant—in those days they both took long hours and constant work for granted, but somehow they made time to be together.

Seven years later, Jean finds that she sees less and less of her husband. He works even longer hours, frequently stays late for meetings, and, when he's home, catches up with paperwork in his downstairs office. She feels abandoned and indignant. She often thinks of divorce. He tells her she's overreacting—he wants to be a good provider and to have a few luxuries as well.

Harvey's compulsion was planted early in life. His father was an alcoholic salesman, often unemployed, who gave scanty support to a wife and four children. Since he was quite young, Harvey has been trying to prove to the world how responsible he is.

In contrast, Jean came from a well-to-do New Jersey family. Her father never put in an hour of overtime, and there were no money worries. At about the age of nine, Jean suffered from a severe illness and spent a long time in the hospital and subsequent months in a health sanitarium recuperating. This meant a prolonged separation from her mother, who was emotionally as well as physically distant. A six-figure income means a lot less to her than it does to Harvey—but deep in her memory is the sense of abandonment by someone she loved.

The overtime compulsion is especially hard to moderate or change because, as we've suggested, workaholics/money addicts are, without realizing it, striving against their anxieties. If money suddenly became worthless and work no longer accomplished anything, they would still go on accumulating bank notes and laboring overtime. Even when they can be brought to realize the truth, it is extremely hard for them to give up this means of dealing with their peculiar kind of stress.

Realization is the beginning of liberation. If workaholics can absorb the lesson that working twenty-four hours a day and a hundred billion dollars in the bank will never rid them of their self-doubts, there is some hope. The lesson will stick only if they understand the emotional force that drives them to work ever harder. It might be their desire to emulate a parental model; it might be a desire to differentiate from a parental model; or it might be a constant seeking for reassurance as to their competence. The next step in therapy is to get them to redirect their focus from the external solution of money/work to inner satisfactions.

The greatest truth they must discover, however, is that time is more precious than money.

Define the Two Roles

The man brings home the paycheck, and the woman controls the household finances—that has long been the simple, traditional division of money responsibilities. Most dual-career couples, seeking better management efficiency, break the assignments down into more logical parts—according to competence. Perhaps he has a good accounting background, so he would keep the books. Or she has worked in a brokerage house, so she oversees family savings and investments. Because he knows a lot about cars, buying one is his sole responsibility. Or she has a good background in legal matters, and thus she handles property purchases and any necessary dealing with lawyers.

This is productive role specialization, and it is something clearly agreed on. Detrimental role specialization is agreed on only implicitly, and it appeals to a couple's weaknesses rather than their strengths. This was the case in the unhappy bargain between Carol and Sy, in which Carol traded off her individuality in return for his economic support, and Sy enjoyed having control but felt martyred by having to be the sole mainstay of the family.

Another root for the money quarrel is something that might be called "pseudo-authorization." For example, the husband gives his wife ostensible control over the checking account but constantly finds fault with the way she manages it. In an oblique way, he is expressing the thought, you are incompetent; you can't be trusted.

There is a difference between entrusting a responsibility to someone and copping out. If a husband asks his wife to handle some part—or all—of the family finances because he knows she is shrewd with money, he is saying simply, "I trust you." If he asks the same thing of her because he thinks budgets and bookkeeping make a boring job only fit for a clerk, he is copping out.

In contrast, a woman's cop-out is usually for other reasons. One common pattern I find is that of a woman who avoids financial responsibility because she really wants to put a father surrogate in control of that part of her life or she senses that her husband cannot tolerate her acting as his equal. She then feels loved, secure, taken care of.

Whenever there are conflicting ideas about roles—a wife might suspect that her husband is undermining hers or he might suspect that she is encroaching on his turf—there is bound to be trouble in the marriage. On the premise of "You haven't kept your part of the bargain, so okay, I won't keep mine," people often turn deceptive. The traditional example is that of the wife who disguises her luxury shopping bills somewhere in the household budget.

Couples usually arrive at a balance of roles sooner or later, but they should then stop to examine what that really means. They should ask themselves whether they have produced this stability out of matching strengths or matching weaknesses. If, for example, he is the big spender and she the saver, they fight over the way they allocate their income. They know they are going to fight because it has become a part of their marriage routine. And the fights have a strange kind of usefulness. They are a psychic rationalization for the pair's ambivalent feelings about saving and spending.

Cop-outs, passive resistance, ritual battles, undermining, thoughtless patterns of behavior—these are the attitudes that make for a precarious balance of roles. As I have suggested, the better way is for a couple to examine the question and to make conscious choices about how their roles should complement each other. What should come out of this is a real-

THE SEVEN BASIC QUARRELS OF MARRIAGE

istic dovetailing of roles—each one does the part of the money chore that he or she is good at; furthermore, they agree that they will take any truly formidable problems to a professional financial consultant.

Sharing Versus Keeping It Separate

A common treasury or separate accounting? This is one of the first questions couples have to face, and the decision involves some of the emotional issues of the marriage pact.

Pooling all income has some advantages, but what if one partner, let us say she, feels that she is giving up some of her hard-won independence? No joint accounting, she says. To him, her refusal reads in a different way. He's seeing her message as, I'm still suspending judgment on this marriage, and I don't want to commit everything until I know if it's going to work.

The two systems of finance will reflect the agreed-on systems of the marriage: the traditional pact is heavy on mutual trust, sharing, a complete merger of interests; the egalitarian pact emphasizes an alliance of individuals with freedom of choice in many areas.

Rosanna Hertz in *More Equal than Others* quotes one wife who says:

> If somebody wants to go out and buy something really stupid—and we all do that—why should the other partner be upset by it? And the only reason they are is when it's *their* money going into it. So if you work it out this way [meaning separate accounting systems], he can do what he wants and he feels better about it, and I can buy what I want.

Hertz also notes that some couples have three accounts—two separate and one joint—with elaborate tests for determining who pays for what and what is to be split.

Some dual-career couples prefer entirely separate accounts, as do quite a few wives who have unearned income of their own. Whatever way serves to minimize conflict is a good way. There is, for example, that first-of-the-month moment when the checks get written—occasion for a regularly scheduled fight in some families. Perhaps that occasion can be dropped from the agenda. As one woman told me:

> He knows I spend more money than he wants me to on clothes and, in fact, we've roughly budgeted what it should be. But by our labeling that as my money, I don't have to consult him and he doesn't even have to see the bills. We've eliminated that regular source or irritation and minimized how much we fight about it.

A couple's roles should complement each other and dovetail—that is true, but people should also allow for a certain self-determination in financial matters. However it may work out in detail, whether through separate accounts at the bank or budget apportionment, the principle is important to observe in practical ways.

For one thing, the psychological benefits of being nonaccountable at times are subtle but real. Every marriage should have a certain amount of privacy in it—privacy from second-guessing and criticism. She should have her own authority to buy that too-expensive coat. He should be able to make some bets in a poker game without being scolded if he should lose. The instances themselves are not important—the agreed-on financial privacy is.

One of my clients gave me another interesting reason for having that area of separateness. He said that it gave him the power to buy a real gift for his wife. To use some of their pooled money would somehow depreciate the gift; to buy it from his own resources made it genuine.

Make a Treaty over Money and Power

The more money one partner contributes to the family income, the more relative power he or she will have in the marriage. That seems to be a well-established fact. The first power decision in marriage is most important, and it comes early: who sets the priorities and makes the policy? This should not be left to chance or drift; it should be negotiated and firmly understood. That is the only way that the partner in the weaker position (usually the woman) can get any recognized voice in financial decision making. And it is the only fair basis on which later and lesser money negotiations can take place. When the woman in my previous example got her husband to agree on a clothes budget over which she'd have sole discretion, she was establishing policy.

Of course, there are financial decisions that belong properly to him and others that belong properly to her and, in between, the ones that clearly ought to be mutual. The big money decisions American middle-class families make in the course of a lifetime are: buying a house, a cooperative apartment, or a condominium; building a capital reserve in savings or investment; educating the children; revising the financial plan when something drastic happens (severe illness, death of one partner, divorce, retirement, etc.); and bequeathing the estate. These decisions should be mutual, and they should be decided on well in advance at family summit conferences.

Working-class families will have roughly the same problems, accentuated by the facts that they have smaller incomes and less financial cushion. Decisions, therefore, are usually dictated by necessity—these families don't have the same choices about house-buying, investment, or education.

Breaking the silence, negotiating openly, and arriving at understandings remove unhealthy secrecy and a temptation to make power plays from the money question. This is the difference between diplomacy and war.

Confront Problems in Giving, Receiving, and Sharing

Reciprocity—or lack of it—can be another area of trouble. There is the familiar type who guards his or her property jealously, gives grudgingly, and is always sharp-eyed to find somebody else cheating him/her, even by a penny. His/her nearest relative is the person who lives by the maxim "What's mine is mine; what's yours is negotiable." Both of these need special handling.

Then there is the natural socialist, the born sharer who seems to have no sense of private property at all. He or she will not only give away his/her own belongings but will wear your sweaters, lend your books to mere acquaintances, give your coin collection to the kids, or hand over your carefully maintained car to a teenage driver.

They should not marry each other.

These are extremes, of course, but most of us have something of one or the other in our natures. The healthy arrangement any couple should come to is a "line of credit," a store of goodwill, about borrowing, gift-giving, or sharing anything of value. This line of credit is based on the confidence that if he gets the bigger slice of pie on one occasion, she will eventually get her turn, and things will always even out.

Actual gifts are a special subdivision of the problem. As we noted previously, giving has its ethics; there are good-motive gifts and bad-motive gifts. A shrewd scrutiny of motive will reveal which kind any particular gift might be. The objects themselves are of little importance, but the kind of reciprocity and thoughtfulness in marriage that they symbolize is all-important. One of the moral points made by folktales from the earliest times is that any gift is useless, even harmful, if the recipient refuses to share it. Good marriages are constant exchanges—of love, companionship, caring, trust, fidelity, pleasures, ideas, humor, and many other things. All are given freely and without ulterior motives.

Quarrels come when the exchanges are meager and grudging or when the purpose behind the gift is self-serving. In an interview, Rosanna Hertz made the point that in their various transactions about money, couples are usually trying to arrive at some equitable outcome. If that does not happen, and if one or both feels unfairly treated, the basic money quarrel will go on endlessly. Hertz points out that couples usually don't decide what is fair or equitable on the basis of dollar value. They are interested in balancing "what I really want" against "what you really want."

Reconcile Not Having Enough or Having Too Much

For people above the poverty line, having enough money is largely a subjective matter. Most of us seem to fall short of what we'd like to have or think we could use. This can be a good stimulus if we're on an upward income track. If, as a couple, we've reached the point of diminishing returns and lessening prospects, however, the shortfall can be depressing and the relationship is usually under stress.

In this world of dissatisfactions, affluence can be difficult as well. Nick and Polly are a good example of it. They both came from blue-collar families with conservative ideas about money and limited aspirations. Nick first worked in a factory, later as an auto mechanic; he was not very successful. Then, in an odd twist of his fortunes, he took a course and became a real estate salesman—and, as it turned out, a highly successful one. Suddenly, the family income doubled, and then doubled again.

Nick bought a BMW and began shopping at Brooks Brothers for his suits. After a couple of years, he bought a new house with a swimming pool. He was exuberant. You could almost see the sign on his lapel that read, "Look! I've made it!" After years of failure and self-doubt, he was now a different man.

All this made Polly extremely nervous. Her guilt feelings operated overtime. She had come from a family with seven children where everything had to be strictly rationed—you even shared your ice-cream cone with your sisters. Her mother bought clothes that would wear well, wouldn't show the dirt, and could be handed down to the next kid. The BMW, the swimming pool, silk shirts, and expensive suits struck Polly as crazy extravagance—and she didn't hesitate to give Nick a hard time about them.

Nick forgot to give her a present on their tenth wedding anniversary. The question that came back to her again and again was, "How can he spend so much money on flashy things but never give me anything of himself?"

No one can really furnish an answer to "How much is enough?" because it is not so much a question as a subjective problem for each person. The only way to handle it is to go to the root of the matter. A couple should reexamine their whole set of preconceptions about what their marriage economy should be like. What is really essential to their happiness and what can be foregone? What goals are reasonable and expectable and what goals are castles in Spain? Once they understand each other on these grounds, they will not have to worry about "How much is enough?"

Don't Avoid Responsibility

Some people can never decide how to decide. They are unwilling to define their own financial functions and even unwilling to take responsibility for their reluctance. By default, one member of a couple takes to writing the checks and the other complains about being left out. Nobody has made a conscious choice; both have avoided any negotiation on the matter; each hates his/her own role but doesn't want to take on the other's. Dr. Turkel comments that some people are so afraid of acting independently that they are incapable of making decisions or accepting responsibility. Whenever they have to take some action having to do with money, they either try to pass the responsibility on to another person or else make a mess of the matter so that someone else will come to their rescue.

The couple in this predicament have never agreed on any guidelines; they never discuss; they go eternally from argument to argument. Those arguments are settled simply by one of them giving in, not for any logical reason but just to restore peace. They constantly wish that financial problems would just go away.

Their muddle very likely comes from a general inability to decide any difficult issue—emphasized by the fact that they have a particular distaste for money questions. First of all, they have to find within themselves some means of coming to a verdict, and, along with that, they must make an effort to educate themselves about family money problems and solutions.

Finesse Money Entanglements
A couple's financial issues aren't, of course, limited to those of paycheck, budget, and monthly bills. Almost everyone has further involvements of various kinds. One couple may be engaged in a lawsuit; their next-door neighbors await an inheritance; their friends across the street are repaying a loan from her parents; the couple on the corner are buying a business franchise. Some of these involvements will turn out well and others badly, but even catastrophes can be survived if the fate of the marriage is not inextricably bound to the fate of outside events.

I remember Vincent's sad story, unfortunately a fairly common one. He had built a shopping mall in a neighborhood where many new apartment developments were projected and had overextended his finances. The developments were slow in getting started, and Vincent had fewer leases than he'd counted on. He secretly took out a second mortgage on his house, borrowed money first from friends and then from his father-in-law, and exhausted all his resources. Nothing worked. Finally, he had to file for bankruptcy.

Maria, his wife, had stuck with him loyally for a long time, despite doubts about the enterprise. As things grew worse and Vincent stubbornly refused to admit it, they quarreled more and more often. She accused him of gambling with their money—and her father's as well—and he accused her of being disloyal. When bankruptcy became inevitable, the marriage was emotionally bankrupt as well.

Vincent had made the mistake not only of annexing assets in which Maria had a legitimate share but also in violating her allegiance to her father. He had, in effect, robbed his own family and so intermingled his marriage with his project that the failure of one destroyed the other.

In an article titled "Emotional Mortgage," Raymond J. Sauer gives an example of another kind of money-family complication. He describes a family of six who lived rent-free in a house divided into two apartments and owned by the husband's mother. The mother kept the telephone in her own name, but the couple had an extension in their bedroom.

In the course of time, the couple spent thousands of dollars remodeling the apartment house in hopes—but with no guarantee—that it would be theirs some day. The husband had asked his mother about this a number of times, but she had always answered vaguely, without committing herself. The husband's brother, supposedly his mother's favorite son, was the question mark in the matter. It was a good guess as to whether she would do right by the couple or leave the house to the brother.

From her vantage point on the first floor, the mother controlled the family upstairs. When they got a telephone call, she monitored it. She enlisted one of the children to inform on his parents. The wife hesitated to spank any of the children for fear of what her mother-in-law would say. This woman had become an awesome figure by virtue of the emotional mortgage she held, and the couple had no idea how to deal with the situation.

Sauer comments:

> The real purpose of such arrangements is continuation of tight parental control over and involvement with a married child after he [or she] has left the family of origin. Vagueness of the contract and hope that parents will eventually give the property to them drives the couple to extreme submissiveness and emotional enslavement. They do not seem to realize that [they are paying a price] in terms of human freedom and independence.

I have never encountered a case quite so extreme, but there are many lesser examples of the ties that bind too tightly when parents give gifts or dangle inheritances.

This is, of course, another one of those problems that comes from family-of-origin loyalties, and the advice about freeing oneself from the effects of the loyalties that handicap is appropriate here.

To recapitulate, I suggest five guidelines to avert or defuse a basic quarrel over money:

1. Break the Code of Secrecy but not of Privacy

Secrecy about money matters may protect people from anxiety, but in the end is no guarantee of security or satisfaction. Money secrets are often dangerous secrets. Even if they are less than dangerous, they create an area of darkness in a marriage, leaving certain habits and preconceptions unknown and unaddressed.

Privacy is a different matter. It provides for a discretionary use of certain money without question or interference from

husband or wife—and it is useful as a way to avert unnecessary quarrels over details. Secrecy is like a numbered Swiss
bank account, all knowledge of which you keep to yourself.
Privacy is like an ordinary checking account in a local bank—
your husband or wife is aware of it and how it is used but, by
agreement, can't draw money from it.

2. Identify Each Person's Values and Hang-ups About Money and How They Interact

For example, when a big spender and a tightwad are married
to each other and constantly quarrel about money, they may
not realize that they are having a checks-and-balances quarrel, a productive quarrel. This situation could escalate, however, with the risk-taker baiting the security-seeker again
and again and the security-seeker reacting by exerting more
and more control.

Another precarious situation is when one partner demands total control over money matters and the other gladly
concedes in order to escape responsibility.

3. Conduct Financial Affairs on a True Partnership Basis

This implies that decisions are mutual and are freely arrived
at, that each person has rights and responsibilities of equal
weight.

4. Insist on Fairness

Nickel-and-dime quarrels degrade marriage, but sorting out
principles of what's fair and what isn't in money matters is a
first priority. Making sure that each ends up with some acceptable measure of what he or she really wants is the goal.

5. Ask Professional Advice

A couple is in trouble when they won't seek consultation
with a professional. When they do their own tax returns,
work out their own financial plan, or avoid seeing a therapist

about a basic money quarrel, they are taking chances with their marriage. The more immune they are to outside thinking and advice, the more likely they are to be unrealistic and inflexible in their ideas about money.

The malice can be taken out of money questions by acting on these five points and by stripping away the ostensible dollars-and-cents reasons for trouble in order to find the true source of the anger and anxiety.

CHAPTER FIVE

POWER

On May 1, 1988, Bob Sullivan retired after thirty years as a pilot for a major airline. On May 6, he took delivery on a luxurious new Bluebird camper. On May 10, his neighbors in Kansas City gave a backyard-barbecue retirement party for Bob and his wife Elizabeth. Everybody said how wonderful it was that they could spend some real time together after all these years of semiseparation Bob's schedule had dictated. They were off for their long-anticipated trip west. They smiled happily as they waved good-bye and set off in the gleaming Bluebird.

That mood lasted just about twenty-four hours. The first rift came over the itinerary. Bob had decided they should go south after Denver—Mesa Verde National Park, the Grand Canyon, Las Vegas, and Los Angeles. Liz thought that it was much more exciting to go by way of Aspen, Salt Lake City, Lake Tahoe, and San Francisco. Since they had several hundred miles to argue about it, they didn't decide right away.

The next difference of opinion came over Bob's driving. She thought it was a little too fast and reckless. She wanted to take over at least half the time. Bob said, for God's sake, he'd been bossing a lot bigger machines than this for thirty years. None of his other passengers had criticized him.

Then it was the choice of overnight halting places—she always wanted to look for a regular camper park; he preferred any convenient location off the highway. She wanted to have dinner in restaurants, at least sometimes; he thought that was a waste of time and money when they had perfectly good cooking facilities in the Bluebird.

And so it went—push and shove, one argument after the other until each of them began to wonder what had happened to their successful marriage, let alone their second honeymoon.

They were caught in a quarrel they hadn't anticipated. It had been dormant over the years largely because the Sullivans had divided family power between them in a pragmatic way. Bob brought home a good paycheck and handled the finances and investments. Liz managed the household efficiently, brought up the children, and took care of the civic and social duties. (She had served, variously, as president of the school PTA, chairwoman of the neighborhood association, and as a member of the Republican party state committee.)

Bob was used to being captain of his plane; Liz was used to being chief executive of the household and a community leader. He wasn't used to having his judgment questioned, and she had a habit of being in charge. Until they got into their camper and headed west, they'd never had to work out authority-sharing in the same arena—until now.

The Sullivans, like a great many American couples, found themselves locked into one version of the power quarrel. Our uses of power, the ways we assert it or decline it, the bargains we make in sharing it, how it shapes the whole history of our marriages, are crucial matters. As Phyllis Rose, author of *Parallel Lives*, says, "Marriages go bad not when love fades—love can modulate into affection without driving two people apart—but when this understanding about the balance of power breaks down, when the weaker member feels exploited or the stronger feels unrewarded for his or her strength."

Power is not a simple word. It has many sides and many shades of meaning. Those include our sense of mastery in a situation, our feelings of security or vulnerability, the degree of control we have over another person, or ourselves, and the amount of weight we carry in making decisions or fixing on goals. Having power not only helps us to make things work the way we want them to but gives us the inner reassurance of command.

Power relationships in the world at large are something most of us can perceive, at least in their general outlines—policy debates between the two parties in Congress, competition between big companies, international rivalries. And there is an important connection between the public world of power and the private one of marriage. As Phyllis Rose says, "On the basis of family life, we form our expectations about power and powerlessness, about authority and obedience in other spheres, and in that sense, the family is . . . the building block of society." There is, nevertheless, an important difference of quality. In personal relationships, power operates in many more subtle, more emotional, and more covert ways.

We are most sharply aware of power issues in the ways couples deal with money and sex, but those issues underlie all other transactions of married life as well. Our inklings of that are expressed in such common phrases as, "He's a henpecked husband," or "He's got her wrapped around his finger," or "She wears the pants in the family."

If you look at any marriage closely enough, you will see a number of power clues in names: A woman doesn't take on her husband's last name but keeps on using her maiden name. Another woman insists on a hyphenated family name

(Mr. and Mrs. Smith-Jones). A husband insists on keeping the house, the beach cottage, and the investments in his name alone. Or, she requests a joint checking account with both their names on the checks.

There are a myriad of other signs and hints: who settled on what kind of birth control they would use, who decided on the car to buy, who chooses whether they'll go to *The Magic Flute* or the wrestling matches, who always interrupts whom, who metes out punishment when Billy or Susie merit it, who balances the checkbook, who is more active in choosing their friends, and so on.

Many of the couples who come to my office for therapy have a major problem with power, and, as usual in basic quarrels, they are far less concerned with what they seem to be fighting about than about "giving in." They usually lament the fact that their quarrel seems to be a kind of circular madness; they have gone around again and again until they have lost hope of escaping it. At the same time, they haven't given up some vague hope of winning—often, one or the other will try to enlist me on his or her side, either subtly or overtly. When this happens, I can deduce the kind of power manipulations that must go on in that marriage.

It is likely that neither of these people could say what the stakes are, what there is to be won. They feel powerless to change. The only power they have at their command is destructive power—to deny something to the other, to wound, to interfere. Those are costly tactics.

My first effort is to get them to look carefully at their conceptions of power, and at the ways it has been operating to harm their relationship. Since all of us have had our power encounters—and have been either bruised or benefited by them—we tend to think that everybody agrees on what power is and how it works, but that isn't true. Men and women envision it quite differently. As individuals vary, it plays a different role in each marriage. Its means are as diverse as its ends. It has so many facets that for thirty years therapists and researchers have been trying to analyze its dynamics in married relationships.

DEFINITIONS AND DESCRIPTIONS OF POWER

Most analysts of the subject seem to agree that control is one main element of power. Controlling power can be felt in the form of an action (Jack slaps Jill to make her stop arguing with him), in the form of authority (Jack says, "Don't argue with me; I'm the head of this household."), or as some threat held in reserve (Jill tells Jack, "If you don't stop drinking so much, I'm leaving you.").

The wide range of meaning in the word *power* can be seen in the different verbs used to activate it: power to influence, to modify, to affect, to control, to impose one's will upon, to organize, to choose, to master, to force, to have impact on, to set the agenda, to define. Each of these has a different intensity, and each suggests a different manner of wielding power.

Just as the means of power are complex, so are the aims. The two basic goals are self-control and control of others. In some cases, for example, the objective of power is to control your own emotions and the emotional behavior of your partner or family. In another case, it might be to impose one version of reality on partner or family. Again, it might be used simply to establish the priorities of your marriage.

In another, larger sense, power might mean recognizing territoriality—that is, spheres of influence or control. Since 1920, natural scientists have recognized the territorial principle among most living creatures—the impulse of each to stake out a private living space. When those creatures mate, the territorial rights belong to the bonded pair.

Robert Ardrey, in *The Territorial Imperative*, says:

> As scientific thought developed, it became apparent that
> the private territory held by a pair is a prime reinforcement
> for the bond between the two. Sexual attraction may initiate
> the bond, as it does in man . . . and continued sexual activity
> may reinforce [it] . . . but it is the private territory of a breed-
> ing couple that provides most reliably that the children will
> not be neglected. Through its strange enhancement of pow-
> ers in the male proprietor, energy not otherwise available is
> placed at family disposal. And through isolation of the two in
> their little world, and their joint antagonism for all others of
> their kind, nature keeps the pair where they belong—at the
> service of the next generation.

The "territory" of a modern marriage is much more complex than the primate couple's patch of the jungle—or even
the settler's farm and cabin. It's a diverse estate made up of
various intangible assets along with the protected little world
that insures security for children.

Within the human pair-bond territory, there are subdivi-
sions. Traditional female areas of power have been household management, nurturing the children, tending the sick,
religious observance, and other private matters; male areas
were work and providing, indoctrinating the male children,
and serving public functions in war or government. Even
now that the subdivision lines have been blurred, there are
still a few physical spaces, such as the kitchen and nursery,
where the wife governs; and there are still places, such as
garage or workshop, ruled by the husband. It is the non-
spatial areas of power where the lines are unclear and the
basic quarrel begins.

In my therapy work with couples, I'm often faced with an
interesting question about the nature of power in marriage.
Sometimes it seems to be a matter of individual characteristics—for example, if one of the pair is strong and the other

is weak. Or power could be a feature of the marriage itself—for economic or other reasons. My conclusion is that marital power is always relative. For example, in the case of the Sullivans, Bob produced the entire family income and held an upper-scale job; that tipped the power scales in his favor. But Liz came from a wealthy and influential family, and she was a community leader. That gave her a certain edge. Some power springs from individual character, some is drawn from the outside world, some derives from interaction between the two.

Power takes many forms. It can be secret—"the iron hand in the velvet glove." It can be legitimate or illegitimate or pseudolegitimate—that is, openly agreed on by a couple, simply commandeered by one of them, or ostensibly granted by agreement and later undermined. It can be hidden in the passive disguise known as the "tyranny of the weak," which draws on such tactics as sulking, crying, taking ill, and playing the martyr.

In some couples, characteristic ways of behaving can be clues to power attitudes—for example, the person who is "bossy," demanding, indifferent, or timid. More baffling, a man or woman who is a terror in the office may be Mr. or Mrs. Milquetoast at home.

Power can be actual or symbolic. The difference is put very well by the husband who says, "My wife decides the little questions, such as what furniture we buy, where we go on trips, when we go out to dinner, who our friends are; and I decide the big questions, like whether Israel should recognize the PLO." Many power quarrels are more about symbolism than substance. One wife I know of wanted to buy a BMW to replace an aging Buick. Her husband said no. He had nothing against BMWs, but his unexpressed reason was that he didn't want her to make the decision. For him, this would have meant a redefinition of their power relationship, with him as the loser. As Jay Haley has pointed out, many a basic quarrel is not about content but about who establishes the rules.

Male Power and Female Power

To make the matter even more complicated, there are different gender conceptions of power. Two writers on the subject define them:

Anthony Astrachan in *How Men Feel* notes four kinds of traditional male power:

First is "the power to name and define," or the authority to determine the relative importance or urgency of anything. This would include the power to establish agendas and priorities—from a husband's setting the family budget to the secretary of state's determining United States foreign policy.

Second is the power to hurt, or "the power to mobilize destructive aggression—the intention to kill or harm others." This would range from the wife-beater to the four-star general.

Third is "the power to organize life—society, economy, and polity—for destructive and constructive ends." That would extend from the father who lays down rules for the family to the president of IBM.

Fourth is "the power to direct others' use of their skills, to command others' manipulation and control of the environment, to select what is to be changed, to choose the desired goals, to measure efficiency and effectiveness." This might span the distance from a farmer allotting chores to his children to the scientist in charge of a huge cancer-research project.

As for the female conception of power, the psychiatrist Jean Baker Miller says that although "in our culture . . . we have maintained the myth that women do not and should not have power," women actually exercise a kind of power that "is difficult for the world to comprehend, for it is not how 'the real world' has defined power."

This could be called the power of enhancing. She says, "One instance is in women's traditional role, where they have used their powers to foster the growth of others—certainly children, but also many other people. This might be called using one's power to empower another—increasing the other's resources, capabilities, effectiveness, and ability to act."

There are entirely different psychologies of power in men and women, and therefore entirely different goals: on one side, to organize and command both society and nature or, on the other side, to maximize human potential—to order our present world or to insure that our world has a future.

It isn't only that women have different power goals, Miller believes, but they have a profound aversion to those of men. She says, "When women even contemplate acting powerful, they fear the possibility of limiting or putting down another person. . . . To act out of one's own interest and motivation is . . . the psychic equivalent of being a destructively aggressive person. This is a self-image which few women can bear." And once having shown such destructive aggression, the unconscious logic continues, she will be abandoned by those she is close to—and that is unthinkable because a woman's very identity requires close relationships.

One interesting research project was based on observation of girls and boys as they took part in team sports. When the game produced a disputed decision—such as whether a runner in baseball was safe or out—boys would argue for about seven minutes on the average and finally arrive at a compromise that would permit the game to go on. The compromise was most often some form of a replay. Girls involved in some equivalent dispute, however, would end the game and go home. The most apparent conclusions from this would be that the boys loved the aggressive competition so much that they would always find a way to make it continue while the girls, fearful of competition and of damaging their overall relations of friendship, avoided the danger by quitting.

The difference in the ways that men and women define legitimate power is, in itself, a central power struggle in marriage—the question as to whose values will have the upper hand.

STYLES OF POWER: WHAT RESEARCH REVEALS

The pioneer studies in the subject of marital power were done by Robert Blood and Donald Wolfe in 1960. They questioned wives as to which spouse usually made the decision in eight areas of married life such as the choice of the husband's job or whether or not to buy life insurance. The researchers used the answers to divide the couples into "husband-dominant," "wife-dominant," or "egalitarian." Egalitarian couples were further separated into groups of those who made decisions jointly and those who made an equal number separately. In the final rating, the egalitarian marriage with joint decision making was ranked most successful and the wife-dominant marriage least. (Critics have pointed out that Blood and Wolfe gave equal weight to questions of unequal importance—that choice of home and job are more serious and long-range than choice of a car or a vacation spot.)

Subsequently, clinicians such as William Lederer and Don Jackson defined three power types: the "symmetrical" relationship, in which people give and take directions equally and have equal status; the "complementary" relationship, with contrasting roles and one partner (usually the husband) dominant; and the "parallel" relationship, in which spouses alternate between the first two patterns. As for potential troubles, the observers noted that symmetrical relationships are likely to produce competition, complementary ones to produce resentment by the partner of lower status, and parallel ones to be the most satisfactory.

The Blood and Wolfe findings were questioned because they rested on the testimony of wives alone and because they were "self-reports." Researchers, beginning to realize that people often distorted results by telling the questioner what they thought he wanted to hear or what they thought socially acceptable, became more sophisticated. Such researchers as Dr. John Gottman have used physiologic measurements, complicated coding methods, and statistical techniques.

While the new, observational kind of studies are likely to be more accurate than the old self-report method, they are still far from an exact science. Take, for instance, the hypothesis that the mate who talks more is the more powerful in the marriage. That ignores the everyday fact that some people are naturally more loquacious than others. We have those long-familiar characters, the silly chatterbox and the strong, silent type. Another hypothesis suggests that person A, who makes the most decisions, is the more powerful partner. That can be totally misleading when B, the other partner, is devious enough to shift the burden of decision making onto A, but makes sure that the decision is the one B wants.

The results of the self-report method and the observational method often contradict each other as well—couples who report one pattern of power will show another when they are under observation. Even the terms *power* and *marital satisfaction* are so vague that various researchers define them in different ways.

When your favorite magazine reports this month that the "latest research" finds this or that to be true about marriage, beware. Next month's issue is likely to bring you a quite opposite opinion.

A result is valid only after many investigations have confirmed the same pattern of findings. Here are the most consistent of those patterns thus far:

- *Wife-dominant relationships are the most likely to be unhappy ones.*
- *Egalitarian relationships have the best chance for success.*
- *Coercion (threats, manipulation, etc.) usually make for an unhappy marriage.*
- *Blaming the other partner is always detrimental.*
- *Believing that you have little control over the conflicts is a sign of serious trouble.*

In order to put these results in perspective, we have to understand some of the central issues in the dynamics of power in marriage.

MODELS OF MARITAL POWER

Investigators have looked at the question of why one partner holds the stronger hand and whether that makes for a more or a less satisfactory marriage. There are overlapping research studies, contradictions among them, and different levels of analysis. This is a relatively new field, and no one yet has come up with a unified theory. Here are some of the most useful insights that have come out of the inquiries thus far.

Economic Power

One explanation of this, known as "resource theory," proposes that the partner who contributes more resources (and that usually means more money) to the marriage has the upper hand. Blood and Wolfe added the idea that the more prestigious the husband's job, the more weight he had in making decisions.

Historically, women in general have had neither of these resources, and therefore less authority. As women acquire more economic power in today's world, there is evidence that the balance changes in their favor. For example, one study reports that the higher a wife's income relative to her husband's, the more housework the husband is willing to do. People seem to accept marketplace values, because wages are concrete and quantifiable, as a standard of worth and so as a yardstick of power.

Traditional Beliefs

There are other standards beside money and job status, and a look at each spouse's W-2 forms won't tell us everything about comparative power of the two people in the marriage. Tradition, too, is part of the equation, because in our culture the male has always been the head of the family. If the wife was employed at all, her income was considered a supplement to the budget.

Partly because of traditional feelings, the wife-dominant marriage seems to rank as the worst of three power patterns. Some wives seize power and some have power thrust upon them because their husbands are passive or less competent. In the second case, I have found that many wives and husbands are distressed by the "unnatural" format of their marriage. This often leads to the wife putting pressure on the husband to be more involved and assertive and the husband withdrawing farther into his shell.

Many old fortresses of traditional belief remain unconquered. The perception of equality between the sexes is relatively new, and the habits of male domination go back at least as far as that primate-ruled patch of jungle. What we are seeing today is not so much role change as role strain.

Women, for instance, have to go outside the marriage to acquire a power base. Most commonly, that base is wages; more rarely, it is some technical skill or some accomplishment in the arts that gets recognized by the world at large. In matrilinear societies, by contrast, wives have a power base in their families of origin—and thus more power in their own marriages.

The main liberation battleground has been on male turf, where women have succeeded in acquiring traditionally male authority both in the workplace and the home. At this point in our social history, women's big handicap is the family-of-origin loyalties to role models. Both women and men feel uneasy at rejecting the images of the mother-and-father relationship they knew as children. As power shifts and relationships change, a new generation will have a different kind of role-model loyalties.

Rosanna Hertz points out that a wife's having a job isn't necessarily going to give her more power. To gain it, she has to control some discretionary money and insist on a share in financial decisions. Paradoxically, some women who have a strong position in the outside world will compensate by accepting a subordinate role in their marriages—which is a good illustration of Jean Baker Miller's observations about women's fears of taking on male power. Some would call these fears neurotic; others would call them well-founded, given the fragility of the male ego.

Remaking a marriage into an egalitarian form is a high risk/high gain gamble. It it doesn't work, the failure can lead to a basic quarrel. If it does work, the bargain demands a high level of collaboration, which is all to the good. Many traditional marriages may be unsatisfactory, but they don't demand much creativity or effort. A sound egalitarian marriage is a working marriage—that is, it requires the kind of constant effort democracy calls for, not the passive acceptance a tyranny exacts.

Justice and Equity
Some people operate out of a naive egotism that tells them, "What's good for me is good for the marriage." That means that they feel compelled to dominate the other person, either for conscious or unconscious reasons. They think, I'm not to

blame for asserting myself—if I don't run things, he/she will take over, and what a mistake that would be!

For those who lack the ability to trust, relinquishing control means making themselves vulnerable to control by the partner. In this fearful logic, one action almost inevitably follows the other, the world is a great either/or proposition in which it's dangerous to disarm unilaterally.

That defensive urge usually comes from some painful past experience in the family of origin, in a love affair, or a previous marriage. The mature person is one who can absorb those shocks of the past and be willing to trust his or her partner with a share of control.

There is also the unequal relationship in which neither is able to assert effective leadership and any attempt at dual control is a failure. For example:

HUSBAND: What do you want to do tonight?
WIFE: Anything you like, dear.
HUSBAND: Well, I don't know. You have anything in mind?
WIFE: I haven't thought of anything. You decide.
HUSBAND: I suppose we could go to a movie? What's on?
WIFE: Are you really in the mood for a movie?
HUSBAND: I suppose we could just stay home.
WIFE: You decide, dear.

In another scenario, the couple works out an agreement that incorporates some part of the first two examples—reaching a "partial equity" by enlightened self-interest. They acknowledge the demands of ego but try to balance those with a standard of fairness.

Looking for what couples would consider their "equity point," researchers find that people in the worst marriages have the most divergent ideas of what each considers fair. When the husband earns a higher income than hers and the wife wants an egalitarian partnership, the gap is widest. This is the unequal match between a power base and a plea for justice.

George Homans says that many people consider justice "a curious mixture of equity within inequality." There is no such thing as an absolute standard of fairness between two people; like most of the premises of marriage, it's a matter of perception. When I read research indicating that egalitarian marriages are the most successful, I take that simply as a reflection of marriages where there's an agreement on equity. "We have our problems, of course, but we both believe in fair play, and that's what saves us," one wife says.

An outside observer might find a strange contradiction in some marriages between this show of satisfaction and an obvious disparity between the husband's power and the wife's. In such cases, the explanation is either that one partner has no urge to have an equal share of power or that there are other trade-offs and compensations in the marriage that produce this contentment.

Personality
When we think about power relationships, we must think about individual characteristics. Some people are born to exert power; others shun it. Some people use power well; others bungle it.

Americans generally regard power-users as chosen people. Saints, martyrs, contemplative thinkers, artists, or idealistic dissenters may be interesting to us, but we believe they have little impact on the real world. It is no wonder that the American feminist movement views economic and political power as a major force to gain social equality. Our past stereotypes of marriage have been either one of the strong patriarch with the dear, sweet wife or—though we acknowledge this less often—the powerful matriarch married to the charming, ineffective man. Part of the turbulence in marriage today springs from the fact that many women have emerged as stronger than they would have been perceived in the past and many men as comparatively weaker. This can produce an unfortunate kind of confrontation.

Women have learned to exercise traditional powers of men in recent times, but not vice-versa. When men try to use the forms of power that Jean Baker Miller has defined as characteristically female, they often feel inept and ill at ease. They cannot cope with the embarrassment of being a "house husband" nor can they find articulate expression for feelings of sadness, vulnerability, or shame.

There is a form of basic power quarrel when one of a couple is forceful and the other merely ambitious to be forceful. That is, the natural leader faces a demand for power-sharing from a wife or husband who has less talent for leadership. Tradition has taught men that they must be the dominant sex. Women's liberation has taught women that they must be competitive, share command, act independently. What if she can't live up to the model of her new role, or he can't live up to the model of his traditional role?

David McClelland has traced the development of the consciousness of power as humans mature. He says that, in the first stage, we depend on another person for our power—as a small child depends on the mother to make things happen. Later, we discover that we can develop our individual power—as the adolescent boy who takes up bodybuilding develops his muscles along with the self-discipline it takes to stick to the schedule.

The third stage is where we use power to direct or influence other people. The final stage is where we can put ego aside, identify with some greater authority than the self, and draw our power from it. That power comes from dedication to service.

These stages, or phases, have an application to marriage. The person who remains arrested in the first phase is heavily dependent on his or her partner, perhaps dangerously so. One who is arrested in the second phase may have achieved internal confidence but is narcissistic—unable to realize how his or her pursuit of satisfaction affects the partner. Those in the third phase may be able to collaborate but will demand control as the price. Those in the fourth phase can be—at the extremes—either saints or fanatics. For them, questions of control are subordinate to a mutual vision of some new order of things. More normally, people who have reached this final level of maturity can dedicate themselves to their marriage and invest their power in cooperation and singleness of purpose.

Rules

Jay Haley believes that the most serious power conflict in marriage is over who sets the rules. Some of the rules of living together, as he sees them, would determine who keeps the checkbook, what is the protocol with in-laws, or what criticism of each other is permissible. Battles over rules are not merely legalistic—they are intense and deeply felt because, ultimately, they involve whole patterns of behavior. Those fights pit his idea of his basic rights against her idea of hers. Listening in to such dialogues, we might hear:

"No more of those scenes in front of the kids. If you're sore at me, let me know and we'll talk in private."

"If you're going to borrow from the housekeeping kitty, leave an IOU in the cash box and replace the money when you get your next paycheck."

"No more wisecracks about my housekeeping."

These are not simply regulations for isolated problems. The first suggested rule deals with the question of how to handle family strife; the second has to do with financial accountability; and the third would define permissible criticism. Most rules, less explicit and unwritten, have evolved in the course of time and argument.

Haley also outlines two kinds of relationships—the "complementary," which is a trade-off of different kinds of behavior, and the "symmetrical," which is an equal exchange. For example, Mary has had a painful argument with her sister, and by the unspoken rule, John must sympathize and soothe her—a complementary situation. The next week, they must decide whether to buy a condominium in their building or move, and, by the rule, they make a joint decision—which is symmetrical.

Trouble comes if John and Mary can decide on questions like the condominium purchase but fail when it comes to "complementary" giving and receiving. Or, on the other hand, if they have no trouble giving and taking but misfire when they have to act jointly, they are in just as much trouble.

If the rules in Haley's two different areas of behavior seem to contradict each other, the trouble is compounded. Say that one day Mary says to John, "Don't be a wimp, John. If I were you, I'd get rid of that lawyer, and then we should find somebody who'll take the case to court and not settle outside." She's blaming John for being a wimp and also telling him what to do, which is complementary; at the same time, she's saying that they should take joint action, which is symmetrical.

It is paradoxical communications like these that make for power confusions. All in all, we could compare this to a game with two players. When one or the other changes a rule from time to time, when one player applies two contradictory rules at the same time, or when the two constantly debate over the fairness of certain rules, the outcome is likely to be a basic quarrel.

Tactics

The ways of getting your own way are not very numerous, and all of them are well known on school playgrounds and in family living rooms everywhere. There are six of them, and they are of two kinds: weaker toward stronger and stronger toward weaker. The first set would be:

- *Manipulation: You drop hints, flatter, seduce, remind the other of past favors.*
- *Supplication: You plead, or cry, pretend to be ill, act helpless.*
- *Disengagement: You sulk, make the other feel guilty, play the martyr, lock yourself in the bedroom.*

The second set would be:

- *Bullying: You threaten, insult, ridicule, or become violent.*
- *Autocracy: You claim to be better informed, or you assert authority.*

The final one would be:

- *Bargaining: You reason, negotiate, compromise, offer trade-offs.*

The tactics you use will define your power position, regardless of your gender. If, for instance, you try flattery and seduction, you cast yourself as the one with the weaker position; if you try negotiation—even though you may have the weaker bargaining hand—you are starting out with the premise that the two of you are peers.

I could cite the case of the couple who had a disagreement over investment of their small nest egg. He had accumulated the money from his company profit-sharing program and had invested it in government securities. He guarded that capital possessively and had an emotional resistance to disturbing it.

She saw that it could be more profitable as an investment in some attractive real estate she'd learned was for sale. She bypassed the debate about whose money it "really" was,

compiled information to show how promising the land purchase would be, and put her case objectively. Treating the
matter as a negotiation rather than a debate, she made the
playing field level, and she finally won her point.

POWER AND ITS PROBLEMS

Role assignments, or as Hollywood terms it, typecasting, can
be a kind of stabilizer for a marriage. Husband and wife
always act true to form—but the form itself may be an act. In
the old TV series *All in the Family*, Archie Bunker played the
tyrant, and Edith, his wife, played the helpless, rattlebrained
dingbat. The series joke was that Edith, beneath all her flus-
ter, usually turned out to be wiser and more levelheaded
than Archie. But she was comfortable playing her dingbat
role, and he could be comfortable in no other role than that
of living-room honcho. Such acting keeps many marriages
together, but its fatal flaws are its inflexibility and its good
chance of failing in a crisis.

I remember the example of Dorothy, who always played
the part of an impractical, artistic soul in her marriage, and
Don, who played the role of patriarch. Don, an engineer,
was injured in a plant accident and was left an invalid for a
long period of time. Insurance and compensation helped,
but the two children of the family were in expensive colleges,
and the budget got badly out of balance. While Don was
helpless, Dorothy took charge of the family destiny.

She finished work for her master's degree at a nearby university, found a good teaching job in a high school, and took
on the role of a disciplined, responsible head of the household. Don couldn't stand it. He complained and pontificated
from his wheelchair constantly. To his dismay, Dorothy had
broken out of her old role and had assumed an equality that
he couldn't understand or accept. His deep misgivings about
his own power—suppressed before—had suddenly become

reality. As for Dorothy, her childlike dependence on a father figure was suddenly no longer possible. Ironically, what had been a stable marriage now came under severe stress.

Tit for Tat

There is a certain kind of contentious marriage between two managers. Each tries to control the other, and each keeps books on the other's behavior. Although this may result in a kind of equity—a bickering one—each will feel controlled and manipulated by the other. The situation is worse if there are no rewards exchanged, if the books show debits only. Neither has the courage to make a concession even once.

The Power of Violence or Its Threat

It was only a few years ago, in the 1980s, that the public—and mental-health professionals as well—became aware how frequent and numerous are the cases of battered wives or children. When men feel that the marriage is slipping out of their control, some of them react with violence. This kind of man is aroused by some change he suspects in his wife. He feels that she has begun to reject him, either by showing a new independence or by getting interested in another man. Like Dorothy, she seems to be escaping from her helpmeet role.

His only resources are the two male power tactics—violence and autocracy—because he hasn't the skill or flexibility to try negotiation. The result is another battered wife.

In some marriages, there is little or no real violence, but the threat is always there. Marilyn and Fred were a case in point. Fred was a former athlete who, after his playing days were over, landed a job as scout for one of the National Football League teams. This meant that he was on the road a lot, assessing possible draft choices among college athletes. Fred liked parties, and he drank.

Marilyn hated the absences and excessive drinking and

was never diffident about telling him so. The main ties that kept her from leaving Fred were their two daughters, but when one daughter married and moved away and the other went East to college, Marilyn began to feel depressed and desperate. Fred promised to reform, but he never did. One weekend when he was golfing, she took an overdose of sleeping pills, and only by the best of luck a neighbor discovered her in time to get her to the hospital.

Fred was sobered and shocked enough to promise to change his ways. His ways were changed for him, instead. Marilyn insisted that he give up scouting, take a minor job in the team's front office so that he wouldn't be on the road, and give up drinking. The outcome is that Fred still has longings and temptations, but he lives in dread that Marilyn might actually kill herself on another try. She has successfully used threat-of-violence power tactics against him, but at the cost of a never-ending basic quarrel.

Power and Intimacy
Some power quarrels have their showdown in the bedroom, and often a sex boycott has been a convincing weapon. But sexual evidence of the power struggle usually comes out in far less conscious ways. Many dysfunctions—anorgasmia, impotence, or premature ejaculation—may reflect a deep-seated fear of loss of control. To have satisfying sex, both partners must voluntarily give up control in favor of the shared experience. (There will be a more extensive discussion of this in Chapter Six.)

Power as Thought Control
There are some people who have a compulsion to impose their own version of reality on their partner. No two people, of course, ever experience events in quite the same way or have an identical recollection of them—especially if their emotions have been involved. A husband recalls a skiing

vacation in Aspen as a glorious time—leisure, good company, good food, and challenging slopes. His wife, who is not a good skier, recalls it as a bore—falling down a lot on the beginner's slope, aches and bruises, too much anxiety, and too many uncongenial people. He insists that she is wrong. Everybody else, he says, had a wonderful time. For some reason, she's forgotten how much she enjoyed it. But if that's the way she feels about it, maybe they'd better skip a vacation this year.

She can either submit to his view or cling firmly to her own, but there seems to be no chance for an unprejudiced version. This kind of dissension about the truth, about what actually is or was, can produce a power struggle in more important areas of the marriage than vacation memories.

Power as Coercion to Role Models

As we have pointed out in the chapter on loyalties, everyone brings to marriage a set of role models and expectations (most of them unconscious) about behavior and attitudes. The effort of one, or both, of the couple to make married life conform to those established ideas often develops into a no-win power dispute. It is no-win because, if one partner succeeds, the other is likely to have guilt feelings about abandoning her or his loyalties and will feel a traitor to the old affiliations. The paradoxical result is that neither can take charge of his or her own destiny—even the winner is the slave to old allegiances.

Power and Authorization

We have an instinctive distrust of people who try to exercise power unless we're convinced they have proper credentials. It's why policemen have badges, doctors put their diplomas on their walls, and colonels wear eagles on their collars. Unauthorized use of power is considered coercion. In marriage, there has always been a certain authorization through tradition—the husband was recognized head of the household, and he delegated specific powers to the wife. Today, authority is more likely to be assigned by voluntary agreement, with the limits understood and the power defined. If a wife takes on the assignment of buying new furniture for the apartment, obviously she must take their family budget and her husband's tastes into account, even though she is exercising her own judgment.

One of the worst games of power antagonism is delegation followed by undermining. She has, for example, chosen the furniture and described it to her husband because he was too busy to go with her on the shopping trips. She has shown him the illustrations in the brochures, and he has agreed with her choices. When the furniture is delivered, however, he finds that he hates it. It's too expensive; it's badly built; it's the wrong style, he complains.

This is a classic case of pseudoauthorization. He has an unconscious wish to undermine her authority role; between the lines, he's saying, "See, if I authorize you to do something, I can't trust you to do it right."

Along with this misuse, there are such examples of bad management as the grant of responsibility without any real power or the assignment of vague or ambiguous power.

The delegation of power has to be more than conscious and voluntary, it must be a full legitimization. The person you authorize must have the power to act not only on his or her behalf but on yours as well. It is similar to granting a legal power of attorney. Such an understanding requires true teamwork and comprehension of each other.

Power and Inconsistency

Changing the scenario back to the beginning, let's say that the wife heads for the furniture store but gets led astray by a show window displaying a model kitchen with many new and interesting features. She enters the store, is pleased with what she sees, and thinks, "Our kitchen is long overdue for remodeling. We need that much more than we need new furniture—in fact, I could probably hold off on the furniture for another year. Maybe there will be a big sale in January. I think I'll go ahead and order the kitchen redone now."

This is an inconsistent use of her power. Role should be defined in relation to task. If there is an agreed-on, equal division of authority in the marriage, then any attempt to exclude the other partner from important decision making is an inconsistency and a violation of the basic premises.

The Power of Symptoms

One secret weapon in power battles is the symptom. It is so secret, in fact, that even its user is unaware that it is psychogenic (originating in the mind, not the body). Ed and Jenny have a Saturday night argument over which one is to pick up Aunt Margaret and take her to the airport bright and early Sunday morning. It goes:

"After all, she's *your* aunt."

"Yes. And she's planning to leave most of her money to *our* children."

"Hasn't she ever heard about taxicabs?"

"Yes, but she says she can't depend on one to come when she wants it."

Jenny loses and reluctantly agrees to make the Aunt Margaret run. When they wake up in the morning, Jenny has such a terrific migraine that four aspirins have no effect. She couldn't even drive around the block. Her pain is real enough, but the headache is psychogenic. And so are many other temporarily disabling symptoms. Their effectiveness as power-struggle weapons lies in the fact that they are—on the conscious level—involuntary.

Even symptoms of perfectly real, somatic (bodily) disorders can be psychological power weapons by means of something known as "secondary gain." I remember the case of a factory foreman who hated his work. One day, he suffered a real-enough back injury. Long after the doctor pronounced him cured, he continued to have backaches so painful that he couldn't think of going back to his old job or getting another.

Power Triangles

Allies, accomplices, backers—the contestants in a power struggle very often try to draw others in to support their positions. The most common forms are these:

- *One parent draws a child in on his or her side.*
- *One partner allies with a parent or in-law.*
- *One or both calls on the testimony of a third party. ("Sally's your best friend, and even she says you're being selfish about this.")*

The last is the most destructive tactic because it is so difficult to defend against hearsay, and because it tries to isolate the victim—supposedly, even her best friend won't take her side.

The most extreme way of finding alliance is to begin an extramarital love affair. "My wife doesn't understand me, but I know you do," he says, asking for a secret support and a prop for his ego.

His new friend replies, "I don't know how she can treat a wonderful man like you that way."

The Power of Manipulation

In any relationship of love or affection, it is natural for us to give gifts, say agreeable or flattering things, do favors, and be especially sensitive to the other's wishes. When we make such benefits into pragmatic quid pro quos, however, they become a kind of emotional extortion. In one case I recall, a successful man with an oversized ego used to abuse his wife in nonphysical ways. He neglected her, was sarcastic to her in company, scorned her friends, derided her interests, and ignored her wishes.

The wife had grown up as an only child, and her well-to-do father had lavished every attention and many expensive gifts on her. The effect had been to give her a love of costly things—especially clothes.

Every now and then, her husband would give her a "makeup" present. It was always luxurious and in perfect taste. Obviously, he had put a good deal of thought and effort into its selection. The wife used to be delighted and grateful because it recalled her father's gifts. Then she would feel guilty about her earlier resentments against her husband.

Eventually, she began to realize that the gifts were not really meant to ask forgiveness but were subtle demands for a quid pro quo. Sooner or later, after the presentation, he would have an assignment or an undertaking for her, generally family or social obligations he wanted to avoid. Once this was clear to her, she lost interest in his gifts. Before long, she decided on a divorce.

One could imagine a similar case in which fine gifts and pampering did not demand a direct quid pro quo but were used as a kind of manipulation—as a substitute for any permitted autonomy.

The Imbalance of Power

A great many marriages, perhaps the majority, are unequal. One partner brings greater abilities or greater resources to the union. There is often a similar—sometimes connected—imbalance of commitment. As the old maxim goes, "There is always one who kisses and one who offers the cheek."

In cases where this was true, I've observed the more committed person in the relationship put up with all sorts of emotional violation—extreme rudeness, physical abuse, alcoholism, workaholism, or infidelity. The reasons for not demanding a change are always much the same: a divorce would be too hard on the young children; or he's lost his job and depends on her financially; or her best years are past and she could never make another marriage; or he would be helpless without her to run the house.

The Power of Secrets

This can be either the power you retain as long as wife or husband doesn't know certain things, or the power you get from knowing certain things about her or him.

A number of times I've treated compulsive gamblers who had managed to keep their addiction—and their considerable debts—from their wives. In most of these cases, it would have been possible for the gambler to confess and win his wife's understanding. That was unthinkable for him, however, because it would then shift much of the control in the marriage to her. She would have to take on a role as guardian of the finances and overseer of his habits. Worse, if she was vindictive, she would never let him forget his weakness.

In this way, husbands or wives—sometimes both of them—use a knowledge of embarrassing secrets either for blackmail or harassment. One husband exploited the fact that his wife, long before she met him, had borne an illegitimate child. By this time, she had become a respectable suburban housewife, and she wanted the past forgotten. Although he never told anyone else her story, he did remind her of it from time to time with just a hint that he might make it public if she didn't agree with what he wanted.

Power Control Through Affect

Anger, tears, a loud voice, a tantrum—expressions of affect—can be weapons to make the other feel either threatened or guilty. Traditionally, these have been in a woman's arsenal. The cold shoulder, the silence, the poker face, the forbidding frown, the way of looking through you, have been men's weapons.

DEFINING POWER IN RELATIONSHIPS

In order to get a clearer idea of how power works in your relationship, you should examine how you and your partner think about power, how you seek it or avoid it, and what power tactics you use. Here are some questions whose answers will help both of you spell out thoughts and feelings.

- *How do you see yourself in relation to other people and events? Do you see yourself as having an impact on things, directing a course? Or are you largely acted upon and controlled by events, by other people, or by fate?*
- *Where does the center of control lie—in which one of you? Both? Neither?*
- *Looking back at "Personality," page 146, where would each of you place yourself in McClelland's stages? Do you think of having power* over, *or power* with? *What does each of you want from power—to feel strong and self-sufficient? To dominate? To be taken care of?*
- *What are your power bases?—That is, who has the stronger voice in decisions? The one who contributes a bigger share of the income (or wealth)? The one who has more special expertise or knowledge? The husband just because he is the husband? One of you because of some special circumstance in the marriage (e.g., one person is an invalid, or much younger than the other)? The one who has some powerful outside support (influential family, social, or establishment connections)? The one who is clever at intrigue, persuasion, and seduction?*

Or does your power derive from your ability to work as a team?

———

- *What are your typical ways of taking on some power? Your ways of keeping it? Do you use weak or strong tactics? Do you change tactics according to the issue being faced? Do you change tactics when you're under stress? How do you react if he/she gets very emotional? How do you react if he/she gives you silence and a cold shoulder?*
- *How do you feel when you have to give up a certain control? Or when you have to agree to share it? Do either of you feel vulnerable and anxious when making such concessions? Do you have a problem in trusting the other with a specific kind of control?*
- *Is one more committed to the marriage than the other? Is one more dependent than the other? If so, does this affect his/her freedom to express disagreement? To assert himself/herself in any way?*
- *Do you each think that your marriage has been fair to your wishes and aspirations? (This is the "equity point" discussed under "Justice and Equity," page 144. It is the perceived state of ideal parity.) If not, to what degree has it been unfair? What does each consider the best marriage arrangement —one dominant? Equal but separate? Equal and joint? Egalitarian?*
- *Have you authorized power in a clear-cut way? How sharply are your roles and tasks defined? Do you exercise your power just as both of you have authorized and defined it?*
- *Who makes the decisions about how money is spent? Is your accounting separate or joint? Who keeps the accounts?*
- *Who holds the balance of power in sexual relations? Who decides what and when—one? Sometimes one, sometimes the other? Both together?*

DEVELOPING MATURE POWER RELATIONSHIPS

Here are some conclusions that emerge from all that we have said on the subject. Take them as guideposts toward a mature power relationship:

- *No power arrangement suits every marriage. Although research tends to show that egalitarian marriages work best in general, that doesn't apply to all couples. Some people—often those with working-class or ethnic backgrounds—are happier with the traditional scheme in which the husband is dominant. The important thing is to find the right equity point for both partners.*
- *Be flexible enough to change the power arrangement if a different situation seems to require it. Sometimes it is best to divide power, at others best to share it.*
- *Reward, don't punish: using negative tactics to control—blame, threats, and violence—is harmful and costly. Positive tactics of reward and ingratiation (although they can sometimes be manipulative or subtly coercive) are always better.*
- *Negotiate fairly: what follows are four good rules for successful negotiation:*

1. *Separate the personalities from the problem. Attack the second, not the first.*
2. *Focus on interests, those on both sides, not predetermined positions.*
3. *Invent some options that permit both to gain, which means find a way of making the pie bigger before you divide it.*
4. *Concentrate on keeping the process of negotiation fair rather than debating details of substance. If you reach agreement on a fair way to divide the pie, no one can then complain about getting the smaller piece.*

These negotiation rules are derived from *Getting to Yes* by Roger Fisher and William Ury. They are the tactics for working out specific problems. Beyond them are some more strategic rules that make it possible to avoid difficult negotiations most of the time:

- *Authorize the use of power: that is, agree on how power will be assigned to carry out the tasks and roles of the marriage, such as financial chores, house management, social obligations, and child-rearing.*

- *Use power mutually: two people can combine aggressive power, or "male" power, with enhancing, or "female," power to reach certain important goals. This means finding ways of making the two partners' sets of capabilities interact. Remember that the "male" and "female" labels are generalizations. A man can exercise enhancing power, and a woman can use aggressive power when she foresees the result as beneficial.*

The general power shift in American marriages has resulted from women working outside the home, producing part of the family income, being less child-bound than ever before, and attaining new rights and status in the world at large. Research has found that men have more respect for and communicate more significantly with wives who work. While Americans rejected paternal rule as a form of government in the Declaration of Independence, it took 144 years before they extended democratic civil rights to the female half of society. The democratization of the family has begun only recently. Copartnership and dual power in marriage are its manifestation. People who didn't grow up in a Victorian-style, patriarchal family can scarcely realize how radical this idea has been.

True partners are people with a power-sharing arrangement and agreed-on goals. One important principle in their relationship is that they are both, in a sense, marriage professionals. A professional attitude toward problems and goals means that people have standards of what is correct and what is just. They do not let emotions overrule their judgment. They understand how to negotiate. And they know how to accept and live with the results of negotiation. For them, power becomes a rational agreement, not a matter of maneuver or hidden manipulation.

All of this sounds quite practical and unromantic. And it

is. One of the old problems of the marriage arrangement in our culture has been the adoration of romantic love, the idealization of (powerless) women, and the sentimentality over children. All of that has been a mask for servitude. There is no reason why a power-sharing, professional attitude toward marriage should diminish its traditional pleasures and rewards. All brides can still be beautiful, all husbands respected, all babies adorable—it's just that a modern dual management treats these things with more realism.

CHAPTER SIX

SEX

Sex, in one of the great ironies of marriage, can bond two people in warm intimacy and yet drive two other people apart. Its main complication is that it involves much more than two bodies. It involves two humans—two sets of personal anxieties, inhibitions, family cultures, and youthful experiences. These are the impedimenta we bring to bed with us, and because of them a simple animal need becomes a complex human encounter. The psychoanalyst Irwin Hirsch goes so far as to say that "one's sexuality is primarily a metaphor for character" and other analysts regard the bedroom as a stage for a drama in which all our unresolved interpersonal problems are acted out. Yet other therapists have said that good sex is less a matter of deep emotional understanding than a matter of learning the right ways to touch and communicate.

Case-history scenes from different marriages show us some of the common puzzles:

The couple were newly married. She hoped that he'd get over his seemingly constant need for sex once the honeymoon period was past. For her, a little went a long way. He didn't change, though, in the course of the first year, and she began to feel under continual pressure, always aware of his silent reproach. For his part, he felt rebuffed and deprived. He wondered what he had done to hurt her or to turn her off after a happy and satisfying courtship.

The timing was always bad for a second couple. She had to be in a mood of closeness, love, emotional warmth, before sex. If she wasn't, the attempt always failed. He, just the opposite, wanted sex in order to restore his sense of loving warmth. Daily, they got along well, but in bed each would have the feeling of wrong time, wrong place, wrong person.

Another couple gradually had less and less sex. She felt that he had rejected her, and, paying him back, she would refuse when he was in the mood. She gave all her energies to taking care of the children and the house. He felt that she had rejected him, and so he spent more and more time at the office or with friends. Her deep suspicion was that he was having an affair. His deep suspicion was that she was having an affair. Their real problem was that they had built up a slow-burning anger against each other, and sex became its focus.

Another pair had a good relationship, except for one re-current moment. She had a small birthmark across the lower part of her neck and upper back. It was noticeable only when she undressed, but when she turned her back to him in the bedroom, he felt a physical repulsion that made sex disagree-able. One underlying reason was that he associated the turned back with his mother's coldness and indifference. The birthmark was no more than a symbol for the rejection he subconsciously expected.

*   *   *

The basic quarrel arising from serious sexual problems afflicts at least half of all American marriages, according to original research by Drs. William Masters and Virginia Johnson that was later supported by others. Alfred Kinsey, in the 1950s, found that a surprising number of married people—50 percent for men, and 25 percent for women—had engaged in extramarital sex before age forty. Philip Blumstein and Pepper Schwartz discovered that little had changed by the 1980s—30 percent of husbands and 22 percent of wives had been unfaithful within the first ten years of marriage.

The paradoxes of sex are many; there is no one pattern of relationship problems, and sexual issues can grow sharp in an otherwise trouble-free marriage. Some marriages have a general tenor of anger, mistrust, and tension that exactly matches the sexual anger, mistrust, and tension. In contrast, there are some marriages in which sex is the only good contact between two unhappy people.

For some fifty years, sex therapists and researchers have been trying to find the secrets of these and other contradictory patterns. We have come a long way in learning about the psychology of sex, and while most couples have become much better informed, there is still a great deal about sexual behavior that remains obscure, and many questions are yet unanswered. In this chapter, I will give an idea of what has been discovered and offer some answers to those unresolved questions that incite the basic sex quarrel.

One of the areas of confusion is the connection between intimacy and sex. It's a question of whether couples absolutely must have a close and tender understanding before they can have fulfilling sex. This is the dilemma of the case history couple who kept feeling that sex always came at the wrong time, wrong place, and with the wrong person.

Another question is about the mystery of sexual excitement. It may flourish with the night, the wine, and the music, and ebb away when children have to be read to at bedtime and the alarm clock set for an early start to office and school. His excitement may revive vigorously when he goes on a business trip with the young woman whose office is just down the hall, or hers may rally with the college friend who looked her up again when he moved to town. Obviously, circumstances make a difference.

Margaret Mead has noted that in some cultures people get sexual stimulation from a particular context or particular body exposure—in some Islamic countries the woman's face is taboo but her navel, in the belly dance, is permissible and exciting. In other cultures, arousal comes from more general promptings. Whether two people can use the knowledge of general or particular stimuli to solve their sexual difficulties in marriage is another question I want to deal with.

How hostility or anxiety affects sexual behavior is still an open question debated by experts. The sex therapist Helen Singer Kaplan thinks that those two unfavorable states have the same general effect as a cold shower, while psychiatrist Robert Stoller thinks that a certain sense of risk and antagonism makes for excitement. This chapter will discuss that issue as well.

Finally, the most important and inclusive question asks how we ought to seek solutions for sexual problems, in whom we should confide, and what kind of knowledge we really need.

SEXUAL STUDIES AND FINDINGS

One of the earliest books of sex advice in English was Daniel Defoe's *The Use and Abuse of the Marriage Bed*, which recommended that couples have sex with "a temperate affection" and that they refrain from "violent transporting desires, or too sensual applications."

In the late nineteenth century, there were two pioneer sex

surveys, one of women born between 1850 and 1880, and one of a group born a little later. Ignorance about sex, guilt, and anxiety showed up in the majority of the answers, and the overwhelming opinion was that the only excuse for sex was to have children. Katharine Davis, one of the survey-takers, commented that the wedding-night shock for the uninstructed bride made for long periods of readjustment and a large number of unhappy marriages.

Early in this century, Sigmund Freud horrified many people with his theory that childhood sexual impulses and fantasies lasted into adulthood and that repressed sexuality was an important source of psychopathology. Gradually, his ideas came to be accepted, taking sex out of the realm of sin and secrecy, although Freud saw sex more as a matter of instincts than of intimate attachment.

By the 1950s, there had been massive changes among Americans. An early 1950s survey by Ernest W. Burgess and Paul Wallin indicated that most college-educated couples entered marriage with adequate sexual information and few fears. The subject of sex really became part of public consciousness with the publication of Kinsey's landmark studies in 1948 and 1953. The message of his books was that female expectations about sex had grown much closer to male expectations in the course of two generations since the first American survey. Most men had masturbated and had enjoyed sex before marriage, and at least half of the women had as well. Most women no longer thought of sex as a degrading duty. Kinsey did, however, hold the biased opinion that many husbands were unsatisfied because their wives didn't want sex often enough.

Changes in attitudes are also reflected in the popular sex-advice books. In the 1950s and 1960s, these manuals proliferated, coincident with the greater emphasis placed on erotic pleasure, but continued to assign the main responsibility for sexual satisfaction to the man. He had to use emotional restraint and physical control to achieve what was then the ideal finale—a simultaneous orgasm.

The feminist movements of the 1970s to 1980s proposed a drastically different view of female sexuality, with less dependence on men. The most popular of the advice books, *The Joy of Sex* by Dr. Alex Comfort, taught that sex was a fifty–fifty matter in both effort and enjoyment. It encouraged foreplay, imagination, and eroticism. Along with that, feminist books instructed women about their bodies and about how to attain orgasm with or without a partner.

The Problems

Despite all this new enlightenment and freedom, the subject of sex continued to place high on the list of major marital troubles whenever therapists were questioned. The most common problem reported by women, according to recent British and American surveys, was "unresponsiveness"—that is, trouble in becoming aroused—or anorgasmia (inability to reach orgasm). Over half of the women questioned had experienced such afflictions. A much smaller percentage complained of vaginismus (an anxiety reaction that caused the muscles around the vagina to contract) or dyspareunia (pain during intercourse).

Men's chief difficulties were failure to achieve an erection, premature ejaculation, and worries about sexual inadequacy.

Sex therapists and researchers generally have found that specific dysfunctions—such as impotence or anorgasmia—account for only a small percentage of sexual complaints relative to sluggish desire. The sex therapist Bernie Zilbergeld believes that this decreased sexual interest is actually a result of different intensities of the sex drive in people—too often they are mismatched in a married couple.

The Treatment

There are two different approaches to dealing with these problems. The psychodynamic method follows traditional lines of therapy, treating dysfunction as a symptom of emotional problems from unconscious conflicts and childhood experience. It explores thoughts, fantasies, dreams, and feelings with the goal of producing a fundamental change in the way a person relates to other people.

The new behavioral approach, which owes much to Masters and Johnson's *Human Sexual Inadequacy* published in 1970, is more of a shortcut. It tries to change patients' behavior by assigning certain exercises and stressing a benevolent and permissive attitude toward sex.

One behavioral exercise, for example, is a series of tasks called "sensate focus" in which the couple first give each other massages without touching breasts or genitals, then gradually increase erotic contact to orgasm. The undemanding pace and the chance to identify where mental blocks exist are meant to free the couple from anxiety gradually.

More recently, Helen Singer Kaplan and others have attempted to combine the two methods. She believes that behavioral methods can deal with immediate dysfunction problems but that a long-term change—particularly in couples with infrequent desire and difficult arousal—depends on exploring deeper feelings and attitudes through traditional techniques.

At first, the innovative Masters and Johnson therapy seemed to have startling success with a variety of dysfunction problems—a 90 percent cure rate. After a while, however, skeptics began to take a closer look, and they didn't like what they found. According to them, Masters and Johnson tended to select highly motivated, close-knit couples who suffered from little more than ignorance and inexperience with sex. These people adjusted quickly. The critics also noted the experimenters' careless handling of their evaluations and vague definition of "successful treatment."

My belief is that while Masters and Johnson made a real contribution to sex therapy, they vastly overstated their case.

The most common complaint is diminished interest in sex, and all forms of treatment for it have had no more than limited success. Treatment is less likely to succeed if the problem has lasted a long time, if the couple do not love each other, or if one or both have a psychiatric disorder. If the couple has once had a good sexual adjustment, still find each other attractive, and can agree on the nature of the problem and goals to be reached, treatment results are much better.

EIGHT PROBLEMS

The Nature of the Problems

Many couples I see professionally describe the signs of a slow-burning quarrel that is gradually consuming their marriage. They make sure not to go to bed at the same time; others sleep in separate rooms. They cannot touch each other without feelings of despair and resentment. They avoid any discussions that hint of affection.

When such a couple comes to consult with me, my first step is to try to learn where the anger and anxiety originated —from a remote source in the past or from a more immediate context. Helen Singer Kaplan describes the remote causes as childhood experiences with sex or problems of love and intimacy within the family of origin. Immediate causes come from sexual failures, of whatever kind, in adulthood. Whether the anger is old or new, it destroys desire. Both sets of causes must be dealt with.

I see eight different areas of difficulty contributing to sexual quarrels. Sometimes a relationship will have more than one of these troubles; sometimes each partner will suffer from quite different ones. They are:

The Fear of Intimacy
The Tug of Invisible Loyalties

The Dangers of Control
The New Ignorance
The Delusion of Command Performance
The Prohibition of Pleasure
The Role of Aggression
Issues of Identity and the Game of False Selves

The Fear of Intimacy

Alice and Sean were an example of a complicated basic sex quarrel. When they first talked to the therapist, both had drifted into affairs with other people. Both wanted to end the affairs and revive their dying marriage.

Alice's reasons for disaffection could be traced to her dislike of what she considered "too much damn togetherness" in the first years of the marriage. She thought she had lost all independence while playing the role of loyal wife. What she didn't recognize was that her family experience had conditioned her to recoil from any show of love or intimacy—and sex was closely associated with those feelings. She bore grudges, too. She felt that Sean had let her down as far as sexual gratification went. Even though she was afraid of intimacy, Sean's brusque and rapid sex approach left her unsatisfied—she almost never reached orgasm—and feeling brutalized.

Sean's "remote" problems stemmed from too much of a temptation toward intimacy. His father had been a reserved and unapproachable man, but his mother had been a beautiful, emotionally generous woman whom he adored. He was capable of love and warmth, and even tried hard to show it in the first year or two of marriage, but he also associated sex with incestuous desires. Although he did not realize it, marrying cold Alice was a defensive measure. What he was painfully aware of was his symptom of premature ejaculation.

Alice's and Sean's affairs satisfied several of their

motivations—to create a comfortable distance from each other, to retaliate for disappointments, to gratify sex in a less "loaded" relationship, and for each of them to reassure themselves about sexual adequacy.

Wallace and Shirley Ann were mismated in quite a different way. In childhood, she had suffered from the absences of her father and the constant criticism of her mother, and this had led to a desperate seeking for reassurance in adulthood. She sought approval for her good looks and good deeds. Although she had flirtations with other men, she remained faithful to her husband—but put relentless sexual demands on him.

Ironically, Wallace's problem complemented hers in an unfortunate way. He had, from his boyhood, deep misgivings about his sexual adequacy, and these now emerged as frequent episodes of impotence. All this added up to a basic quarrel of grand proportions because Wallace and Shirley Ann were both wounded in the most vulnerable points of their self-regard. Her pressures made him feel more anxious and less capable of sexual accomplishment, and this in turn made her feel even more rejected and undesirable.

All relationships have swings between closeness and distance. Most marriages have a shifting equilibrium because two people rarely feel just the same need for intimacy over the course of a day, a week, or a year. This shows up in the common phenomenon of the couple who, living together, have a satisfying sexual relationship but, after they marry, have a bad one. In their case, intimacy may set up an emotional overload of associations with a family of origin, or it may signal the closing of an escape hatch—the end of a more casual and voluntary relationship.

Women and men who shy away from sex-related intimacy usually have different involuntary reasons. With women, it is frequently a sense of vulnerability and a fear of being rejected or abandoned. With men, it is more likely to be a dread of being trapped, a foreboding that they will lose their independence.

The broad and general rule—notwithstanding the exceptional case of Alice and Sean—is that males usually find something threatening about intimacy, while females feel just as great a threat in impersonality.

The Tug of Invisible Loyalties

Couples are often unaware that immediate sexual dysfunctions stem from fears and inhibitions planted long in the past. The chapter on loyalties pointed out that the marriage ceremony is a ritual that is supposed to supplant old allegiances with new ones but that such drastic uprooting is psychologically impossible. Sex in marriage may not recall specific childhood sexual incidents, but it does recall body warmth and intimacy with parents and kin. What messages of reassurance or comfort those ghosts of the past come bearing or what messages of warning or fear they carry are entirely dependent on the individual.

Psychoanalysts describe the period between birth and approximately age five as the "pre-Oedipal" period in which the child learns basic trust, realizes itself as separate from other people—especially its mother—and makes distinctions in its relationships among different people. In the "Oedipal" period, a girl's experience is different from a boy's, but what they have in common is a realization that she/he can't have exclusive possession of the parent of the opposite sex. At this time, the child also forms an identification with the parent of the same sex. As a result, the child learns to manage a triangular relationship among itself and the two people most important to it.

A person who has never succeeded in becoming emotionally independent of the mother is still trapped in a pre-Oedipal conflict that may frustrate sexual expression. Such people are fighting their own tendency to merge with or be engulfed by the loved other person. They also fear that any anger on their part could destroy the one person they cannot live without. Such a person can either suffocate his or her spouse with this desperate need to cling or else flee from closeness because it seems to spell dependency.

It may happen in just the opposite way—someone who felt a lack of mothering in childhood may also have sexual problems. This person is likely to have such desperate and exaggerated longings that nothing the partner can do will satisfy them. That is what psychoanalysts call a "pathological need state," a desire so unrealistic that it will always be unrequited.

People with Oedipal problems either feel a strong need to compete or are shackled by sexual taboos enduring from their formative time. A boy who thought of his father as a frightening or distant figure can neither identify with him or quite give up his exclusive claim on his mother's affection. The case of Sean, given above, is a good example. He could not allow himself to enjoy sex with his wife because his pleasure was mingled with an incestuous guilt.

One couple who came to me complaining of a "communications problem" eventually confessed that they had stopped having intercourse after marriage and that they were completely puzzled as to why. I suggested the "sensate focus exercise"—the nude massage mentioned earlier. At the next session, they reported that during the exercise, the woman had a panic attack. She then told me that she had been sexually molested by her father when she was an adolescent. This memory had never interfered with her sexual life until now, when she felt committed to one man.

Unfortunately for the chances of a cure, her problem was complicated by the fact that the man criticized her unduly, was unreliable, and like her father, had a drinking problem. This was too much trouble to overcome, and the relationship ended in divorce.

The sexual part of marriage can carry pleasure or disappointment, be a bond or a bondage, but there will always be a basic quarrel when sex bears too heavy a burden of unsolved questions from the past.

The Dangers of Control

Sex quarrels can be intricately tangled with drives for power or control. The need of one partner to dominate the other may arise from a fear of being neglected—but it may also come from a fear of that other person's power. Thus: "Better I control you than be controlled by you." Or tit-for-tat patterns may persist: "Since you reject me, I'll reject you." Or one of the two—usually the man—may resent it when the other takes a sexual initiative.

In one case I was acquainted with, two promising young actors had a marriage that was rapidly going sour. They each expressed great respect for the other's talents and personal charm but confessed that their sexual encounters were always irritating and unsatisfying. They believed that they were cursed with some mysterious sexual incompatibility.

Some exploration through therapy showed that the actual basis of their quarrel was not what they seemed to think—it was actually a power quarrel and a career rivalry. True enough, they respected each other's talents on the stage, but that respect was heavily colored with envious rivalry. He could not stand to watch her triumph in a role, nor could she bear to hear him praised. Once they understood this and made an effort to separate their professional lives from their marriage, they enjoyed sexual harmony again.

The full experience of sexual passion requires freedom. True lovers must be taken over by feeling and erotic sensation. If either one is anxious about loss of control or self-control, the encounter is almost certain to fail.

I find that people who have experienced that failure are usually at an impasse. They are powerless to change things for the better, and their only remaining power is to make things worse. In the crisis mood of sexual frustration, they condemn and criticize each other. Each may win a pyrrhic victory by this act of rejection, but it will really be a self-defeat.

The New Ignorance

We usually assume that Victorian ignorance about sex is a thing of the past, therefore we overestimate our modern sophistication. In this era of sexual education in school, plentiful sex manuals, and teenage sex, everybody is supposed to be experienced and knowledgeable. Few but the therapist realize how many people, married or living together for some time, have come to think of sex as part of the household routine, slightly more exciting than washing the dishes but often more difficult.

It isn't so much an ignorance of the mechanics as an inability to communicate feelings and desires. My work with couples has shown me that many people are reticent about conveying their exact wishes or reactions. Vague messages, impatience, and embarrassment all add up to a kind of modern stinginess about pleasure quite as senseless as Victorian moralism.

One couple, married for more than twenty years, came to me for a treatment of her anorgasmia. After a little questioning, I found out that she had, in fact, been faking orgasm for many years. Her husband had sensed something wrong, but they had never discussed the matter.

Further questioning brought out the fact that she was capable of orgasm by squeezing her legs together when she was alone, although she never masturbated. Once all this was out in the open, the treatment involved the woman's reaching orgasm alone by her own manual stimulation, then with her husband present, and last, teaching him best how to stimulate her.

In the early stages of a sexual relationship, there is so much passion and novelty that people usually have little trouble pleasing each other. As habit takes over and unrelated problems impinge on sex, the partners stop being curious about each other. They follow a routine, and the routine becomes impersonal. The sexual deadening that follows usually makes each partner feel inadequate, and that leads to blaming and withdrawal.

Sometimes people don't know what they want. They are afraid to imagine any sexual variation because it might make them feel guilty. Others may assume that the partner doesn't really care about pleasing him or her. Judith Jordan notes that many women are confused about their true desires because they sense that their men aren't interested in finding out more than they already know. When we are in a relationship with someone who isn't responsive to our needs, she writes, we are likely to be confused ourselves about what those needs are.

The Delusion of Command Performance
The sexual equivalent of stage fright is performance anxiety. He or she feels called upon to be a capable lover and is therefore beset with worries. He thinks, Will I get an erection? Will I come too soon? Or take too long? Will she be disappointed? She thinks, Do I seem seductive to him? Will I have an orgasm? Can I have one at the same moment as his? Will he be satisfied with me? This is the kind of anxious wariness that Masters and Johnson call "spectatoring." People who ask themselves such questions become critical spectators in the bedroom, not carefree lovers.

When two such critics get together, they have an organized, goal-oriented view of sex. They take it like a ladder, step by step up to the obligatory orgasm. There's little intimacy or enjoyment, but there is satisfaction in a job accomplished. Once again, attractiveness, adequacy, and potency have been tested and proved. Self-esteem is reassured. The only trouble is that one day the system, under this inordinate burden, breaks down, and a dysfunction appears.

I treated a couple who had gradually abandoned sex altogether. They traced their problem back to a period when they were trying to conceive a child and had to go through an arduous and embarrassing fertility workup. For a number of years, they had to engage in a patterned and monitored sex life with such requirements as measuring basal body temperature and frequent intercourse at the time of ovulation. Eventually, the wife did become pregnant, but at the cost of all spontaneity and playfulness in their sex life. For them, sex had become associated with tiresome routine, anxiety, and failure.

The Prohibition of Pleasure

It is only about thirty-five years since sex began to be openly discussed and openly portrayed in American popular media. Victorian attitudes about sin still linger in many people, and internalized judgments that sex is shameful or dirty still derive from family-of-origin attitudes. These are usually expressed in parental prohibition against a child's asking questions about sex, masturbating, or indulging in sex play with other children. Alternatively, some adults suffer powerful inhibitions about sex as a result of improper stimulation as a child, exposure to the sexual activity of parents, or sexual abuse. As adults, they still subconsciously associate their arousal with being shamed, violated, or punished, and they are frightened.

In my clinical practice, I have been impressed by the volume of reports of childhood sexual abuse. Freud used to discount most such memoirs as fantasies reflecting unconscious wishes or fears, but recent experience has made us believe that we have far underestimated the frequency of abuse and incest in families.

Sometimes the heritage of inhibition, surprisingly, urges people to more sexual action rather than less. Judith Felton reports that many people who chose sexually open relationships in the 1960s were not so much audacious free spirits as they were people struggling to overcome their internal prohibitions about sex.

I once treated a couple who attributed their rapidly declining sex interest to the presence of their five children. After dealing with the kids, there just wasn't time, energy, or opportunity, they said. In the palmy days before their population explosion, they used to go skinny-dipping in their pool and have wonderful sex afterward. That was no longer possible.

I began to suspect that the children had become an external focus for their own inhibitions, and I questioned them more closely about the household. I found out that they allowed the children to come into their bedroom without knocking, that they were careful to avoid any display of affection in front of the kids, and that each went to bed at a different time from the other to avoid any intimation that sex might be in progress.

The first thing I had them do was put a lock on the bedroom door. The real treatment began with an exploration of the family origins of their own sexual inhibitions.

The Role of Aggression

Anger is one of the primary barriers to sexual performance, comments Helen Singer Kaplan. It can be overt, but more often the basic quarrel that causes sexual dysfunction is hidden. Enduring anger is like a circuit breaker that turns off desire automatically; memories of the argument at breakfast or a refusal to take one seriously—things that have nothing to do with sex—shut off the current of responsiveness. The circuit breaker then acts as a passive-aggressive weapon, whether consciously or not. It is a way of saying, in effect,

"You've been impossible to live with this week, and now you want to have sex? Well, not with me. I'm turned off completely. I think it's time for a little revenge."

Male sexuality is usually typed as sadistic and aggressive— a view supported by a great deal of pornography—and female sexuality as masochistic. When the aggression thesis was tested in the Sexual Fantasy Project at the Columbia Psychoanalytic Center, the old stereotype got substantial support. Of the men questioned, 11 percent had fantasies of torturing their sex partners, 20 percent fantasized about whipping or beating partners, and 44 percent imagined forcing their partners to submit to sex acts. Answering the same questions, women scored zero on the first, 1 percent on the second and 10 percent on the third. Clearly, the part aggression plays in sexual excitement is radically different in a fairly large percentage of males and females.

Whether many men are inherently sadistic or whether their hostility toward women is conditioned culturally is an open question. The psychiatrist Ethel Person believes that these male impulses to dominate are not inherent but are compensation for feelings of inadequacy. Men have the urge to dominate women as a reprisal for their rejection by women. This suggests a corollary conjecture that male sexual hostility may be vented only partly on the wife or lover and partly on a persistent memory—of a mother, former wife, or girlfriend, or any woman who played some important role.

Sexual dysfunction may arise as a guard against one's own supposed potential for sadism and aggression. For example, a man might subconsciously fear that he hurts a woman with his penis and, as a result, would avoid sex.

Aggression may also show up as competitive—as resentment or jealousy of the other person's pleasure. It may also take the passive form of frustrating the other's wishes. Withholding sex is a power play or a revenge play, whether it is consciously done or not.

As Otto Kernberg points out, the female invasion of once-male territory in business and professions has increased a generalized aggression against women. The man who finds himself taking orders from a woman at the office, store, or factory may take out his resentment on his wife after he gets home. Kernberg thinks that the level of male sexual hostility, taken as a broad societal fact, has risen in recent years.

Aggression is not, however, quite so simple as I've presented it this far. We have seen that some couples are unable to have sex because they fight and some couples fight in order to avoid sex—but there are those others who fight so that they can enjoy sex. Surprisingly, hate is not the chief enemy of sexual love, but indifference is. There has been too little study of the passionate relationship in which hostility is one element of sexual excitement. That may be a violent relationship, but at least it is in balance—for the time being. The *Kama Sutra*, the ancient Indian book of sexual instruction, compares sexual intercourse to a quarrel, "on account of the contrariness of love and the way it leads to disputes."

Issues of Identity and the Game of False Selves
First, we have to be able to trust, which makes it possible for us to create a firm identity for ourselves. Knowing ourselves in this way, we can go on to a mature sexual relationship. The psychoanalyst Erik Erikson comments:

> Where an assured sense of identity is missing, even friendships and affairs become desperate attempts at delineating the fuzzy outlines of identity by mutual narcissistic mirroring: to fall in love often means to fall into one's mirror image, hurting oneself and damaging the mirror.

Sex combined with love is a merging experience. That experience can be risky, as Erikson says, unless we have a secure sense of self we can refer back to. Another risk is the fiasco, or unsuccessful sex, which can shake self-confidence, making us feel inadequate or unappealing.

Gender identity plays a complicated role in our sexuality. Most people think of the intensity of sexual response as being a test of whether one is adequate as man or woman. We often look to sex to give us reassurance about our identities, and such overdependence often makes us insecure.

Sex, more than any of the other six quarrel causes, makes people put on disguises. Adopting a false self usually begins in adolescence, when the apparent sexual response of a person is often no more than a pose. Adolescent boys and girls are likely to begin sex either as a way of getting rid of nervous tension, or as a way of showing they belong to their peer group, or from the stimulus of dreams manufactured by the commercial culture. Judith Jordan notes that women in their teens or early twenties may actually want a love affair—an emotionally satisfying bond—but end up behaving as a sexual object because that seems to be the only chance to connect with boys. It is no news, on the other hand, that boys create a false self and play the romantic lover when their intentions are purely physical—or show bravado when they are most insecure.

The result is that people often begin to perceive sex as a game of false selves that has to be played to maintain a relationship, and that persists into adulthood. The girl who got accustomed to using deceptions in adolescence may become the wife who fakes orgasm. The boy who counterfeited gallantry in college days may become the husband who only pretends emotional involvement in sex. My own belief—although there seems to be little professional discussion of the subject—is that the game of false selves is the cause for a great deal of sexual dysfunction. When a wife or husband is unable or unwilling to have sex, it's a signal that somewhere in the subconscious a voice has said, "This is all a fake. Stop pretending!"

This kind of behavior is not necessarily pathological, but there are a pair of problems that are more severe—"pathological altruism," or masochism and its counterpart, pathological narcisissism. The altruist gives all but can never receive anything; the narcissicist always takes but cannot give. I once observed such a match. The woman seemed thoroughly grateful that a "special" man had chosen her. She fed his vanity, agreed to all his requests, flattered him outrageously, and never had a thought of her own. In return, he gave her lavish presents but nothing of himself. One day, without getting his permission for fear of a refusal, she made a trip that she considered unavoidable. This small, independent action infuriated him, and no matter how repentant she was, he beat her. He couldn't stand the thought that he was not the center of her life.

THE STEPS TO IMPROVEMENT

Discussion

Persistent and seemingly insoluble sexual problems call for the counsel of a third party, usually someone trained in sex therapy, but there are improvements that can come from our own efforts to sort out problems and talk them over as a couple. Today, there are many good books and even sex-instruction films that will help to define the issues clearly. If things are not going well, here are some of the quite ordinary facts of daily life in a marriage that should be assessed anew for clues of contradictions and misgivings. As part of this self-assessment, couples might ask themselves these questions:

1. *How does each partner define the sexual problem, and how would each like to change?*

2. *What things most tend to influence the frequency and quality of sex?*

3. *Do foreplay and other intimate contacts always lead to intercourse?*

4. *How much pleasure in physical (but nonintercourse) contact and sensuality can each of you allow himself or herself?*

5. *What were each of your childhood and adolescent experiences of physical contact and pleasure?*

6. *Can each partner let the other know what he or she finds most pleasurable sexually?*

7. *How comfortable is each of you with nudity and with bodily functions such as defecation?*

8. *How and when does each person turn himself/herself off sexually? What kinds of things are turn-ons, what are turnoffs?*

9. *What is your foreplay like? What do you do or avoid doing, and have you negotiated the matter?*

10. *Are you able to say "no sex" if you don't feel inclined?*

11. *How does it feel if your partner says no, and how do you handle that?*

12. *Who initiates sex and how? How does either communicate sexual arousal; how does either decline?*

13. *Can you bring each other to orgasm without intercourse?*

14. *How concerned is each of you about gratification for both? Is there a balance, or is it one-sided?*

15. *Who is the dominant person in the sexual relationship?—or is it equal?*

16. *How much concern and caring is expressed in your sex and in the overall relationship?*

17. *How comfortable are you with your own body and your partner's body?*

18. *What would happen if sex improved?*

19. *What kinds of things tend to interfere with sex (e.g., children, illness, work, fatigue, etc.)? How have you tried to deal with them?*

20. *Have contraception and fear of or inability to become pregnant been problems?*

21. *How were sexual matters handled in your family while you were growing up? What were your impressions or fantasies about your parents' marriage and their sexual relationship?*

22. *When did your sexual problems begin and what reason—or reasons—does each give for them?*

23. *Has the frequency and nature of sexual contacts changed?— and what may have contributed to this?*

24. *Do you feel free to express your sexual desire at any time?— and what kind of a reception do you expect?*

25. *What are the kinds of things you find most sexually exciting?*

26. *Is the pattern of sexual problems in this relationship similar to those that occurred in past relationships? Why or why not?*

27. *Do you each tell each other what you like or dislike—both sexually and otherwise?*

28. *How do you handle disappointing sexual experiences?*

29. *Do you still find each other physically attractive?*

30. *Do you have a difference in sexual drives—if so, how do you handle it?*

31. *What do you most value or admire about each other? What do you most dislike?*

32. *How important is sex to the overall relationship?*

33. *Was there a time when sex went better? What has changed?*

34. *When either of you can't seem to get aroused sexually, what feelings are you aware of? What are the things either is anxious or angry about?*

Help from Sex Therapy

As useful as it is to try to define sexual problems by this kind of questioning, deeper problems and chronic dysfunctions demand the help of a therapist. As I have suggested before, behavioral treatment has its limitations. It doesn't work very effectively with people who resist any change in their habits of life or who have little motivation to solve their problems. For the more intrepid and adaptable, for those with a basically sound marriage, it can be rewarding.

The therapist can be helpful in identifying the true problem. There is the common case of the wife who can reach orgasm by masturbation but not in intercourse and yet rejects stimulation by her husband because she is too embarrassed. Another couple thinks their problem is premature ejaculation—he can't persevere longer than five minutes. The therapist can point out to them that their goal of simultaneous orgasm is unrealistic and will point out alternative ways for him to satisfy her.

Sex therapy is based on the notions that both man and woman deserve gratification; sex is a natural act that is sometimes constricted by negative attitudes rooted in the past. The therapist respects the power of personal history, but tries to soften old inhibitions with a spirit of warmth and reason, rarely through individual therapy alone, usually through couples therapy, and sometimes through a combination of the two.

At the same time, the therapist is looking for what Helen Kaplan calls the immediate causes—life-styles and personal styles. The couple with the heavy work schedule and two-year-old who loves to jump into the parental bed, the angry couple who drag their resentments to bed with them, the spouse weighed down by depression, the missionary-position couple who have reached the point of total boredom—these people are all subject to short-term therapy. The sex therapist prefers to treat the marriage itself as the patient rather than one or both of the partners as distinct from it. If the therapist singles out one partner alone for treatment, that person may feel blamed and humiliated. This doesn't bar the therapist from occasional one-on-one therapy. In the above-cited case of the woman who had to overcome a fear of manual genital stimulation, for example, the therapist discussed the problem with her alone in the beginning. The object will always be to work toward an eventual bridge that will bring both partners into the process and emphasize their shared responsibility for change.

The object is to get husband and wife to stop asking, "Why are you making this trouble for me?" about their sexual problem and start asking, "What have we been doing to cause trouble for each other?" The ultimate responsibility for improvement then lies with each person, resting on shared hope rather than one-sided blame.

Earlier, I referred to the anxieties we bring to bed with us as one major cause for sexual disagreements or indifference. Helen Singer Kaplan believes that we have a much freer choice about our sexual feelings than we realize. She maintains that we can train ourselves to banish negative thoughts and images—the irritating incidents of the day, some angry observation about our partner, guilt about something done or undone—if we make the effort. When people can't let go of the inhibiting thoughts, they require longer-term therapy in order to understand the reasons.

The folklore of sex is full of fallacious notions, and one of them is the idea that orgasm is something like a winning touchdown and multiple orgasm a championship. Couples should look at their hours for sex as times for relaxing, for sensuality, for sharing agreeable and frivolous talk; it is a time when there are no faults, no mistakes, and no guard fences.

In contrast to the "ladder" idea of sex mentioned earlier, the sex therapists Robert and Patricia Travis propose an ideal "circle of intimacy," in which sex is not separated from daily living but is always present in a kind of "foreplay" that isn't necessarily a prelude to intercourse.

To make such intimacy possible, there must be a clear and direct exchange of feeling—the invitation to sex, the response, and how each will stimulate the other. Judith Jordan points out, however, that this isn't simply a matter of saying "touch me there," but a whole vocabulary of intimacy, almost like a private language.

SEX, INTIMACY, AND CHARACTER

Intimacy is an enigma. It often happens one person will have an affair—and far more passionate sex—with someone he or she knows far less well than wife or husband. Intimacy, it seems, can be either an aphrodisiac or a cold shower. This paradox underlies the debate between the behavioral and the psychodynamic therapists—how interdependent are sex, intimacy, and character? Behaviorists argue that it's not their job to try to change character. It may not be necessary or it may require a long, drawn-out, and expensive analytical process. Advocates of psychodynamics say that the frequent failure of behavioral cures shows that sex has to be dealt with in the context of intimacy and character. Some even believe that it may be "natural" for some couples to give up sex altogether, and therapy, in those cases, is only a form of artificial resuscitation.

The psychodynamic partisans even have differences among themselves in the sex-intimacy-character debate. Freud thought that sex was largely a matter of instinct, a discharge of tension through lust. The British theorist W.R.D. Fairbairn—whose approach is called "object relations"—believes that our first need is to form a relationship with someone (in his term, the "object") and that erotic experiences are only "signposts" that point toward this end.

Erik Erikson believes that the mother-infant relationship establishes basic trust, which is the foundation of personal identity, which in turn is essential for mature sexual relationships. This is a strong endorsement of the view that intimacy, character, and sexuality are bound closely together.

Harry Stack Sullivan, in contrast, wrote that intimacy and

lust are not necessarily related. He saw three primary human needs—for security or freedom from anxiety, intimacy, and lust. These can be combined in some relationships, but in others they may be trade-offs. That is, a wife or husband might give up some sense of personal security in order to have full intimacy. Sullivan also thought that our capacity to be intimate first develops with friends of our own sex.

My own clinical experience tells me that it is often hard to distinguish cause and effect in relationship problems. I know on one hand that intimacy, commitment, and tenderness can contribute to a richer sexual life, but on the other hand I also know that different people have different needs. Some couples can be satisfied with less of one element and more of another. Marital guidebooks advocate various "ideal" sexual relationships. The question is, ideal for whom?

There are gender differences in those desires. Men generally seem to fit Sullivan's theory of dissociation between lust and intimacy; Fairbairn's theory best describes women's desire for closeness and empathy above all.

I believe that the fallacy in most theories about an ideal marriage lies in the assumption that marriage is a steady-state affair. It isn't. The relationship between intimacy and sex will probably change in the course of time. It becomes a basic quarrel only when no compromise is possible.

SEX AND PSYCHOLOGICAL EXPERIENCE
If good sex depended just on absence of anxiety, we would search out the dullest mates we could find and never have love affairs. The sex and intimacy of the present is inevitably linked in the mind with old prohibitions, past loves, good and bad memories—and such comparisons are usually disturbing. In love, we are looking for an escape from that past to a more distant, innocent, pre-Oedipal past, according to the British psychiatrist Henry Dicks. He believes that mar-

riage is akin to the "original parent-child relationship," making couples "able to regress to mutual, child-like dependence, without censure or loss of dignity."

One of the ways to make that escape would be through intimate play. Here is an example as related by a wife:

> One time before we were married, we went swimming in a secluded mining pit that had filled with water. I had rather long hair then, and I put it up in pigtails. After we got out of the water, we lay on the blanket nude, waving at an inquisitive small plane that flew overhead a couple of times. I said something about feeling like a little kid with my pigtails. Chet laughed and said that I did look pretty young, and it made for a great fantasy. I played along, acting like an innocent little girl. It made for one of those magical days together.
>
> A few months later, there was a thunderstorm when we were at home and I was frightened. Something just came over me, and I ran and sat in Chet's lap and he comforted me as if I were a little girl. Every so often now we play at me being a little girl. I suppose it makes me feel protected and cared for.

Taking a somewhat more complicated view of the return to childhood, Dr. David Scharff, in *The Sexual Relationship*, writes that we associate good sex with the remembrance of a loving and generous parent and unsatisfactory sex with a parent who frustrated or disappointed us. Into the image of the bad parent, he would incorporate guilty memories of stimulus and excitement and ultimate disappointment. Such recollections are not conscious memories but feelings of association that make us react to our partner as we would react to the "good" or the "bad" parent.

In a good marriage, gratifying sex acts both as a kind of amnesty from the onus of past mistakes and failed relationships and as a commemoration of happy and bountiful experiences. It is an occasion for joining past and present in a fusion that repairs and renews.

The Symbolism of Sex

The true erotic experience is stimulated by novelty and subtlety. We are seduced by innuendo and quickly bored by crude and literal exposure. A nudist camp after a while becomes about as sensual as a sales convention, while in the city an unanticipated glimpse of an inch of flesh is exciting. The women's fashion business thrives because its designers understand mystery, illusion, ambiguity, and tantalization.

Erotic appeal is, nevertheless, a matter of taste. One man's or one woman's titillation is another's boredom. What no one, in the literature of sex, seems to have expressed is the idea that eroticism is in fact a metaphor. We are excited by something that has the power to evoke a delicious memory—perfume, dress, picture, bodily shape, or body language, or a sexual approach. These, not chemicals, are the real aphrodisiacs, and their strength is the strength of a private metaphor.

The behaviorists haven't recognized this because they have concentrated on banishing anxiety and giving positive reinforcement, to the exclusion of the personal element.

The psychoanalysts have missed it by defining sexual desire as a complex of instinct, unresolved childhood frustrations, conflict, and early gratification. Both of these theories are incomplete. The metaphorical reference to the past is exciting because it adds richness to the present; adult sexual arousal has layers of meaning rather different from simple, first-time experience.

Crossing Boundaries

When one's sex drive is blocked from winning its desired object, according to Freud, romantic love is the result. The European medieval and Renaissance philosophy of courtly love—possibly the most extreme version—glorified the idea that a knight could love a lady not his wife with passion but without sex. Unrequited love was one of the great themes of the Romantic poets and novelists a few centuries later.

In 1896, Alice B. Stockham's *Karezza*, a popular marriage manual, recommended:

> Given abundant time and mutual reciprocity, the [sexual] interchange becomes satisfactory and complete without crisis by either party. In the course of an hour, the physical tension subsides, the spiritual exaltation increases, and not uncommonly visions of a transcendent life are seen and consciousness of new powers experienced.

Anthony Storr has written that sex achieves its primal importance because it is the only major aspect of life that is not overtly consummated in the family. That is, because it is concealed from the child as he or she grows up, the result is a lifelong quest to heal the split between love and sex. For the psychoanalysts, the great barrier taboo between lover and object is the Oedipus complex, which is activated by family prohibitions against early sexual behavior.

I prefer Otto Kernberg's view that sexual passion arises from defiance—a rebellion against various taboos of which the Oedipal taboo is only one. As I have noted elsewhere, "Our fascination with the forbidden and out of reach is not just a matter of our unresolved incestuous wishes. Every secret carries within it the wish to conceal but also the captive wish to reveal."

Loved One Versus Love Object

There is a profound distinction between a loved one and a love object. Martin Buber labeled them I-thou and I-it relationships and considered the sexualization of love as a form of I-it. Robert Stoller, writing on perversions, says that when one person transforms another into an object, as it were, that act of dehumanization is an unconscious revenge. It is a revenge against the adults who long ago frustrated him or her as a child.

A graphic example of I-it is in fetishistic behavior, where, for instance, a man may dote on a woman's shoe in lieu of the woman herself. Stoller points out that a similar psychological process takes place with pornography. The male viewer feels that he is looking at something forbidden and that the woman pictured is somehow forced to display herself in this way. From that, he gains a victory over the real women who have rejected and humiliated him.

The opposite of this is the mature experience of sex as self-transcendence, the almost spiritual merger of two selves, the ultimate of I-thou. It might seem impossible to see any connection between these polar extremes of perversion and self-transcendence, but I believe that there is a continuum.

Can a couple weave both hostile and loving elements into their relationship, and thus have a richer and more passionate sex life? Stoller answers that hostility is essential to sexual excitement, and it's a rare person who has nothing but tender and altruistic impulses. Kaplan disagrees. She says that hostility is the chief impediment to successful sex.

I am convinced that most couples move back and forth between I-thou and I-it, and I think that this is not necessarily destructive. I agree with W.R.D. Fairbairn in his definition of maturity as the ability to use multiple pathways to make contact. It seems to me that, at certain times, one partner may need to view the other as an object or an actor within a private fantasy in order to work out internal conflicts. If both indulge in such fantasy and if they relate well in other ways, this flight of fancy may even abet sexual intimacy. As George Goethals says, "A perversion is something that two people do but only one [of them] enjoys."

Playfulness

Playfulness is a part of intimacy and sex that has had little attention from therapists and researchers. In my own investigation of it over the past fifteen years, I've found it to be one of the great values in marriage. Playfulness—by which I mean teasing, private language, jokes, and shared fantasy—is a unique way of relating. Couples who play successfully show a deep trust in each other and a deep respect for each other's vulnerabilities.

Sex as a deadly serious matter becomes merely deadly. In foreplay, the emphasis should be not on the "fore"—which is a goal orientation—but on the "play," which is spontaneity, relaxation, creative lovemaking.

Conclusion

Sex, like money, should carry a warning label: do not attach unrealistic needs or expectations to this product. I consider a sexual relationship a flexible affair, subject to change. There is no permanently satisfactory form that a couple can draw up and expect to be final. Kernberg says that mature relationships are always ambiguous and mysterious and that there are only two essential constants in them: intimacy and discretion.

CHAPTER SEVEN

PRIVACY

Privacy is the quiet region of marriage. Since we tend to consider it a personal, subjective matter, we seldom contemplate how much good a subtle balance of intimacy and separateness can contribute to a relationship—or how much trouble can come from misapprehensions about what we should share and what to keep to ourselves. When any pair begin to live together, they should realize that two sets of private boundaries have to be redrawn and redefined.

We can see a balance of privacy rights and concessions in the larger arena of society. The Constitution guarantees us no more than the freedom from unwarranted search and seizure and from having troops quartered in homes, yet the principle of protection of privacy runs through many of our laws. The right of a citizen to vote in secret, of a jury to deliberate in secret, of a lawyer or doctor to claim privilege for his or her conversations with client or patient, of a person to refuse to testify against himself, are some of democracy's guarantees. Society limits or infringes on privacy when it demands to know the amount of our incomes, requires us to serve in the military, or regulates our behavior by law. When it punishes us, it deprives us by putting us in prison, but when it punishes us severely, it gives us total privacy—in solitary confinement.

Marriage, in certain ways, is also a regulated affair. The government both licenses it and dictates how it can be dissolved by divorce—and no-fault divorce laws in certain states protect the privacy of people in divorce proceedings. On the other hand, there are even some cases of absurdly unenforceable invasions of privacy. New Hampshire and a few other states rule that only a married couple can have sexual intercourse, and in 1953, Alfred Kinsey reported that a number of states still decreed which positions in intercourse were legal and which illegal.

One paradox, a cause of many basic quarrels in marriage, is contained in the notion that privacy may be a right but free access is just as much a right. When two such irreconcilable rights meet head-on, the marriage will surely go wrong.

MARRIAGE AND PRIVACY

Within any marriage itself, the partners have to make successive decisions about privacy. First there is the determination about individual privacy within the relationship, then there is one that concerns other people—parents, relatives, friends—outside the marriage, and finally there is the decision about sacrificing individual privacy and couple privacy as a consequence of having children.

Marriage, strange compromise that it is, forces us to give up certain personal areas in order to create a new area of intimate privacy. This is the isolated world of the couple as a unit, distinct from all other roles, relationships, or obligations; it is the inner, dual sphere that constitutes the heart of marriage.

The sociologists Peter Berger and Hansfried Kellner have noted that people commonly make the mistake of entering marriage with the idea that they are simply adding another person to their individual world when, in fact, the marriage creates an entirely new reality. In the past, that creation was relatively simple. Newly married couples relied on a whole network of extended family, community, and religious and ethnic relationships to provide the outer circumference that defined their inner privacy. Today, with those supports diminished or lost, the limits of privacy tend to be defined by more impersonal forces such as the law, geographic isolation, and one's employment.

Real family privacy is a relatively new development in the modern world. In the eighteenth century, the king of France was alone only when he said his morning prayers and put on his breeches—the rest of the day he was surrounded by a crowd. As for the working class, the artisan's apprentices usually lived in the house with his family. The houses of the well-to-do or rich were full of domestics—even as late as 1910. One householder complained, "With servants living in our home by day and night, confronted with our strange customs and new ideas, having our family affairs always before them, and having nothing else in their occupation to offset this interest, we find . . . this arrangement as far removed from privacy as could be imagined." Boarding in private houses was another practice that lasted well into the twentieth century, and, if there were no boarders, there were usually elderly parents or other relatives in residence.

In our own day, such crowds of observers and interlopers have disappeared, and most nuclear families inhabit their own house or apartment in a luxury of isolation—and with a much more intense dependence on the success of their private world. One of the basic quarrels of marriage arises from a failure to achieve this mutual privacy, a shared balance of separateness and union. Whether the failure comes from the intrusion of outsiders and outside interests or from the couple's own inability to attain that balance, it is damaging. It is also one of those failures that most couples find hard to express in words.

There are probably two main viewpoints about the part privacy plays in marriage, and both of them are value judgments. One opinion asserts that marriage should be without secrets; each person should be totally honest and accessible to the other. Another holds that while the sharing of certain secrets is a part of intimacy, it is a mistake to make marriage confessional; each person must retain some areas of autonomy and detachment.

I believe that either of these theories could be detrimental when applied too zealously. One should never underestimate the importance of "islands" of privacy in a marriage—areas of the mind where no other person is allowed—but never to be mistaken for a mainland.

The sociologist Robert F. Murphy puts it well when he says that when people come to know each other more intimately, they must strengthen the defenses that guard "certain residual private spheres." In other words, the more intimate the relationship, the greater the need to keep a certain distance and a certain guarded area of privacy.

As reasonable as this seems, the myth of marriage as a total exchange of thought and emotion persists. The sociologists Robert M. Laufer and Maxine Wolfe compare this attitude to superstitious beliefs about devils and witches. We tend to think, they say, that "what is hidden from us . . . [is] potentially harmful." Any knowledge not shared collectively suggests the possibility of "conspiracy, deviance, and intimacy."

THE MEANINGS OF PRIVACY

Four Kinds of Privacy

There are four different kinds of privacy: of space, of time, of thought and emotion, and of property. We hear them referred to in such common expressions of need as, "time to think this out," "a room of one's own," "in strictest confidence," and "what's mine is mine."

Privacy in marriage is not a simple No Trespassing sign. It is more like a two-way regulation process that controls the flow of confidences—decreeing seclusion when people need it and intimacy when they require that. Couples tend to misunderstand its nature because all four of the elements are mingled in the mind and because the need for privacy usually fluctuates. Most privacy quarrels spring from such a misunderstanding.

The phrase "I need time to think this out" points to the element of time in privacy, as does the complaint "You're always rushing me." As I've noted before, people live at different personal tempos. To try to force someone into acting or making a decision before he or she is temperamentally ready is an invasion of privacy. The reverse can be true as well—a wife or husband who seems to procrastinate needlessly while the other is impatient to move forward can be just as guilty.

The idea of pure meditation time is alien to many Americans. As Edward Hall says, "Just plain sitting, trying to capture a sense of self, is not considered to be *doing anything*." This accounts for the person who says, "You don't seem to be doing anything, so I guess I'll take this chance to talk to you awhile."

"A room of one's own" is a key to the sense of spatial privacy. The instinct to single out some small piece of the world for sole possession goes back to the idea of territoriality described in Chapter Four. Because of that instinct, songbirds sing to mark their territorial boundaries, bears claw bark from tree trunks, and wolves leave urine as an olfactory signpost.

Although humans have a more mobile and less standardized perception of their private space, we all have some re-treat where we can escape from the pains and confusion of the human world—in other words, to shut out the overload of stimuli from observation, communication, and obligation. As children, we find it in a treehouse, a tent, or a nook under the stairs. Later on, in marriage, the need for privacy may get expressed in twin beds, separate bedrooms and bathrooms, and separate studies or workshops. Writers often mention the lack of privacy in the "ant heap" of modern urban-suburban life, yet Americans probably have more keys to spatial privacy than ever before in history. Philippe Ariès notes that European houses had no rooms with specialized functions until the eighteenth century. There was no family privacy of the kind we now have. To enter a certain room, one might have to go through one or two other rooms. Beds or dining tables were moved from chamber to chamber whenever the householder was in the mood for a change. Strangers walked in and out at will.

The modern house, with rooms marked for particular func-tions, rooms opening onto hallways, and separate bathrooms began to take form in the eighteenth century. Whether the change came from a new yearning for privacy in the family or whether the functional arrangement helped to produce that yearning is difficult to say.

Another private area is the personal space we carry around with us—in Edward Hall's memorable image, our "space bubble"—which, for Americans, has an intimate distance of about two-and-a-half feet. We are uneasy if any stranger violates that space, and even more uneasy if touched. Amer-ican culture, unlike some others in the world, is not a "touch culture."

As for the privacy of thought and emotion—"in strictest confidence"—we probably discover this as children when we tell our first protective lie. The next manifestation might be the diary with lock and key, or the private language children sometimes make up to exclude adults. Psychological privacy is defined by the sociologist Alan F. Westin as "The right of the individual to decide what information about himself should be communicated to others and under what conditions." I would propose a somewhat more inclusive definition by saying that privacy of thought and emotion is a sanctuary to protect our sense of autonomy, identity, and vulnerability. We take refuge there to recover self-esteem, to mourn, to envision possibilities, to nurse secret loves or hates or ambitions.

"What's mine is mine" touches on private property as distinct from mere possessions. Such property, as sociologist Barry Schwartz points out, has something of the self in it, and, he adds, "Some private objectifications of self may be observed by family members, but some may be observed by *no one except the self.* There is no doubt that these latter objects have a very special meaning for identity; some of these are sacred and must not be contaminated by exposing them to observation by others; some are profane, and exposure will produce shame, but both . . . represent an essential aspect of self and, from the possessor's point of view, must not be tampered with." The family car is something owned; the bundle of love letters is private property.

Often such private property is purely nostalgic and symbolic: a lock of the baby's hair, Mary's second-grade crayon drawings, the nude pictures Mom and Dad took of each other on their honeymoon in 1963, or Dad's old marine uniform. In fact, physical property of this kind usually has more connection with personal experience and past emotions than do the immediate privacies of time, space, and psychology. It is a part of the history of the self, and to violate it—say, by destroying the love letters—is not a momentary interruption in the present but the invasion of a whole life.

Definitions: Four States of Privacy

The four different states or conditions of privacy noted by Westin imply some of the subject's complexity. He distinguishes them as solitude, anonymity, intimacy, and reserve.

In *solitude*, a person is free from observation, but hardly suspended in nothingness. He or she still has stimuli from seeing, smelling, touching, or tasting surrounding things, and he or she still may suffer heat, cold, pain, thirst, or other sensations. Most important, one is still prey to memory and emotion. Solitude is an escape from other humans, not from humanness.

Anonymity is the avoidance of identification or surveillance in public. In a physical sense, that would be to remain unrecognized in a crowd or in some open place like a park or a street. In another sense, "avoiding identification or surveillance" can mean staying nameless as instigator, perpetrator, or author of something, whether a charitable gift, a book, a poison-pen letter, or a crime.

Intimacy is a shared privacy between two people or a very small group. Those who collaborate try to reject any outside influences by people or events and nurture intense interpersonal relationships. This is the privacy of cultists, conspirators, happy families, and lovers.

Reserve, according to Westin, is the most psychologically complex of the states. For the individual, it is a matter of refusing to reveal aspects of himself or herself considered too personal, shameful, traumatic, or undignified. In a group, it is a matter of maintaining it oneself and respecting it in others. Once very evident in marriage—a nineteenth-century lady might refer to her husband as Mr. Jones (or whatever his surname) all their lives. The modern preference is for intimacy as the better kind of marital privacy, although reserve still has its place in marriage—but without the Victorian formalities.

Privacy Versus Secrets in Marriage

In ordinary usage, the distinction between privacy and secrecy has become blurred. People will often use the two words interchangeably, but there are important differences. We hold something secret either because we know that, revealed, it would be unacceptable to some others or that it could be used to our disadvantage. Secrets are covert in a way that privacy is not. Privacy is usually a neutral thing— "that's my own business"—while a secret is usually provocative, kept a mystery because it might become part of someone else's business. Its content is usually not neutral. Those who share secrets are engaged in a conspiracy of silence, while those who share privacy simply deny intrusion into their closed world. It is possible, however, for something private to be transformed into a secret, and vice versa.

Most marriages have a measure of both. In successful marriages, there will be a maximum of privacy. In quarrelsome and difficult marriages, there will be a predominance of individual secrets. Unshared secrets in marriage may be indicators of guilt, distrust, or selfishness or signs of immaturity. The other side of that coin is the relentless need to know, the continual suspicion that the other person is holding back something. There is the husband who denies his wife any detailed knowledge of family financial assets, even to the provisions in his will; and there is the wife who secretly goes through her husband's clothes looking for some clue that he has been with another woman.

Georg Simmel studied the nature of secret societies, and some of his findings are relevant to marriage. He notes that a secret society is relatively free from the laws of the general society, and yet it imposes its own internal laws and rituals. Just the fact that the members participate in group secrecy— no matter how trivial the secrets—binds them together.

Marriage has a similarity to those societies in that it is a small, closed system with a special bond. Some marriages may even have their own internal rules and rituals to compensate for their freedom from the norms of the bigger world of society.

Types of Privacy in Marriage

Couples work out their areas of privacy in one or more of four different ways:

They can allow privacy to develop without preplanning, according to the natural pattern of their day. Times for intimate communication and times for silence, what they share with each other and what they withhold, all fall effortlessly into some accustomed routine. This might mean, for example, that they have an unspoken agreement not to talk about certain problems at the dinner table in front of the children but will wait for a relaxed half hour before going to bed.

Alternatively, they can evolve their guidelines by reaction to what either one considers an intrusion. As a simple example, if she likes to start a conversation while he is trying to listen to the news on television, they can then set up a privacy rule about that kind of trespass. It's a trial-and-error method that depends more on assertion of "rights" rather than discussion. His right to an undisturbed half hour with the network news becomes a part of the common law of the household.

Again, they can define their privacy as keeping secrets from each other, maintaining a certain reserve, and independently deciding what part of their relationship is combined and what part separate. She does not tell him that she was sexually abused as a child; or he does not tell her that he once had a homosexual fling; or she does not tell him that there have been many deaths from cancer in her family; or he does not tell her that he has been arrested for drunken driving. Unlike these, there may be secrets that are not guarded consciously—sometimes we are only dimly aware that we have a sensitive area of memory that must not be touched verbally.

Finally, they can establish their domains of privacies by agreement and collaboration. For instance, couples who follow this reasonable approach may concur that their separate bank accounts are not subject to review by the other; that each can make investments or own property singly; that each can have friends of the opposite sex without hints of jealousy; that either can take a solo trip or vacation—always without getting approval from the other.

PRIVACY QUARRELS AND THEIR CAUSES
In the following examples of basic quarrels over privacy, one theme runs throughout: people who initiate such conflicts are usually those who cannot tolerate ambiguity in situations and who have pronounced views about privacy, either for or against. It takes tolerance and a sense of security to be able to work out mutual agreements that will, necessarily, close off some areas of a partner's life from the other person.

Suffocating Togetherness
One couple I knew ran an office-supplies store together and had to deal with each other all day long as well as after work. Another pair were both tax lawyers, and although they worked in different firms, they constantly discussed tax problems and compared notes in their hours together. A third couple, two psychotherapists, left no aspect of their relationship unanalyzed—as if they were each other's patients. In another couple, the wife was a confessional personality—the type driven by guilt or hostility—who insisted on admitting her every fault, flaw, or misstep to her husband. Early in the marriage, he listened sympathetically; as time went on, the confessional became oppressive.

None of these people suffered from any basic ill-will toward his or her spouse, but all endured a steady, low-grade irritation. They had consciously opted for an extraordinary congruence in their marriages, forgetting the old maxim that there can be too much of a good thing. When they quarreled, they quarreled about unrelated things, but their actual problem was that they had destroyed all privacy in their marriages and most—if not all—of them subconsciously resented it. "Good fences make good neighbors" in marriage as well as in Vermont.

Intrusions

One husband, shortly after marriage, had the habit of walking into the bathroom and pulling back the curtain while his wife was taking a shower—which she resented as an inroad on her right to be alone. He protested that they had been intimate for some time, and he'd never noticed any inhibitions about nudity in the bedroom.

A wife was used to reading her husband's mail. When he objected, she said that she'd never seen anything secret or shameful in it and that she had a right to know what was on his mind.

Another wife would visit an astrologer about once a month. When her husband found out, he was indignant—he said it was a waste of money on a worthless exercise and it made her look gullible.

Each of the victims had the same reply: "Stop it because it's none of your business." Sometimes that simple and inclusive declaration of the right to privacy says it all.

Betrayal

One example of betrayal concerned a couple who were having sexual problems. Looking for a sympathetic ear, the wife confided all the details to a woman friend. On discovering this, the husband called it an act of disloyalty and said that problems between themselves shouldn't be passed on to others.

A betrayal quarrel is probably the most serious of all privacy quarrels because it involves the felt violation of a basic trust. It is not always so clear-cut as it might seem, however, and it can have a number of different motivations. An overly suspicious or overly sensitive person can demand unreasonable limitations on what can be said or done outside the home. In another instance, a betrayal of confidence can be— either consciously or unconsciously—a hostile act. Its intention then is to wound the other person deeply. For such betrayals, forgiveness comes hard.

Mistrust

In an article on intimate play, I cited the case of a young couple who liked to play a childhood game. One would hide and then unexpectedly jump out and scare the other. As time went on, the game had a peculiar effect—all their trust in each other began to deteriorate. One of them said, "When I go home to what ought to be an empty apartment, I can't feel sure that I'm really alone. It's hard to relax." Then, to make matters worse, the wife had a secret hiding place where she kept something valuable. After she had repeatedly refused to tell him the location, her husband was furious. He said that she was treating him like a child.

Issues of trust are less dramatic than betrayals, but they, too, can have destructive outcomes. Most people get married with a sense of confidence about trusting the other completely. If that confidence begins to erode, the marriage erodes proportionately.

Privacy Fears

I have often treated marriage partners of whom one had become pathologically jealous. Almost always, the jealousy took the form of sexual suspicions—he or she was convinced that the other was having a homosexual or heterosexual affair. One woman, after several years as a housewife, got a job working in a tourist agency. She had a close female friend who worked in the same agency, and occasionally they had to take a business trip together. In another case, a husband was helping a new business venture get started in another city and so was often away from home overnight. Spouses of both these people were tormented with suspicion, although there was not the slightest indication that either the woman in the first case or the man in the second had done anything wrong.

The fear of infidelity, then, was no more than the outward sign of deep-running insecurity and mistrust. In actuality, the accusers felt threatened and angry because their partners had reserved an area of privacy for themselves.

There can be many different reasons for a near-pathological inquisitiveness. In one case I knew, a wife had been previously married to a philanderer who had managed to keep his affairs secret from her for several years. In another case, a husband had grown up in a family that was constantly moving from city to city for reasons that were obscure to the children. As he grew older, he learned the secret—his father couldn't keep a job, and his mother was enraged by such shiftlessness. In both cases, the people I knew suffered feelings of desperation because of their past experiences of being denied the truth. In married life, both began to have overwhelming feelings that their spouses were hiding some momentous, devastating secret.

Self-deception

Some people insist on designating certain actions as private when those actions are in fact matters of double deception. I knew of a man who speculated constantly on dubious stocks and get-rich-quick business investments without ever telling his wife. Over several years, a good part of the family income was lost on penny stocks and wildcat oil drilling. He explained his deceit by saying, "It would really break her up if

I told her. She just couldn't handle it." His deception thus had led to a self-deception, and the whole family suffered as a result.

This again, can be called a hostile act in that the husband declared, in effect, that his wife was too fragile to accept bad news, and hostile in that he was holding back information important to her.

Sometimes people are actually able to hide the bad news from themselves, never quite consciously acknowledging that they have done something wrong. They have mentally camouflaged the unpleasant fact so that they won't have to face it—and the rationalization they give themselves is that they must protect their own privacy.

Lies

I have seen pathological relationships in which lying, on the part of one or both, was routine. I treated one case in which the wife was having a long-term illicit affair. Whenever something happened to arouse her husband's suspicions, she protested innocence—when she went out in the evening, it was always to see women friends or to have a drink with some coworkers. One day he found an incriminating Valentine's Day card from her lover, and eventually the truth came out. The husband said, "I guess I really knew all along, but deep down I thought that I would always be the only one for her. Somehow, hearing her say it [that she'd been unfaithful] feels different." Once she'd confirmed his belief in words, he was ready for a divorce.

Lies that are deliberate, cynical, and self-serving are the ones that cause basic privacy quarrels. In my experience, there is some amount of lying in almost every relationship. Small social lies or face-saving lies are not a sign of pathology or a bad marriage. We are all engaged in a certain amount of normal, human concealment and self-deception. The crucial thing is to distinguish between the white lie and the destructive lie.

Pretending

When either husband or wife can't understand the subtle balance of intimacy and privacy, the other is often driven to a kind of playacting. The woman who always faked orgasm, mentioned in Chapter Five, was a good example of someone who could not assert her right to privacy. In pretending to feel something she did not feel—in order to flatter a man—she surrendered something of her own private, inner integrity.

Dissociation is a psychological mechanism that creates an area of privacy when there is no other way to have it. When we can't retreat physically, we cut ourselves off from our feelings. If this happens often enough, we grow permanently numb to feelings.

Seduction

Therapists dealing with privacy troubles are aware of many kinds of manipulation. One example is the person who confides some special information of his or her own in order to disarm another. He or she then exploits the sympathetic response and good feeling to extract even more confidential information from the other, only to put his or her own guard up soon after. In this way, intimacy can be used as a seduction and a confidence game.

Another manipulative ploy I have seen is the minor confession offered as a decoy to avoid making the major one—a small embarrassment, perhaps, in lieu of a serious admission. This is usually not a conscious effort to deceive but a fairly customary effort to save face.

Then there is that awful phrase "I'll be frank with you." It automatically alerts me to a coming lie or else warns me that my interviewee is, uncharacteristically, about to tell the truth.

Territory and Isolation

As I've noted before, disputes over personal space—a desk, one side of the bed, the bathroom, a favorite chair, dresser drawers—are one of the significant and consistent forms of privacy battle.

If we insist on too much privacy, we can make ourselves victims of a fortress mentality. As John Archea writes:

> To illustrate the architectural dynamics of privacy, consider a solitary person surrounded by thick stone walls which allow virtually no sound transmission. With a single, unlocked door . . . one would . . . assume that a high degree of privacy exists. . . . Yet if someone approaches the door from the other side, the barrier to sight and sound . . . may diminish the privacy of the person in the room because he or she will have no way to anticipate the . . . intrusion. The . . . surprise . . . created when the door is thrown open could easily be more intrusive than if a thinner barrier had permitted a few moments of prior warning.

Secrets

Some secrets, if revealed, can be devastating for a marriage. I have known of wives who had long-standing love affairs with their husband's business partner and husbands who have been sexually involved with their wife's best friend. Except in rare cases of forgiveness, revelations of such behavior usually destroy a marriage, if not in the courtroom at least in the heart.

Even a previous bad experience with a nonsexual secret can influence a marriage for the worse. I recall the case of the woman who, as a child, had her pet dog disappear, and no amount of searching succeeded in finding it. Later, she found out that her father had given the dog away for fear it would bite her small sister. When the woman was grown and married, she was hypersensitive about the possibility that her husband might be keeping secrets. He took this as a sign that she didn't trust him and from that came their privacy quarrel.

When another couple came to me for help with severe sexual problems, I discovered that the husband's anxiety came in part from an old secret. As an adolescent boy, he had engaged in some fairly innocent sex play with other boys. His parents had learned of it, and their reprimand had left him with guilt feelings. He had never dared tell his wife about this because he knew of several times when she had passed intimate information on to her friends. It is a good example of how an old, guilt-tinged secret and insensitivity about keeping a confidence can combine to mar a marriage.

Outsiders

The aged mother-in-law who comes for a visit or to move in; an old college friend who overstays his welcome; the "au pair" who, though great with kids, has some peculiar habits; the teenagers' friends who arrive with their stash of pot and their favorite CD rock music—all of them diminish a couple's privacy in both obvious and subtle ways. It should be noted that it's likely that each partner of the couple will react differently here because people have varying thresholds of tolerance to nuisance. The wife, for instance, might get thoroughly irritated with the careless au pair girl but simply smile at the teenagers' commotion.

When the discomfort level rises too high, however, the couple usually begin to quarrel, one the accuser and the other a defendant. Until this happens, we are never quite aware of how much outsiders and their individual voices, noises, movements, and habits can encroach on our private space. It is no wonder that one of the householder's most cherished maxims is "Fish and guests spoil in three days."

Gender Differences

The cultural stereotype to the effect that women tend to disclose more of their thoughts and feelings than men is substantiated to a degree by research. These differences in outlook underlie a great many of the quarrels over intimacy and privacy.

Most therapists are likely to view a man's greater reserve as a grave deficiency that has to be modified. When he is faced with a wife's complaint about her husband's uncommunicativeness, the therapist usually tries to help the man change. The therapist's goal—to make the husband more affective and communicative—is a tacit acceptance of the feminine definition of intimacy. That definition can be just as tyrannical as was the old stereotype that women are simply creatures of their emotions. In many cases, this male reserve about self-disclosure is not a problem that can be rectified but a fundamental gender difference that needs to be understood as such.

Trade-offs

People use various mechanisms to insure privacy: by staking out personal space, avoiding eye contact, refusing confidentiality, hiding true feelings under a social veneer, withdrawing emotionally, remaining aloof from others' problems, withholding information, and telling protective lies.

Georg Simmel believes that most people have a natural ratio between the privacy they seek and the openness they desire. The ratio between the two remains constant, but there can be changes in the kind of privacy they demand. There was the case of the couple who were lovers for several years before they were married but lived in separate apartments. Neither minded an unannounced appearance at 2:00 A.M., telephone calls at the office, or a spur-of-the-moment request to go somewhere. After they were married and living together in a new apartment, they underwent a physical withdrawal that seemed to reflect an emotional withdrawal—it meant twin beds instead of the double one, a separate dressing room for her and a study for him, and negotiated agreements on their social schedule. It was as if after losing the privacy of living alone, each compensated by putting up barriers in the new, jointly inhabited place.

WHAT RESEARCH SHOWS ABOUT PRIVACY

Privacy by its very nature resists psychological observation, and thus the research has been sparse. We must rely largely on insights from anthropology, ethnology, sociology, and child development.

The research and clinical observations from different disciplines tells us how complex this subject is and how it operates in intricate ways to regulate boundaries among people. Privacy has several tension points:

- *Separation from and connection with other people*
- *"Stage" and "backstage"*
- *The wish to hide and reveal or to know and yet not know*
- *Identity as created by connection and role versus identity based on autonomy and aloneness*
- *Love and work*

In contrast to those of other primates, mankind's territorial requirements are flexible and symbolic. Researchers have learned something about human spatial behavior from the investigations of interpersonal distance, small group ecology, and crowding. Evidence shows that people's space preferences are decidedly different from one culture to another—and individuals within the same culture can vary considerably as well.

When two people are together, the distance they maintain corresponds with how they feel about each other, what their relationship is, and what their transaction of the moment might be. Edward Hall has divided these distances into four: intimate, personal, social, and public. As for crowding, investigation has identified no particular pattern of response, although a crush of people does induce stress.

Mark Baldassare has pointed out an interesting facet of space privacy. He notes that people who accept severe spatial limitations feel little pressure if they also have some freedom of choice or control. Someone in a crowded elevator might begin to feel desperate and claustrophobic in contrast to someone who sits on a crowded porch but who can always step outside or inside if he wishes.

Position, authority, and social role have a great deal to do with privacy rights. A surgeon has supreme authority over us in the operating room, the judge in court, the coach on the playing field, or the priest in the confessional. Sociologists have noted that we tend to surrender certain rights of privacy to these authority figures on one extreme and to servants on the opposite. We grant concessions to doctors, lawyers, et al. because their functions are arcane and because they are often bound by a code of ethics that includes confidentiality. Servants, on the other hand, are in our pay, and we have a measure of power over them. We also tend to think that they, sharing our lives, are loyal to us. As a corollary, control over territory is associated with high status and lack of control with low status.

My own speculation is that when people marry, many yield some of their privacy to partners either in the role of privileged figures or as servant figures. That is, invaders of our privacy usually have to be idealized and authorized in one case or devalued in the other.

Barry Schwartz has observed, "The invasion of various degrees of privacy may be a duty, a privilege, or a transgression, depending on the nature of the interpersonal bond." Intimate acquaintance plays a large part in any spouse's role.

It includes aspects of duty and privilege, but it also has to include an understanding of transgression. How a couple defines privacy determines what a transgression is for them. A husband walking in on his wife while she takes a bath, a wife eavesdropping on her husband's telephone conversation—these could be either privileged or transgressive according to the couple's privacy ground rules. Certain kinds of intimacy are essential to a good marriage, others are not.

Like it or not, we are all involuntary actors because we all play roles in life that are largely written for us. Erving Goffman advances the idea that people need a "backstage" area in their lives where they drop the public masks and are "out of role." Marriage, in a sense, is that backstage. Beyond that, married people need a further retreat to escape each other—a personal refuge beyond the backstage.

We define our lives by love and work. People and activities we love are one half of our identity, and our vocations are the other. It is quite as possible for a person to retreat from love into the privacy of work as it is to do the opposite.

That retreat can be as extreme as the example of the merchant mariner who leaves his wife and puts to sea for a long voyage or the successful dual-career couple who maintain a house in Los Angeles and an apartment in Manhattan because neither is willing to sacrifice career advantage for togetherness. In many cases, one partner is much distressed by the separation. In other cases, the couple eventually live together again and find the resultant loss of individual privacy intolerable.

Another research finding is called "the phenomenon of the stranger." That term refers to the fact that many people seem more willing to confide personal information to a stranger than to someone they know well. When two people meet for the first time in a bar or side by side in a plane, they may get into intimate discussions and disclose secrets they have guarded at home. Some subconscious logic tells them that the encounter is momentary, the stranger will soon be lost in a crowd, and thus they are protected. The very remoteness of the setting seems to help the urge to divulge.

Anthropologists' studies of privacy in different cultures show that the desire is universal, although the forms it takes are variable. For example, in one Brazilian Indian culture, the village offers little spatial privacy. Thatched huts face a circular plaza, and the paths leading outward are straight and open. The Indians provide for their privacy by making secret paths, by observing taboos against saying anything about the misconduct of another villager, and by observing ritual periods when they seclude themselves. Married couples bathe together, eat from the same bowl, and hang their hammocks from the same pole to show solidarity. They are also discreet enough to ask no questions about a partner's extramarital sex. Attitudes about public behavior and privacy collaborate in this culture.

Other interesting observations come from child-development researchers. They note that our earliest experiences often involve unchosen aloneness and unchosen intrusions—a baby is unhappy at being left by itself or a small child resents an adult suddenly interrupting its play. Negative or positive childhood experiences are the basis for our privacy concerns in adulthood. Those concerns also arise from our early sense of our own bodies, the beginning of modesty in a child is the antecedent of a conception of privacy. Off-limits places and prohibitions—the medicine cabinet or father's workshop—are important to a child's learning that conception. A child's first attempts at concealment such as telling a lie, hiding something treasured, or keeping a secret from parents and siblings are early education in privacy defense. All of these experiences will later be reinforced by experiences outside the home.

Whether adults tolerate the child's privacy or whether they shame the child by arbitrary invasion will be reflected in how the child will interpret privacy in later life, either by rigid defenses or reasonable flexibility.

I know of some couples who argue bitterly about the nature of their relationships with "outsiders," especially about what subjects can be discussed with parents, in-laws, the family doctor, or close friends. Again, this is an example of the long shadow of family-of-origin loyalties and it usually pits loyalty to a close-knit, secretive family against loyalty to an outgoing, uninhibited one.

Investigating our capacity to be alone, the psychoanalyst D. W. Winnicott concludes that this ability is largely based on the infant's experience of being alone yet knowing that its mother is close at hand. He says that this marks the beginning of "the infant's personal life."

Winnicott's point—that privacy is not solitude but a state of apartness and relatedness at the same time—suggests to me the essential meaning of security in marriage. When two people have a good marriage, distances can separate but cannot divide them. Just as the infant child once learned to be alone but not alone, husband and wife carry with them the almost-real presences of each other even when they are far apart.

In contrast, a couple locked in a basic quarrel over privacy are unlikely to feel any such bedrock relatedness. Threatened by the thought of areas of life reserved to the other, one partner may yet feel intruded upon by any attempts at closer connection. I recall a situation revealed in couples therapy when a husband admitted that he had struck his wife because she allowed him no privacy. She would pursue him everywhere, he said, even to the locked door of the bathroom. While it seemed clear that the husband's withdrawal helped to intensify the wife's pursuit, I concluded that his plea for privacy was less a defense than what it professed to be—a request for personal time and space. His desperate solution, though, was an even greater violation of her privacy.

Such intimacy problems reflect people's sense of insecurity about earlier relationships with parents. There is no simple solution, but it is important that partners discern what harm they might be doing to the other's sensitivities—sensitivities formed long ago.

As adolescents, many people come to associate privacy with their discovery of sexuality. It can be connected with masturbation, or the locked door of the parents' bedroom, or the secluded place of early sexual encounters. Thus, people relate privacy to fear, shame, or embarrassment.

As they grow older, they must adjust to a more mature image of the meaning of privacy. The notion of privacy as a kind of defensive wall to hide guilty secrets has to be replaced by the idea of privacy as a combination of defense and security. It is no longer just a protection against being caught in the act. It combines a shield against unwanted intrusions of any kind with that alone-but-related sense the baby develops.

WHY PRIVACY IS SO IMPORTANT

Psychotherapists have focused largely on the first half of Freud's formula for psychological health—"love and work." In his recent book *Solitude*, Anthony Storr notes that independent striving and attainment—work in the broadest sense—deserves a good deal more attention and evaluation. Privacy for the mature person often means a combination of two things: a relief from stress and a freedom to accomplish something individually. The *kind* of accomplishment isn't necessarily significant. It may vary from the composer's symphony written in seclusion to the hobbyist's construction of a bookcase—but any form of creativity is important because the effort is individual. Most work in our modern society requires interaction or cooperation within some kind of a team. That has many obvious rewards—but it also has its psychic stresses. The opportunity to carry out a plan and reach an attainment on one's own is one of the mature values of privacy. Like any other wise use of privacy, it can enhance a marriage. A friend once told me her notion of the difference between her family-of-origin life in this sense and her married life. When she was an adolescent, she frequently took part in this kind of dialogue:

"Linda, will you go to the store for me?"

"Not now, Mother. I'm working."

"What are you doing?"

"I'm writing a poem."

"Oh, I thought you said you were working. Now here's the grocery list."

She said that after she was married, her husband would understand perfectly that "working" and "writing a poem" had a significant connection that should be secure from interruption.

Knowing "True" and "False" Selves

Our outer, social selves are largely created by the people around us. How they expect us to think and act, how they perceive our abilities, how warmly or coldly they respond to us, all get summed up in an image. Those others are a collective mirror in which we see ourselves cast in a public role. In privacy, we escape from the imposition of that role image. As Erving Goffman writes, "Privacy is one of the little ways in which we resist the rule of group commitment and reinforce our selfhood. . . . Our status is backed by the solid buildings of the world, while our sense of personal identity often resides in the cracks."

Clinicians often speak of the false self—one created by external stimuli—as opposed to the real self—one formed by personal feelings and convictions. Each of us harbors a sense that we never quite convey to others who we "really" are, and that if they only knew, they would have a different reaction to us—either a more loving or a more disapproving one. Whether the true self is better or worse than might be assumed is less important, we think, than the fact that it is constant, valid, and central. When someone says, "I want to find myself," or "I need to get in touch with myself," this is what he or she means.

I am not at all convinced. I believe that the so-called false self is a perfectly real and natural part of our character. Our behavior and thought as social beings are quite as valid as our private acts and ideas. Privacy, then, should not be regarded as a way to put aside a false self but as a vantage point for a new perspective on our role in the world of human relationships.

Staying in Touch with Feelings

To become acquainted with one's feelings, one has to be alone with them. Meditation, reassessment, and self-criticism are psychological resources we always have at hand even in a busy world. Simple things like a solitary walk, an hour alone in a room, a weekend in the country; or, if attainable, a long vacation, a trip far away, or a sabbatical year are times that one self owes the other. In marriage, the feelings between two people become so intertwined that these excursions into the inner quiet are especially valuable for thinking in the singular rather than the plural and to rediscover the personal impulse.

Healing Through Mourning

Many cultures deal with mourning through ritual. Our own symbols are the vigil beside the dead, the funeral obsequies, the wearing of black, and—in the past at least—a temporary withdrawal from the world. Solitude is an essential of mourning, and privacy is the condition of healing. When something has been torn from our lives, we need peace to knit again and to reconnect.

I believe that we also endure mourning for losses less drastic than death. Any major rejection such as a disappointment in love, the loss of a job, or the failure of a project are reasons enough. We always have two recourses: either distraction by flight, alcohol, drugs, a new relationship, another project—or recovery through mourning. The same applies to marriage. There are times of deep disillusionments in marriage and thus there are times when we should mourn our former illusions. The archetypal loss of illusion is the realization that the wife can never be the totally loving mother we never had or the husband the all-wise, all-powerful father we once imagined. In order to see our partner in real terms, most of us have to mourn our fictive losses, and this requires a certain distance and a private time.

Guarding the Self

One of the functions of privacy is to protect the self. It provides a refuge where wounds and embarrassments can be forgotten. The capacity to set up this protection, to control how much intimacy we will have with another person, is central to our sense of self—it defines us as well as furnishes us with a sense of personal dignity. It is one of the choices that gives us a sense of independence. To forfeit the right to privacy in marriage is to risk a loss of self.

THE PLACE OF PRIVACY IN MARRIAGE

Boundaries

Boundaries and limits are all-important. In a good marriage, everything is a wise balance and fair division. We draw such dividing lines as symbolic of our respect for each other's individuality. We know that love requires distance as well as closeness. The right to choose the time and extent of that distance reminds us that each of us is a unique human being with the gift of free will.

The boundaries of privacy differ with every marriage. There are the big areas of privacy, such as creativity or mourning. Then there are the minor treasures we all cherish: a personal bank account, the separate studio or office, the freedom to go out with friends, time alone to write a letter or make a phone call, time to listen to music by oneself, lonely jogging, fishing from a rowboat, or sitting and looking at the stars. Georg Simmel thinks that all human relations have a content of secrecy in them. The amount never changes, but a new secret is taken on as another is exposed or forgotten. He says that the secret offers "the presence of a second world alongside the manifest world" and this means "an immense enlargement of life." That "second world" can be either the couple's mutual realm of privacy or the hoard of small secrets they keep from each other.

Negotiations

Almost any apartness can be misinterpreted, and therefore privacy in marriage is usually something we have to negotiate. Privacy is such a delicate matter that surprises can be offensive, even threatening. Mary, for example, tells Tom that she's decided to spend Saturday afternoons alone at the movies and explains that she needs this private distraction. Because she's been so open about it, he understands the unspoken message that her withdrawal is not a rejection.

If, on the other hand, Mary simply disappears without explanation every Saturday afternoon, the case is different. Her subliminal message then is that the matter is nonnegotiable and is none of Tom's business.

Privacies that do not come out of agreement and relatedness will seem threatening. Philip Slater observes that American families tend to attempt privacy by giving each member a separate room, and even a separate telephone, television, and car when economically possible. The result is that people feel more alienated and lonely when they get trappings of privacy that only tend to destroy the familiar patterns of interdependence.

I know of a family with three television sets, one for each parent and one for a teenage son. They came to this arrangement when they discovered that they could never agree on what to watch because they all had favorite programs. They had, in effect, negotiated a kind of isolation rather than privacy. Privacies have to have a purpose that makes sense and that serves the marriage.

Rituals
Couples develop rituals of privacy. These are implicit rhythms and areas of intimacy or distancing. The ritual of reading the newspaper, a special hour for listening to music, the time for taking exercise—there are rituals. The understandings about what subjects must be discussed, what can be kept private, or what need firm decisions—these are more matters belonging to the personal bill of rights.

One worthwhile form of privacy ritual is contained in the old phrase "Let's sleep on it." That is, when some problem is at hand—an argument about finances or in-laws perhaps—it is usually best to stop short at a certain point and give each person time to withdraw and think about the problem alone. Debate pushes people toward more and more inflexible positions; privacy tends to urge people on to new solutions, compromises, and regrets for having been so vehement.

Sensitivity
Realizing that privacy is important to the other person is not enough. Knowing how he or she seeks it and for what special reasons is equally important. For example, we all have

vulnerable areas of vanity, or *amour propre*, that should be treated with tact and gentleness by the other.

One of the common patterns I see as a marital therapist is crowding during a quarrel—symbolized by the common demands to "get out of my face!" or "Get off my back!" Couples interrupt each other. They push each other orally, jump to conclusions about what the other is going to say, and deny each other time and space to talk. It's a good symbol of a jostling, competitive, closed-in marriage that each resents.

I often see the opposite pattern as well in a couple that avoid each other after every painful argument. Then there is another variant in the cheerless marriage where the couple keep their distance, observe great areas of privacy, and preserve a studied detachment.

Power

Privacy has a direct relation to power. When we lay claim to areas of privacy, we limit the power that others have over us. If the couple have separate bank accounts, there is less chance of one dominating in financial decisions. In an office, power and privacy are almost interchangeable—there is an obvious difference in the status of the person you can walk in on and the person whose secretary will take your request for an appointment.

When a couple thinks about privacy issues between them, they must think about their power balance at the same time. The right to privacy includes the right to forbid intrusions, physical or psychological.

Conclusion

People have different levels of need in almost every area I've discussed—in sexual intimacy, family loyalties, uses of power—and so it is with privacy as well. Some see privacy as an inviolable physical space; some see it as a private fantasy life; others see it as a period of time exclusively their own.

Couples should understand that none of this is absolute—an individual's need for privacy of whatever kind follows certain personal rhythms and is not constant from day to day or week to week. One of the hard-won achievements of a marriage is learning to understand and respect each other's rhythms.

Marriages can suffer from a kind of inauthentic intimacy. This means that the couple, while pretending to be completely open with each other, conceal important areas of self. Other couples are frequently engaged in a border dispute with one or both trying to invade and occupy a larger part in the other's life.

In fact, the key word in this chapter is *balance*. That room of one's own is vitally important, but it is just one room in a larger house.

CHAPTER EIGHT

CHILDREN

It is part of our modern mythology that the arrival of children contributes new love and purpose to a marriage. Although this is true in some cases, one of the most frequent reasons couples go into psychotherapy is because of difficulties concerning children. The act of marrying is the first great rite of passage. In rough times, some people find the commitment a comfort and reliance, while others find it a shackle. The second rite of passage is the arrival of children. It alters the emotional equation in much the same way. For better or for worse, each event raises the stakes in life.

Among those couples who are susceptible to the children quarrel, questions of whether or not to have children and when to have them can provoke the earliest disputes. Then come the differences over changed schedules, altered lifestyle, and division of work at home after the first child is born—although sometimes it can be the birth of a second child that puts strain on the couple in unexpected ways. Through the early school years, the turmoils of adolescence, and the departure from the nest to the in-law problems that come with their own marriages, children can become potent causes of—or sufferers from—a basic marriage quarrel.

In the course of my work at McLean Hospital and several child-guidance clinics in the Boston area, I often meet parents who ask help for a troubled child or adolescent without realizing that the child's difficulties—whether tantrums, school problems, drug use, sexual predicaments, or depression—can be traced back to the parents' own basic quarrel. Often a couple can use the child's problems as a mask, a means to avoid facing their own.

Three families I have known in my clinical work represent three complex situations that I've simplified to illustrate typical dynamics:

A traditionally oriented family had an adolescent daughter who had become highly impulsive. In the course of therapy, it became clear that there was a major clash between the older children and the father, who could not tolerate any questioning of his authority. It was plain that the wife had begun to rebel against being cast as a Patient Griselda type, and that the children's struggles against the patriarchal rule mirrored her own. In the typical quarrels with her husband over disciplining a child, she, significantly, always took the side of latitude and tolerance.

Another couple denied having any marital problems themselves but expressed worry about their children's difficulties in scholastic accomplishment. The father, a successful businessman, was frequently absent on trips, and during therapy the children revealed their sense of grievance over his remoteness and his reluctance to share any of their feelings. I sensed, however, that what seemed to be a problem of their identifying with the father was actually a broader problem of a lack of emotional connection in the marriage—again a case of a trouble that mirrored and yet obscured a basic quarrel between husband and wife.

In a third case, the wife accused her husband of being "an angry person," routinely condemning him for any sign of irritation or anger. As a result, he increasingly closed himself off from her and the family. During treatment, it emerged that she had grown up in a troubled family with one alcoholic parent and, as a result, was extremely sensitive about anger, which she saw as always destructive and frightening. One of the children in this family was volatile and suicidal; at the other extreme were children who were obedient and overcontrolled. The mother had, it appeared, tried hard to suppress every normal display of temper in her family, and the father had stifled any show of his own feelings. Their house had been an emotional pressure cooker with no outlet for aggression.

The children quarrel is the saddest paradox of the seven basic quarrels. Children, so welcomed and fulfilling for most couples and so sought after by infertile couples and adoptive parents, usually inspire new energies, reveal new goals and new rewards. In less adaptable marriages, they can become the cause of a basic quarrel largely because the format of life is so changed by their arrival and changed again at several transition points as they grow up. The couple relationship is not flexible enough to withstand the stresses of this process and to accommodate itself to the needs of the whole family. Children can become the focus of conflict because they arouse such strong feelings of love, of hate, or a mixture of the two.

Child-Rearing, Past and Present

American ideas about children and family have changed vastly in the past fifty years. First, the very idea of having children is now an option rather than a given. Efficient birth control goes along with altered attitudes. Young adults' present-day habits of having relationships but postponing marriage and children for a number of years has resulted in a population with many childless people in their twenties or thirties. A certain number of these same people will find it difficult, when they finally marry, to sacrifice their established life-styles by having a family. Joan H. Huber and Glenna Spitze have found that whereas 70 percent of young couples in 1973 thought it selfish to remain childless, only 21 percent held that opinion in 1978. In short, self-consideration seemed to be winning out over the urge to have children.

From the Middle Ages through the Renaissance, children's lives were considered tentative because so many girls and boys died at an early age. Few of them were given proper names until they had reached the age of twelve or so. In ordinary families well into our own century, they were re-garded as living assets—so many sons to work the farm or to apprentice to the craft and so many daughters to perform the household tasks.

As Philippe Ariès notes in *Problems of Childhood*, the view of children has changed along with parents' priorities. The concern now is about child quality rather than child quantity. The large number of books and magazines on child-rearing and parenting; the middle-class concern with school grades, SAT scores, admission to superior colleges or universities and then graduate school, all demonstrate an intense interest in—and intense anxiety about—producing ideal sons and daughters.

As gender-role problems between men and women changed with transitions in our culture, our views of the family itself have changed. There is enormous uncertainty as to how couples should deal with the many issues of upbring-ing. By 1985, nearly two thirds of married women with school-age children were employed outside the home. This means that fathers have felt more pressure to become par-ticipant parents. Child-rearing has become a much more collaborative responsibility than it was in the past, although—as I have noted before—the terms of the collabo-ration are by no means easy to settle on. One interesting statistic that reflects a changing attitude about participation has to do with a father's presence in the delivery room during the childbirth. In 1973, only one out of four elected to do this; by 1983, three out of four were there.

Just as people tend to postpone having children, they also—because of increased life expectancy—spend more of their lives in relationship with adult children. This has its own peculiar difficulties of intimacy and understanding, one of which was reflected in a recent Castle Hill symposium on mother-daughter relationships when the question "When did you become your mother's mother?" was asked. Unfortunately, the problems of parenting at the later stages of life have had scant attention in professional writing.

Transition Problems from Couple to Family
The greatest stress in most marriages will come in the transition from a couple to a family. As the sociologist Alice Rossi observes, pregnancy used to follow close after marriage, and thus a woman reached two great watershed points in life almost simultaneously. Her role was determined almost at once. Today, Rossi says, the period between marriage and pregnancy is probably long enough to permit a couple's relationship to become egalitarian. They have an opportunity to share breadwinning and household responsibilities. When the wife quits her job and the first child comes, the roles shift, and there are new tensions between gender patterns, with strong shifts toward less egalitarian and more traditional roles.

The image of children as a benevolent, uniting influence has truth to it, but many people fail to realize that this is not a blessing that descends gratuitously from heaven—it has to be earned. Soon after the first birth, a couple is likely to find that children add to a family but subtract from a marriage. Psychological research consistently found that children tend to interfere with a couple's companionship and sexual relationship. About thirty years ago, researchers even used to debate whether or not the stresses of parenthood for middle-class people could be classified as a "crisis."

In fact, much of the research seems to have brought out negative and disheartening results. There are, however, questions about the validity of that research. For one thing, many early studies were retrospective, relying on what couples remembered about their reactions to parenthood after the fact. For another, results might have been distorted by the tendency people have of giving researchers what they consider to be the socially acceptable answer rather than a completely truthful reply. Third, the studies were hard to compare because many described families at different periods, with children of varying ages.

Subsequent studies of couples interviewed during a first child's early years were contradictory—one report showing a brief "honeymoon" period after the child's birth, and others showing a negative trend in the marriage just before birth and for several months thereafter. The new mothers found child care an added burden, and the couples' romantic attitudes toward each other declined. Other researchers specified the father's dissatisfactions as a diminished contact with friends, a feeling of being "tied down," money problems, in-law intrusions, lack of sleep, and additional tasks. The mothers' hardships were the unflattering change in figure, physical fatigue from interruptions of sleep, and emotional distress. Researchers describe this transition as a passage from an orderly and fairly predictable life to just the opposite.

Mothers' Work and Fathers' Work

Those inquiries considered the changes in intimacy and life-styles that the child's arrival brings about, but equally important are the ways it affects and is affected by employment. Millions of women have made a commitment to employment or career not just to add money to the family income but for important reasons of identity. What happens when a new, time-taking, and difficult job—in the form of a child—is added to the total work commitment of the family is another subject for research.

Fathers, according to some recent studies, are increasingly willing to share the burden. In 1924, a survey showed that 10 percent of fathers spent no time at all with their children; by 1976, that discouraging statistic had dropped to 2 percent. This result, however, is qualified by other research that shows fathers still allocating the role of primary caretaker to the mother and most fathers beginning to show real interest in children only after they are eighteen months old.

Studies of the home after the birth of a child depict an emotionally complicated situation. A husband who shares the domestic and child-care work may feel good about behaving as a responsible parent, but this is frequently offset by a feeling that he is sacrificing time that ought to be spent on his work or career. He also feels a loss of status as he makes beds or changes diapers.

Wives have mixed emotions of their own. They are afraid of their husbands' resentment at the sharing of duties and at the same time feel a twinge of guilt about not fulfilling all of a traditional woman's role. When this is so, researchers find, the mother will act as a kind of gatekeeper, allowing the husband to spend necessary relief time with the child or children but no more than that.

All of these separate research insights add up to equivocal conclusions thus far. One research project found that fathers in general felt that their contributions to domestic tasks—whatever the cost to their careers—help strengthen their marriages because their wives were more content as a result. Another project, on the contrary, found that fathers regarded marriage as less satisfying because they shared domestic duties.

Gender Roles and Parenthood

Whatever pattern of gender roles a childless couple might have, they are likely to revert to traditional male/female ones after the birth of a child. No matter how they may have modified roles before this, the compound of biological urge and social conditioning begins to operate. Folk wisdom has it that in the early months of mother-infant closeness, the mother through "hormonal priming" bonds with her new child in all the ancient female ways, and along with that, the traditions of our culture decree that she take on the primary role of parenting.

That is the rule, but since any rule has exceptions, there are some fathers who would like to take on the main role of nurturing. Researchers have noted that such fathers can develop bonds with a child that are quite as strong as the mother's—and one clue to this impulse is the fact that these fathers hold the infants in the same soothing, caretaking way as mothers do. In contrast, the more typical father will behave playfully with his child.

The example of those exceptional, nurturing fathers has a fascinating implication—perhaps the traditional gender roles fathers and mothers assume are not so biologically ordained as they might seem. Perhaps mothers have simply acquired more skills at nurturing—along with, as Jean Baker Miller says, a psychological predisposition—and infants respond more to one than the other. Perhaps continual proximity is just as important a factor as "hormonal priming."

We carry society's strong imprint of one or the other gender role. However much middle-class parents may try to diverge from the conservative gender assignments, they feel internal pressures to return to them—the men worried that home duties will be a drag on their careers and the women feeling guilty unless they perform as homemakers and mothers.

Our emotional pasts are always with us and a large part of

those pasts is the identity we formed in our family of origin. Along with that are inescapable images of behavior and attitude we received from our parents. Those images grow stronger and more compelling when we become parents ourselves. Wives influence husbands to be more fatherly, and husbands wish wives to be more motherly.

If the images are positive and if the wife or husband behaves in ways that are consistent with what we conceive as maternal or paternal, the birth of a child is our first step toward a rewarding family life. The loyalties I described in Chapter Two are renewed and strengthened; in a sense, they are the best legacy from the two families of origin.

It is understandable—in this stage of our social history at least—that the motivating images will be traditional ones: mother as primary parent and father as provider. Rosanna Hertz says that our actual roles as provider or nurturer have shifted greatly, while our expectations about roles have remained much the same. Even though Mother may have a nine-to-five job or profession, both she and her husband still have an image of her packing the school lunches, chauffeuring the kids to the Little League game, doing the laundry, and making dinner, just as their own mothers did. She remarks, "This image is the yardstick against which men and women measure childrearing practices."

As for the shaping images a man still draws on, Samuel Osherson says that they are chiefly of competent masculinity, of a father who goes off to work all day for the sake of the family. He regards the domestic scene as a feminine, emotionally foreign world full of strong feelings that he finds troubling. At home, he feels vulnerable, not competent and not in control. At his workplace, he finds a haven and a reinforcement of his self-esteem. He may even exaggerate these sentiments into a devaluation of the home and a perception of wives as second-class citizens.

The economic factor that might affect all this—cited in

Chapter Four—is the researcher's discovery that the higher the wife's income outside the home, the more housework the husband will take on. In short, he will trade part of his gender role for a higher family income. I would add my own suggestion that his traditional assumptions about the male provider role will have to undergo reexamination. This is well expressed in the case described by one husband:

> Margaret and I are both professionals—she's assistant director of a small foundation and I'm in city administration. We love kids and we now have two small ones, which makes for the usual bind when you both have developing careers and children who deserve a lot of care and attention. Early on, we decided on a fifty–fifty division of home labor and I've taken a cut in pay in order to be at home three afternoons a week. We do have a baby-sitter, as well. Margie has talked about quitting her job, but we can't quite afford that along with my time off for sharing household work. There's another factor with her—she's a person of very strong beliefs. She loves the children, and at the same time she has a big emotional and intellectual stake in her job.

In such egalitarian marriages, it is not necessarily the choice of the couple but the dependence on two paychecks that creates a painful dilemma. We could inquire into the situation again from the wife's point of view:

> After the first baby came, I suppose I could have quit my job, which would either end or seriously interrupt my career. But I chose to moonlight as a career woman or, if you like, moonlight as a mother, I don't know which. In any case, I saw strong reasons for not quitting the job, aside from the fact that we really need the income. I'd worked hard and reached a responsible position. If I quit, it would simply prove to the [male] management all over again that a woman hasn't any long-term commitment to her work, and as soon as she is

pregnant, off she goes. If I allowed them to think that, I'd be letting down all the women I work with—women I love and respect. I'd be encouraging the management to say to itself, "One more reason for not promoting them or overpaying them—they're just temporary help."

In many dual-career marriages like this one, traditional role expectations clash with egalitarian standards. Women have more to gain, and men may feel they have more to lose in the new socioeconomic order of things. These situations are fraught with feelings of uneasiness or guilt because— except for the traditional gender roles—society hasn't as yet found other acceptable models for a marriage that incorporates dual careers, home, and children.

Wonderful as children are, they bring with them complications that change every equation in a marriage. The traditional family, with its traditional gender roles—however imperfect in other ways—was well-designed for the rearing of children. Once that organization of the family has to readjust to two-career conditions and equity for women, it becomes less efficient as a child-care, child-development system.

The relationship among gender roles, parenthood, and marital conflict is complicated, shaped as it is by powerful early images, changing social customs, financial exigencies, and the availability of child-care resources.

There are five areas that show some of the new confusions and problems of relationship in this time of transition.

"Identity Tension Lines"
Rhona Rapoport uses the phrase "identity tension lines" to describe the tug of war between one's concept of an "ideal" division of gender roles and all the real-life claims that cause people to embrace traditional patterns or narrow self-interest. For example, a husband is convinced that he *should*

spend exactly as much time with the children as his wife does—and yet he knows that this means he will have to give up or modify certain work or business aims. It is a matter of conscience in conflict with ambition. He knows that a good deal of overtime work will put him in position for a promotion; or he knows that he can raise his efficiency and understanding of his job if he has time for study.

A woman executive drops her three-month-old baby off at Childcare Central on her way to the office every morning and, just afterward, suffers feelings of guilt.

Neither of these people has been able to find a workable compromise between what he or she considers the good obligations of life with children and self-fulfillment.

Perceived Choice

The tension lines are relaxed if people feel that they have some discretion, some freedom of choice in the way they divide their time between home and family and their occupation, according to several studies. If, for example, a wife has no interest in her job except for the income it adds, just the fact that she is employed is likely to be a bone of contention between her and her husband. It may have an upsetting effect on the whole marriage.

Another odd but interesting finding is that men are more happily adjusted if their role in the family is quite different from that of their fathers. If the father participated little in household life, the son will be happiest as an egalitarian husband; if the father was much involved in his family, the son is more likely to shun home and child-care duties. It is very likely that just the idea of having an option and—in this time of gender role ambiguity—rejecting the old patterns of behavior offers psychological comfort.

Congruency: A Matter of Fit

That peculiarly modern compromise of a three-vocation couple—two careers and what sociologist Arlie Hochschild calls a "second shift" of home and children—is precarious to maintain. There is always a real possibility for injustice in the division of labor if the feminine half of the assignment includes the complicated and demanding task of being primary parent. Will this kind of marriage always be at the mercy of frayed nerves, always close to a basic quarrel?

The answer seems to be that what makes any marriage pattern work or fail is agreement, or lack of it, between the partners. A firm agreement on roles seems to permit people to be more flexible. For example, Lucia Gilbert and Vicki Rachlin discovered that a couple freely accepting the idea that the husband's career had first priority could then work out all sorts of compromises in sharing. Rachlin found that the husbands in these marriages were not only more supportive of their wives' careers than the average husband but also more willing to participate in the chores of the home. The pact had freed them psychologically to diverge from traditional gender rules.

Equity Versus Social Exchange

Marital theorists have disagreed about whether people try to use trade-offs—or "social exchange"—to get the best deal for themselves, even if the deal is unfair, or whether they prefer an equitable system.

In a 1985 study, psychologists Sara Yogev and Jeanne Brett pursued this question of perceived justice and found that employed wives felt satisfied if they thought their husbands were doing a fair share of the work of the home and husbands felt satisfied if they believed their wives were doing *more* than their fair share. Their findings, quite likely, reflect the traditional male upper hand—and couples' gauges of what is fair come from a combination of what they learned to expect while growing up and what is expected in the particular social milieu they now live in. While holding on to received opinions, people usually adapt to the prevailing attitudes around them. A couple in a small Tennessee town might have an idea of equity quite different from that of a couple in graduate school at the University of Michigan in Ann Arbor. Both might trade viewpoints if they traded hometowns.

The Problem of Separate Spheres

In this bewildering issue of dividing the labor, working together as a team of two seems to have high emotional value. One study found that fathers disliked to take care of the children alone but when their wives were sharing the duty, they resented it much less or even enjoyed it.

Yogev and Brett added another insight to the theory about cooperation when they noted that when wife and husband both work and time is in short supply, they have a tendency to work out coordinated schedules of routines and responsibilities—a kind of planning that single-earner couples seldom feel the need for.

Couples who separate their roles on traditional gender lines have special problems. Research shows that the more children they have, the less happy they are. The strict division of functions, in fact, may shut husband and wife off into separate worlds by the time they reach their fifties. The psychiatrists Richard Schwartz and Jacqueline Olds suggest that the wife, depressed and feeling imprisoned in the home, becomes defensive and territorial about her role as primary parent—and so effectively excludes her husband. By middle age, each has become a specialist; they have lost all sense of marriage and child-raising as shared tasks.

A study of dual-career families with children in which I collaborated with Schwartz, Olds, Susan Eisen, and Anthony Van Niel found that when both partners of a couple worked full time, they became less intimate and disagreed more often. They were decidedly less satisfied with their lives than couples in which the wife did not work or worked part time only.

Again, this seemed to take us back to the principle of collaboration as a key to satisfaction. Whereas the traditional couple kept to their own separate assignments and felt unhappy, the two-job couple had little time or energy for shared work and felt equally unhappy. They delegated what might have been their fruitful cooperation to day care, baby-sitters, au pair girls, or maids, and thus lost touch with each other as partners.

People who lose touch with each other as partners are likely to become emotional strangers and then emotional antagonists. This is the moral of uncoordinated marriages—separate worlds in the same home. At the least, this means a withdrawal from intimacy and produces the oft-expressed plea, "We can't communicate any longer." At its worst, this means a basic quarrel in which children seem to be the contributing cause but are actually caught in the crossfire.

Intrapsychic Issues in Parenting

Reflections of the Self

A newborn child is a blank page to its parents. They project onto it, as psychiatrist Therese Benedek describes, all their own hopes of self-realization along with fears of their own faults being exposed. If the child shows promise, it becomes "my son" or "my daughter." If the child is an early disappointment, it becomes "your daughter" or "your son." Each phrase is reflective of the speaker. Each has buried within it the possibility of a basic quarrel between two powerful personal projections.

Freud wrote, "That which the fond parent projects ahead of him as his ideal in the child is merely a substitute for the lost narcissism of childhood." All those youthful fantasies of brilliant achievement, glamour, recognition, and wealth that have been diminished by reality are revived and accorded the child. In a sense, the parent falls in love with his or her own idealized image. As it works out in daily life, one parent insists that Joan is going to Harvard and is sure to be an MBA; another calls the basketball coach to try pressuring him into putting John on the school's first team because "he already shows signs of being NBA material."

As becomes apparent only too soon, children are quite as human as their parents and show depressing signs of the parental faults and failings. This is a delicate time if the parents' self-esteem is fragile and they have no reserves to deal with the disillusionment. One of my colleagues tells me that his child invariably finds a way to mirror the worst aspects of himself—a great test of maturity for parents.

When parents cannot deal with such disappointments, they are very likely to embroil themselves in the basic children quarrel. "The report card came today and *your* son is flunking again," or "I see you let *your* daughter use the credit card again, and I just want you to look at the bill." In such cases, the disillusionment is not integrated into the self but the defect or blame is projected into the partner. The wife quoted above has forgotten that she was never much of a scholar when she was in school and the husband has lost sight of his own tendency to buy things impulsively.

The psychiatrist John Zinner notes that certain dysfunctional families behave according to the unconscious fantasies each member projects onto the others—and so the internal conflicts get translated into real conflicts *between* people in the family.

Dependency Issues
Children—particularly infants and young children—make some parents wonder whether their own love can be stronger than their rage. They are touched by the helplessness of the

child, are anxious to provide all that a good mother and father should, and at the same time are full of anxieties about their own ability to nurture this marvelous, fragile, but very difficult creature.

Some of that may come from inexperience, but the significant anxieties stem from their own dependency longings. These can be extremely threatening, especially when they are linked with deprivations or traumas of a parent's own childhood. The real infant in the crib triggers a struggle with the needy child inside the adult's psyche. If adults cannot reckon wisely with that need, they will be hostile to the dependency of children of any age, and will, in turn, incite hostility. I have observed children in some families become chronically angry and given to "acting out" because they weren't getting enough care, while the parents, intolerant of any show of anger, were blind to what the anger meant.

The Split Between Impulse and Prohibition

That "reflection of the Self" I noted above can also be a split image. When a parent is unable to reconcile within himself his contradictory urges, the child may be the recipient of the negative ones, the ones the parent wants to reject. Thus the split image—and the parent can picture his own half as good and the child half as mostly bad.

I have seen this dynamic in families with adolescents who cut classes, get into fights, use drugs, steal, are sexually promiscuous, or run away from home. Some parents are either outraged and try to enforce sterner and sterner controls or get totally discouraged and shrug their shoulders.

On the other hand, the parents may be at odds about the remedy, with one advising tolerance and understanding while the other is all for more discipline. This is the classic form of the children quarrel. The underlying dynamic recognized by the therapist is likely to be what he would term imbalance between id and superego—that is, neither parent has been able, within himself/herself, to arrive at a healthy equilibrium between impulse and self-control. Often one or both parents has imposed a stern censorship over, let us say, the vigor of his/her sexual impulses. Their adolescent child's sexual acting out will then strike them as bad, but they will take a secret, vicarious pleasure in it. Such parents are psychologically unable to conceive consistent rules of conduct for their children and, worse, cannot enforce those rules without using punishment.

Separation and Autonomy

There is a common fantasy that a family sometimes shares— the notion that a child's desire for independence is a hostile rejection of parents and siblings. There is another, less-common family fantasy in which a child's dependence is understood as a leechlike, hostile bent, to be discouraged.

In the first case, the parents are likely to make the equation that being dependent equals being loving equals being good. In the second, independence equals self-sufficiency equals strength.

Often the child responds by alternating between extremes —at one time he or she will reject the family completely and a little later will become infantile and overdependent. This swing to extremes is a mirror image of the parents' own internal conflicts about becoming adult.

I have observed families going through major turmoil as their first adolescent child is about to be separated from the family. This may be a physical move—to college, to a job in another place, to enter one of the armed services, to be married. Or it can be simply an emotional separation: "Mom, that's my own business and I'm not going to tell you about it." If one or both parents has not separated himself/herself psychologically from his/her own family of origin—so that their marriage has either a problem of clinging dependence or cool distance—they will oppose and undermine the child's attempt to depart.

The Return of the Parent

Our parents are ghosts who are always with us in a sentient, emotional form. Becoming a parent oneself is more than a reminder, it forces a kind of reliving of the past, except that Small and Big have been reversed. For many people, all of this has a negative hue, and what remains with them about their original family are its angers and conflicts.

In the best of scenarios, we recognize the mistakes and misjudgments in our upbringing and consciously try to correct them for the benefit of our own children. That is an exhilarating experience, and it fits with my previous observation that the fathers who are best adjusted to parenthood are often those who have taken an opposite tack from their own fathers'.

Unfortunately, a great many people identify so strongly with their parents that their children are forced to relive the mistakes of the past. The most dramatic example of this is the abused child who grows up to abuse his or her own children, but there are many less shocking examples of error perpetuated onto the next generation.

In a figure of speech, I spoke of the "parental ghosts," but the living grandparents may be only too present as they engage with their grandchildren. This interaction can precipitate major quarrels with the middle generation of the family, the parents. The question of loyalties can provide many flash points.

If the family of origin had some crucial shortcomings, there is no way the grandparents can win. No matter how they approach their grandchildren, their children will find it wrong. I can think of two cases that illustrate this situation.

One set of grandparents had been neglectful of their children's emotional needs and censorious about mistakes. When they gradually began to display these old attitudes toward their grandchildren, their son was so angry that he broke off all friendly relations.

Another set of grandparents had brought their children up in near-poverty. In that house, there were no presents for the children, no money for movies, excursions, or treats of any kind. Later on, the husband prospered and, when the couple became grandparents, their first impulse was to indulge their grandchildren with all sorts of presents and pleasures. The daughter of the pair was outraged. She compared her childhood years of deprivation with the bountiful way her children were being treated. She especially remembered how often her father and mother had told her what a morally superior thing it was to be poor.

The Pressure to Be Motherly or Fatherly

Most of us know exactly what a mother is because we've had one—and the same is true of a father. The old saw about husbands who want apple pie—or chicken, or pasta, or anything—"just like the way Mother used to make it" has less to do with remembered taste than with a certain image of a benevolent mother in the kitchen and a hungry child anticipating the wonderful taste of the supper to come.

In this way, a husband might expect his wife to copy that maternal image, and a wife might expect her husband to conform to some idealized recollection of her father. Both of them will associate the image with what kind of a parent they feel the other should be. Each will also associate the image with what kind of a parent the other should be *in relation to him or her*. A husband might view his wife as perfectly congenial as long as they are childless but not quite adequate as a wife-mother when the child comes. She is compared to that model mother of the past and, inevitably, is found wanting.

Time and Its Meanings

For us, children bring with them a new sense of time, either its tedium or its swiftness. When sociologist Ralph LaRossa queried new parents about changes in their lives, he found that almost all of them mentioned a sudden shortage of time. As never before, time for sleep, for conversation, for sex, for social matters, had to be rationed. But then there was the time that stretched out—the time spent waiting for the baby to go to sleep, or the time spent amusing young children.

Especially for dual-career couples, time becomes the scarcest resource in marriage after children are born. This is a circumstance where friction builds up to quarrels—quarrels over a husband's not giving enough time to the family, or a wife's not having enough time for herself, or either one's not having time for personal projects. Young children take first priority in the schedule while parents begin to feel their own years slipping by.

The biological calendar is another place where time presses on us. When to have children? More and more, dual-career couples are postponing it until they have established themselves enough to feel confident about money and their careers. In a way, they are spending some of their best family years to buy security. Over them always hangs a question of whether their decision might come too late.

Children's lives remind us of time passing and our own mortality. LaRossa observes that the way we sense time is through our commitment to long-term matters we hold especially important, and children are, for most people, a major commitment. It is when there are several major commitments contending for our scarce hours that we feel the pull in different directions.

Most of us have a long-range time plan buried somewhere in our consciousness. It is the ideal life course against which we measure our successes or failures. One businessman wants to make his first million by the time he's thirty, one woman wants to have three children before she's thirty-two, one writer wants to have published five books by forty, and so on. Unless we come reasonably close to this calendar of expectations, we are likely to grow disappointed and embittered. Couples can deal with time better if they understand the long-term calendar each has in mind and if they coordinate the two.

The Social Context

Children also bring us into a community, probably unlike any we've moved in before. It begins with extended family, child care, nursery school, grade school and high school PTAs, all the children's friends, and goes on through their college years. At the same time, the fact of the children is likely to make other relationships decline. The young couple on the next street who have two children the age of your own children are now more congenial than the old college friends who have no children.

Research on dual-career couples suggests that women may enlarge their social network through becoming friends with other women with children, while husbands are less likely to replace lost male friendships with new ones. Work and family are, necessarily, the two priorities, but it seems to me important that dual-career couples try hard to eke out some time for friendships. I believe that couples who can keep up old connections and make new ones offer a better life to their children than couples who isolate themselves and rely on each other for emotional sustenance.

Remarriage

Remarriage exchanges one set of problems for another, one possibility of a basic quarrel for a new one. The social worker Lillian Messinger found that couples in first marriages disputed most often over:

1. *The partner's immaturity*
2. *Sexual problems*
3. *Lack of readiness for marriage*
4. *In-law interference*
5. *Differences in values and social interests*

In remarriages, people found that their most common problem was children and the second most common finances.

Messinger defines the major problems in remarriage as "role ambiguity" and "role overload." This means that people who remarry usually enter a whole new family complex—acquiring a new set of in-laws and children from a former marriage—and therefore feel uncertain about their role as outsider in the clan. The prefix "step" is, at first, one of the most awkward in the language—especially since the fairy tales read to us as children frequently contain a wicked stepmother.

Often the old marriage lives on in the psyche and—even though it may have been a very unhappy marriage—the former spouse remains as a kind of imaginary third point in a triangle. This makes for tension. What makes for even greater tension is when the new mate is critical of the way his or her new stepchildren are being raised. One opinion goes:

> When I married Liddy, I didn't realize at first just how spoiled and selfish her eight-year-old boy and ten-year-old girl were. Her first husband must have been some father! The kids are always demanding, won't take orders, and get very sulky when they're made to do something. Don't worry; I've told Liddy that things have to change around here.

Liddy—or any biologic parent—will feel caught between her wish to please her new husband and her loyalty to the children. She feels especially uncomfortable because he is now financially responsible for them. The couples Messinger studied had never come to grips with financial matters in relation to the children; probably, she says, because the pair felt hesitant about committing everything to the new marriage. Many kept money aside in case of another divorce, were reluctant to revise their wills, and avoided new financial arrangements in general. Along with this was the familiar two-family burden, with the father paying alimony and/or child support and, as some said, feeling like "a walking checkbook."

In the original nuclear family, according to psychiatrist Clifford Sager, membership and family boundaries are fairly clearly defined. In the family of remarriage, expectations, roles, tasks, and limitations are likely to be much vaguer. One of the reasons is that at least one partner is likely to be remarrying after a divorce.

At the McLean Hospital Adolescent and Family Treatment Unit, in the case of a man who married a woman with children from a previous marriage, we initially referred to him as a "stepfather." He, however insisted that his relationship with the children was that of "a friend." It was a reminder that both clinicians and families should not take roles for granted—in remarriage, roles have to be negotiated. It was also a reminder of the importances of words and their nuances and how much depends on mutual references.

Sager suggests some specific goals for remarried parents:

1. *Help the children to deal with loyalty binds they may suffer.*
2. *Mourn the original nuclear family.*
3. *Understand and accept that the new family is going to be more complicated than the first family, and look for new values.*
4. *Establish the parental authority of both husband and wife.*
5. *Discuss and try to define each parent's role in the new family.*
6. *Spell out the boundaries in the new family system—that is, specify the nature and amount of contact with ex-spouses and ex-in-laws.*

COPING

Unconscious Agendas

In all of the conflicts and confusions of family life, we may forget that every family has a mission: that mission is to prepare and aid each member to cope with all stages of life from birth on.

That means easing a five-year-old into the school years, preparing a twelve-year-old for the death of a beloved grandmother, and smoothing the transition when a twenty-three-year-old is about to marry and move away. A family is never static; parenthood is always developmental. Because it is a commitment to other lives, it demands the kind of altruism that is the essence of maturity. To have a successful marriage, we cast off a lot of our childhood selfishness. To have a successful family, we cast off much of our couple selfishness. We end up making the lives of those hostages to fortune more important than our own.

To realize this fully, we have to examine and revise our unconscious agendas. Take, for example, the new father whose one chief way of feeling good about himself is his achievement in the company where he works—an agenda so powerful for him that he finds it hard to be emotionally and physically available at home. Take the mother whose agenda of invisible loyalties tells her that her daughters owe father and mother unquestioned devotion and obedience.

To the extent that having children forces us to reevaluate and revise the selfish element of our personal agendas, we have a chance for personal growth. To the extent that having children forces us to work through the lingering conflicts we may have with our own parents and their legacy of loyalties, we have a chance to make a private peace. I remember a patient of mine whose relationship with her mother had a long history of trouble. One day, they discussed whether or not the daughter would ever have children.

253

Her mother said, "I hope that you will."

"Why?" my patient asked sarcastically. "So I'll realize how awful it is?"

"No," said her mother. "Just so you'll know."

In that moment, my patient had a revelation. She felt what she had almost never felt before—a strong sense of connection with her mother.

A Shared Task

Nursemaids, au pair help, daytime or weekend baby-sitters—all are welcome allies for dual-career parents. Just as in the case of the traditional housewife-and-earner duo, their very advantages tend to compartmentalize life for each member of a couple. Parenting is potentially collaborative. It is also emotional hard work. It requires a great deal of negotiation and problem solving, but it produces a shared marriage. The couple who have a wonderful Mary Poppins will undoubtedly enjoy more gracious living than the diaper team down the street, but they will not have the same contact with each other, involvement with family, and the experience of collaboration. Having a nanny does not rule out the need for teamwork.

Part of the negotiation and problem solving will be about roles—who will do what and when and how. Men often learn from their wives how to be a parent and from experience how to function as fathers. In a felicitous phrase, Ernest Abelin speaks of parents providing a child with "a double mirror," by which the child learns about different aspects of himself/herself from each.

Frances Grossman suggests how important it is for couples to work out patterns that complement each other. Men, she says, must learn to act in a parental role that is different from their wives' role but must also learn from their wives the skills a woman has in parenting.

I agree with Grossman. In all this, I think it is important for a father to have a distinct fatherly role of his own and not appear to the children as mother's adjunct or stand-in. It's especially important that he interest himself in their play and school activities and be welcoming to their friends. He should be available when children need to turn away from their mother and look to male reassurance, but he should temper any impulse toward aggression or competitiveness in himself so as not to shame or injure. In his differentiated role, the father can feel that he is making a unique contribution to the child's development rather than being a stopgap or a baby-sitter. Children benefit from having two models, two different kinds of emotional resource—especially when those parental models value each other.

Finding the Connections Between Home and Work

Dual-career couples are pulled away from the family by two powerful vocation magnets. It isn't simply the work itself— that may range from fascinating to acceptable—but the small social world that surrounds it: good friends and valued colleagues, common interests in the enterprise, accomplishments and their rewards. Giving up even part of that may seem a painful sacrifice.

It may be possible to make connections between work and home that will remove some of the pain. Nurturing— especially for women—has a carryover from parenting to dealing with personnel in an office. Many jobs have an instructional element in them. Negotiation and the cooperative working out of problems are also common to workplace and family household. If the skills and attitudes of one can be transferred to use with the problems of the other, both parts of one's life will benefit.

One parent told me that what she had learned from her job about establishing procedures and precepts worked very well—although through different techniques—with her five-year-old. Women have had more practice in finding such connections; unless men find similar links of their own, they will be left with the feeling that the compromise between workplace and household duties is hardly acceptable.

Coming to Terms with Limits and Limitations

The sacrifice will still be there, nevertheless. No agreeable connections between work and home will ever change that. Trade-offs, compromises, and expediency are inevitable. Coming to terms with one's necessary deficiencies as a parent is often a wrenching experience, especially for women. Often not only is there guilt in the present but recalled blame for the parenting failures of one's own mother and father.

The psychiatrist D. W. Winnicott proposes a wonderfully useful realistic figure—the "good-enough mother," which, in today's world, would be "the good-enough parent." The lesson is that a parent can have quite a few shortcomings without being a failure. One can relax and trust natural impulses to carry one through. A man or woman who can accept being a good-enough parent and having a good-enough career probably will never become CEO of the corporation or be selected as Mother of the Year, but is likely to have a successful life in both worlds and a good marriage.

Management skills are just as vital at home as in the office, and organizing work and time—but being flexible about it— is no different in principle in either place.

Choice and Fit

As I noted earlier, the research shows that couples fare better when they feel they are making choices about their structure of work and child care. Negotiating the future between them and thinking ahead are two powerful levers for controlling their life. The old saying goes, "Women hope and men plan." One of the greatest feats in marriage is to combine optimism and objective-setting into a mutual conviction about the future.

Connecting to One's Childhood

One secret of being a successful parent is developing an ability to recover contact with oneself as a child, to regress playfully for a time. Unfortunately, many parents have grown stiff in their adult roles and find it impossible to regain a touch with all that is simple, naive, and new to the world. Even if they glimpse the possibility, they may feel embarrassed to try—or embarrassed to watch a wife or husband being childlike.

It is not wrong or silly. One of the great opportunities of parenthood is the chance to experience childhood and youth again, not simply vicariously but as a participant.

Curiosity

The capacity to be surprised by each other is one of the most enriching features of a good family life. The psychiatrist Edward Shapiro describes this as an active curiosity about one another, not intrusions on privacy but a willingness to look for something new and rewarding in a familiar person. One family may in time become a collection of stereotypes to one another; they have stopped asking questions, stopped listening, stopped perceiving in their own home. A different family will include parents who sense that there is always an enormous amount to be curious about in each other and in their children. They are explorers and discoverers in the best way.

Of all childhood's indictments of adulthood, the most tragic is the remark "My parents were never very much interested in me."

Conclusions

In all this discussion, there are probably three major guideposts that stand out. A true understanding of what they mean is probably the best kind of direction for avoiding a basic quarrel over children.

First, the realization that children add to a family but subtract from a marriage. Arriving here, we realize that the first part of the route—with all its one-on-one adjustments, differences, and true pleasures—is now behind us. Our whole mode of travel is different; we must change a great many of our expectations.

Second, the realization that becoming a parent forces us to relive the past, come to terms with our own experience of childhood, and be aware of the imprint that family role images have made on us. This might be called a fork in the road where we have the splendid chance to take a right direction away from the mistakes and disappointments of our past— and also to be compassionate about our unwitting tendency to repeat them.

Third, the realization that marriage and family, in our time, have to be collaborative. The "team of two" that knows how to share, delegate, negotiate, and decide in an equal way is the new model worth trying to achieve.

CHAPTER NINE

THE BASIC PACT

No relationship is immune from all seven major problems described in this book. These are areas of conflict so common to most American marriages that the quarrels arising from them might almost be called inevitable. Even if inevitable, those disputes will wind up as a healthy part of the marriage process if husbands and wives can find durable solutions. I would be suspicious of any marriage that showed no sign of friction or flare-up; I would guess it to be full of evasion and emotional dishonesty.

The *basic* quarrel is an entirely different matter—it is a bleak and hostile climate as opposed to a sudden thunderstorm now and then, a long-running battle in contrast to a temporary falling-out. No matter how it may manifest itself—in heat or cold, silence or tirade—it destroys the spirit of a marriage.

The argument of this book is that while some causes for friction are always present in a marriage, a basic quarrel is not inevitable or incurable. It can be understood, managed, and coped with. Overcoming it is a triumph that actually strengthens a marriage. In the seven chapters preceding this one, we have conveyed a message about awareness and un derstanding, a great part of the "how to" art of dealing with the seven basic quarrels of marriage. That knowledge is the first part of mastery, but, by itself, is not enough. The second part is the safeguard we term the basic pact.

The Basic Pact

The basic pact is a covenant between husband and wife. Some of its provisions are openly negotiated, some unspoken, and some an almost subconscious affirmation of trust. It is like an unwritten constitution for a marriage, a combination of law and faith. In some marriages, it develops out of a couple's abiding sense that whatever their crises and angers, they will come through whole. For other couples, the basic pact has to be built almost word by word—it is the hard-won understanding distilled from years of adversarial turmoil. I know two examples of deliberately developed basic pacts in different marriages.

In the first, there were two people who had suffered from the failure of previous marriages. Trying to avoid old mistakes, they set down a prenuptial agreement that included everything from a financial understanding to a philosophical expression of their hopes for the marriage. That charter worked well. Over the years, they would look back at it and discuss any points that must be modified or amended. Their marriage was like a wise democracy, and it endured.

Another couple had a tormented marriage for about fifteen years before they decided to separate. They had never had a prenuptial agreement, but now they undertook to create a separation agreement that would be both amicable and fair to their three children. It contained an understanding about social or sexual relationships with others, about a division of assets, about what attitudes could or couldn't be expressed to the children, and, finally, about what kind of a future they would wish if they ever got back together again. Just the process of working out this agreement was a kind of magic clearing of the air. The two of them later described it as the most constructive and intimate time they had ever had in marriage—and, when they eventually decided to live together again, the separation agreement turned out to be a wonderful basis for a new marriage agreement.

For most couples, making the basic pact will not be so formal as this. It will be a whole evolution that involves attunement, problem solving, and negotiation. Just for the purposes of explanation, I am going to describe the pact by its components, as if this were a way to take inventory of a marriage. I have included my own experiences as a therapist along with the experience and research of others cited throughout this book.

Commitment

When I meet with a couple in their first therapy appointment, I try to read the depth of each's commitment to the marriage. It's impossible to build on shaky foundations. Once the work gets hard, a partner with a tenuous allegiance will show signs of bailing out. When, on the other hand, both of the pair show me an impetus to make the marriage work and continue, I recognize the first premise for the basic pact.

Commitment to the marriage includes that one-to-one loyalty described in Chapter Three. It requires that both partners assess visible and invisible loyalties to their roots in the past and renounce—however painfully—the destructive elements.

No Blame, No Fault

In the early stages of a therapy, I often find a couple who have been exhausting themselves in the blame game. With them, finger-pointing and accusation have become almost a way of life. They are like two feudists always trying to extract an eye for an eye and a tooth for a tooth.

I try to convince them that it's no good trying to determine whose was the original sin and try to show them that they have let their marriage become a self-perpetuating system of retribution. They've lost the power to be objective. There will never be a winner.

If either accepts a measure of blame or either tries—however ineffectively—to call off the vendetta, it is usually the woman. This may be because she is more committed to the relationship or because she is usually the underdog in the power order or because men have a greater difficulty in owning up to their failures in a relationship. Historically, women have paid a high price for their selflessness.

Once the blame game has been set in motion, no one-sided effort to slow it down is going to work. The only remedy is for both to take responsibility without blame. Peter Kramer calls psychotherapy "the creation of a context between people in which mistakes are useful." In marriage, the same creativity can be put to work—mistakes can be turned around and made into lessons—lessons about what not to do or say.

Two Truths

You say something came about this way; he or she says no, it came about that way—and if one of you "wins," the other loses. This is one of the pieces of false logic that makes quarrels possible. It suggests that the most important thing at stake is whose version of reality is going to get final acceptance. Each argues the point with an emotional charge far in excess of what the dispute calls for because this is actually a battle over personal validity. He is trying to deny her point of view, even her right to a point of view—or vice versa.

In contrast, a basic pact insures that two different viewpoints can live side by side and respect each other. Each side then understands that the other one speaks from a standpoint of personal, not universal, truth. The stark choice of either/or—the hobgoblin of so many arguments—is thrown out, and the basic pact lets us assume that each in some way is right, each in some way may be wrong. Opponents have to start out by asking themselves, "What is he or she arguing that could be quite true?" By focusing on what could be acceptable as true rather than what seems dubious, the debaters get to an old and magical verity: Truth in personal affairs is relative, approximate, even subjective—which means that compromise is possible.

During couple therapy, I have often noted that people begin to relax when they stop trying to deny, disprove, or dissuade. Once they accept the idea of relative truths, the tenor of their discussion takes on a civil tone. Each hears the other. Although the argument about the substantive problem continues, the argument about "Are you going to reject everything I say?" is over.

Equity
The research results show that most couples believe that equity is essential in marriage—and they also show that couples rarely practice what they profess. However they may define it, they speak up for an ideal of fairness, but it's an ideal shaped by their times and by the prevailing culture. In the 1950s, for example, a middle-class wife and husband most likely made the traditional trade-offs. He earned the income, and she tended the house and children. The rewards were a home in the suburbs, two cars, and a wholesome place for children to grow up. By the standards of the 1970s, this arrangement was not equitable—though many couples still accept it in 1991. Today, both the idea of equity in marriage and the trade-offs are different and will be even more different at the end of the century.

I think that the difference lies with women's sharper sense of what equity is for them and a greater impatience with the traditional kinds of trade-offs. The clause in the basic pact about a fair division of roles and rights will differ with different couples, but every couple has to believe that it is indeed just on both sides. Psychologically, the most dangerous hidden word in any marriage is "unfair!"

Connections

Opposites can fall in love. People with dramatically different characteristics often marry. The classic hysteric-obsessional marriage described in Chapter Seven is one distinct type of polarized personality pattern. The question, then, is how two such human contradictions can reconcile themselves in a basic pact—and the answer is that they must look hard for psychological common denominators. If the hysteric is able to assess her choice of an orderly, unemotional husband and he is able to perceive his choice of an impressionable, spontaneous wife as a dovetailing of characters, their insights have rewarded them.

As Carolynn Maltas has pointed out:

> Marriage can be thought of as a contract to affirm each spouse's sense of self and self-worth, though often in ways that are paradoxically painful and growth-inhibiting. Whether in healthy or disturbed marriages, the spouses sometimes function like a joint personality, making up for each other's deficits, fulfilling each other's dreams, as well as frequently carrying for each other disavowed and projected parts of the self. The sense of completing oneself within the relationship is, for many, the essence of marriage.

In my practice of therapy, I am always looking for points of convergence that lie beneath the overt conflict about differences. Once found, these can explain quite a bit about the roots of the quarrel. One couple had fights that sprang either from his need to keep life in order and under control or from her trait of withdrawing emotionally. I discovered that their covert common denominator was the fact that they were both terrified of anger. They had different ways of suppressing it—his was to pull hard on the reins and hers was to seek an emotional hideout—and they also had different family-of-origin sources for this fear. Her parents had fought loudly and openly, while his had sat tight-lipped, silent, and glaring.

With another couple, the conflict arose over shows of authority. She felt that she was always playing the role of the accused in the courtroom while he delivered a verdict. He felt that she was always playing the role of the stern school-teacher giving orders to the slowest learner in the class. Their point of coincidence?—a mutual tendency to feel vulnerable and sensitive to criticism. Each had grown up with an exacting, critical parent and, under the least pressure, was likely to superimpose that stern image on the face of the other.

A third case was one of mutual recrimination—she argued that he spent money too freely and smoked too much; he argued that she was overweight and drank too much. In the losing struggles to control their self-destructive impulses, they were mirror images of each other—they could recognize and criticize in each other the weaknesses they had been unable to master in themselves.

Once these people could understand that their separate antagonisms had the same emotional root, they were able to make the wonderful transposition that allowed them to see things from the other's standpoint. They now knew exactly what the other meant, and they saw that they were allies faced by a common adversary.

The I-Self and the We-Self
One of the themes of this book has been the gender differences—both biological and socially conditioned—between men and women. The book's quest is for a harmony and reconciliation of those seeming opposites. We all need the feminine "We-self" of relationship and interdependence and the masculine "I-self" of autonomy and self-reliance to

create our identity. The basic pact offers a way for the marriage to give full play to both selves in combination. It insures that neither partner will be a chauvinist proprietor of "I" alone or "We" alone.

Shared Task, Differentiated Roles

In Chapter Eight, I gave the example of child-rearing as one of those possible dividing points in the marriage course where men's work and women's work can either separate to our detriment or continue together to our benefit. There are other important places where the course can divide, and a little farther on I will discuss them in relation to roles and to the five perspectives on marriage.

While the key word for authority and responsibility is "shared," the key word for roles in the marriage is "differentiated." Overlapping or separate spheres of influence give husband and wife equal access to money and power, allow each to possess separate functions and expertise in his/her roles (although this succeeds only if each values the other's special accomplishments). A marriage might be compared to a family business owned by two partners. At times, they must be coworkers operating the plant; at other times, they are equal shareholders in Our Marriage, Inc.; at still others, they are officers of the company, overseeing different but interlocking departments.

The basic pact, in this sense, is much like a set of rules for running a small, modern, prosperous business. Negotiation, reciprocity, and cooperation prevail. It might even be said that this is an efficient high-tech business in contrast to an old-fashioned smokestack industry with some Henry Ford–like tycoon dictating the operation.

Outside Connections

In the chapter on privacy, I pointed out that preserving privacy does not mean that isolation is good. No couple can isolate themselves at length from the world of their culture, especially the family-of-origin loyalties and ideas of gender identity. The basic pact should provide for a mutually acceptable understanding about how each person will maintain relationships—whether activities or human associations—outside the marriage. This would include ideas of how to deal with any problems that might come from those relationships.

Playfulness
In my research and my clinical work with couples, I have found that happy marriages usually have in them some spirit of playfulness. I mean something beyond structured games such as tennis or cards, a wide range of spontaneity and enjoyment. This includes a shared sense of humor, private ways of talking or naming each other, diverting rituals, and mutual fantasies. The capacity for play shows something about basic attitudes toward the marriage. Couples can frolic only when they feel safe, relaxed, and in sync with each other. In contrast, the marriage that is totally serious and matter-of-fact is usually laden with boredom and inflexibility. The basic pact should have a fun-and-frolic clause in it.

Five Perspectives on Marriage
We can look at marriage from five different vantage points—in other words, there are five different ways of examining the basic quarrels. Couples with problems often limit themselves to only one of them, and that means they narrow their options for improvement.

1. Marriage as a System
When couples locked in recurring conflicts come to therapy, I always try to help them look beyond themselves as individuals and see their problem as a dynamic. The dynamic is not A versus B but a process called AB, a complex of hostility-and-retribution that has acquired a life of its own. A can now

instinctively push the buttons that infuriate B, and B's auto-matic reaction pushes the right buttons to inflame A. It is like a war between programmed robots. As we put this in slow motion and watch the exact sequence of strike and counter-strike, the two people begin to see that the problem is a joint creation. That realization and its distancing effect can do wonders.

It is usually difficult for people to discern this pattern with-out the help of a trained observer, but just the act of grasping the idea that they have together become the problem and together can become the solution is the first stage of progress.

2. Intrapsychic Focus

Just as I try to look past each individual person in a marital battle and see what's happening in the space between them, I also try to look into each person to try to see what's hap-pening within. There are, for example, the couple who are accusing each other of being too rigid and judgmental about behavior. I try to shift the focus of the argument by ques-tioning them about other people in their experience who have made stern and autocratic demands on them. Was it a father? A relative? A teacher? A lover? An employer? (Usu-ally at least one is a parent.) Once we have accomplished this, the argument can be transferred from a debate over present sins to an examination of past histories. I can then see what projections each is making on the other and what signals their emotional radar has been tuned to pick up from each other. That is, once we remove the immediate onus from the partner to a more historical figure, we can look for inner conflicts and projections that may be the source of all their anti-authority attitudes.

This shift of focus can contribute to a healthy development in the marriage. The more clearly each sees himself/herself, the better both will understand the source of conflict. That self, as we have tried to show it, encompasses loyalties and gender along with attitudes toward money, power, sex, privacy, and children.

At several points in this book, I have described "projective identification" as the process by which people offload onto each other the attributes within themselves that trouble them. Clinicians usually see the adverse results of this, but I believe that a certain amount of it is a normal part of intimate relationships. As people in therapy come to understand more about this process, they tend to reverse it—to "reclaim" the attributes they have transferred—but I believe it both possible and salutary to allow some to remain with the partner, to be vicariously experienced and admired.

3. Tactics of Conflict

In military history, there is something called a war of attrition—a gradual wearing down of the enemy's numbers and resources with no end in sight except total exhaustion. Something like this takes place in many basic-quarrel marriages. People make no effort to solve problems or even aim toward an armistice; their tactics are character assassination, assaults on the other person's most sensitive points, and something called "the kitchen-sink argument." The latter is the tactic of throwing every unresolved or disputed issue in sight into the argument—which effectively prevents the immediate question from ever getting settled.

A halfway step toward a peace treaty is to call off the attrition, forswear those atrocities of argument, and adopt more positive tactics. One of them is to listen to the other and then repeat back a summary of his or her points, just to establish a basic agreement about meaning. Another is to listen to criticism without interrupting or firing back immediately. Another is to speak only for oneself and make no assumptions about knowing what the other feels.

4. Cultural Effects

Surrounded by our society, we are always affected by the trends of our time. Current views of gender, love, economic forces, and current health and medical developments such as better contraceptive techniques, safer abortion, and AIDS are of vital significance to our marriages. The uncertainties of our time—particularly about gender and sexual issues—thus touch most couples. The therapist—or anyone else involved —must not try to analyze a basic quarrel in terms of individual neuroses or "skill deficits" alone, because there will always be some of society's pressures shaping it.

I find that many dual-career couples are relieved to hear that their difficulties—the sense of never having enough time for fun, for sex, for their children, for themselves—are common to many others. They can then look at their own fights more dispassionately and realize that neither is a villain or a failure as a spouse, but both are struggling with problems almost everybody in their situation faces.

5. Developmental Changes

Marriages, like people, have lives that change and mature. A marriage can be said to combine three timelines— each spouse's and that of the marriage itself. For example, the first year of marriage will be different for two previously married people in their fifties, for a twenty-five-year-old married to a person of forty, and for a pair both in their early twenties. Quarrels often have something to do with a discrepancy in past experience or in future hopes that comes from a difference in degrees of maturity—chronological or emotional.

The more usual marriage is that of two people in their mid-twenties to early thirties. Remembering that all marriages don't develop in a linear, consistent sequence, we can still discern a general pattern of change and succeeding areas of possible conflict. Marriages change according to the problems and challenges that time brings. The first of these is the separation from family-of-origin loyalties and the forging of a special bond with wife or husband. Along with that goes the need to form an intimacy that is both sexual and psychological.

The next of time's milestones marks the gradual integration of the marriage into the outside world of work, friendships, and in-laws. It also marks the beginning of some significant conflicts. At this point, the picture each partner has of the other has changed. It is no longer the romantic miniature in the locket but a much more photographic dark-and-light portrait.

The third milestone is parenthood. Along come the problems of two jobs and dual careers, the renegotiation of gender roles, the necessary sacrifice of some pair intimacy for the child or children's sake, and changed relations with in-laws and parents.

The fourth milestone is the famous "midlife crisis," when people must struggle with disappointments in the marriage, an awareness that certain things will never change for the better, and a temptation to look elsewhere for what they think they have been missing. This time of disillusion and reassessment sometimes leads to divorce and sometimes to recommitment, but it is never without serious conflict. It is the era of the "empty-nest syndrome," when two people face each other alone again and all the postponed quarrels can resurface.

The fifth milestone can, at its worst, mark the boredom of "all passions spent" in a marriage that has never settled its basic quarrels but has simply worn them out. At its best, however, this stage can hold all the delight and satisfaction of having won through one of the strangest of all the trials in life—the conflicts with someone you love.

Marital Touchstones for Survival

I am no believer in a methodical, step-by-step technique for solving marital conflicts. Things are never so simple. I do think that one could imagine something like a set of touchstones—things with a touch of magic in them that would not necessarily cure a basic quarrel but could be used as a reference to remind us how good marriage can be.

Touchstone: Minor Pleasures

I think of such comfort in minor pleasures as:

The two of us—weather permitting—get up early and take a walk while the streets or the country lanes are empty. We avoid all problems, matters of concern, and we talk about something we both love.

Another time, on the spur of the moment, we decide on a weekend getaway. We park the kids and go to the most idyllic place we know. If there's no time or money for that, we make a secret assignation for lunch at a romantic little restaurant or for a picnic in the park.

We make a ritual of having a glass of wine together in some secluded place before we go to bed.

We take time out to read aloud to each other from a book we both admire.

We make a habit of each writing a love letter to the other on birthdays, holidays, or whenever the spirit moves us.

We belong to at least one social group or organization together—something that represents a cause or an interest we share.

In all of this, we swear a profound oath to leave the daily baggage of details, problems, children, and worries behind. We have built a private world just big enough for two people. Sometimes—especially when children are young—it's physically impossible to step into it nearly as often as we wish. But knowing that it's there and that we have the key to it is the all-important thing.

Touchstone: Habits and Rituals

As for the immediate ways of handling and diminishing quarrels, the psychologists John Paddock and Karen Schwartz describe certain "interaction rituals" for dual-career couples. These are repeated symbolic gestures, habits, or codes that reaffirm the couple's connection. One couple they worked with used to get into a fight almost every afternoon when each had come home from work. When questioned, he admitted that he looked forward to a warm welcome, some relaxation, and some small talk about her day and his. Tired of people and talk, she just wanted an hour of privacy and silence. The therapists suggested that they rearrange their schedules so that she could arrive home first and decompress by herself. If for any reason he came home before she had eased off, she would silently touch his index finger with hers, in the manner of E.T., and he would understand that she needed more time. The device succeeded beautifully. It expressed her need for solitude and his for connection, and the fights stopped.

Touchstone: Cease-Fire Signals

In the United States Congress, there is an old custom of referring to an opponent on the other side of the aisle as "the honorable and distinguished senator from Illinois" (or wherever) before a speaker begins to attack that gentleman's views. Absurd as this sometimes seems, it is a good custom—it is difficult to proceed by saying that the honorable and distinguished member is a total idiot and corrupt to boot.

In couples' quarrels, when all courtesy is dropped and the matter becomes a runaway fight, they have created a mental whirlwind that has to be calmed before a therapist—or any counselor—can discern the real causes. It's similar to treating an alcoholic. He or she has to be sobered up and brought to his or her senses before the reasons behind the drinking can be explored.

If such a quarreling couple can halt for a moment, it's possible that they can escape their obsession. My version of the old "count to ten" device is to have some couples agree on a stopper, a key word or phrase such as "Time out!" It's a signal that the quarrel is escalating out of control. It means that they have to cease and desist from any talk about the issue for at least half an hour.

The trick is to recognize the danger signs of escalation, such as character assassination: "Your problem is simple: you're a habitual liar." Another is overgeneralization: "Why do you always ignore me?" And another is a kind of random counterattacking: "No, I didn't forget to walk the dog, and why haven't you started to paint the house yet?"

Touchstone: Conflict Management

For the past fifteen years or so, therapists have relied heavily on teaching compromise as the best way to settle marital quarrels. Some surprising light was shed on that approach when Dr. Samuel Vuchinich videotaped fifty-two families at dinner in their homes. He found that family fights end in compromise only 14 percent of the time. Sixty-one percent of the fights ended in a standoff with the opponents tacitly agreeing to disagree. Twenty-one percent stopped when one member conceded. Only 4 percent ended when one contender left the room.

The conclusion drawn was that any family will have a natural mode of conflict management, a mode that isn't consciously planned but that permits a healthy amount of conflict with no blood on the floor in the end. This suggests that therapists might be wise to try other methods of conflict management in addition to compromise.

Most therapists have long favored having partners lay all their feelings on the table even if that made for bruised egos. The rationale for this was that many couples who suppress their angers and avoid conflict end up totally alienated from each other.

John Gottman, a psychologist, tested this reasoning by an experiment. He and his colleagues used newspaper ads to recruit two separate groups of couples: one group that admitted to having marital problems and one that simply agreed to take part in a research experiment.

The researchers hooked each couple up to heart monitors, videotaped them, and coded every tone of voice and every clue of body language as they talked. Gottman's conclusion was that "automatic system arousal"—persistent patterns of rapid heartbeat, sweaty palms, and signs of anxiety—is the best indicator of marital trouble.

Howard Markman speculates that such couples are constantly revved up because they anticipate conflict. Their negative feelings are on hair trigger, and there is nothing they can do to change: "We know what the fight will be like and how it will end. But here we go again—we then have the fight anyway." This escalation is the telltale sign of a problem relationship, or one that will become dysfunctional later on.

Contrary to the therapists' idea of getting every feeling out in full view, Markman says that ventilation is only helpful if the other person is listening and able to validate you. It doesn't work if both are ventilating at the same time. The conclusion is that couples should call a halt, get feedback from each on what's been said, summarize for each other what messages are in the air, and discuss the discrepancies.

This is a good—though theoretical—method of conflict control. Still, all of this is very well for two professors of logic, but a difficult trick for a husband and wife in the midst of a hot war.

Touchstone: Awareness of Gender Differences

Gender differences are a kind of hidden factor in the usual marital-quarrel scenario. When a man withdraws from the quarrel, the woman will usually accuse him—whether or not she uses these exact words—of fleeing from intimacy. In fact, he could just be escaping the conflict. Markman laments the tendency to define intimacy from a female viewpoint, as a sharing of feelings: "Men and women define intimacy differently. Men define it in terms of doing things together. . . . It's important to realize that sharing feelings indiscriminately may lead to destructive conflict and *less* intimacy."

It is even quite possible that there is a physiological difference in the way men and women handle conflict because evidence shows that men and women operate on different emotional thermostats. Once men get upset, they have greater trouble calming themselves down, and unless their wives or lovers soothe them, they are likely to avoid a fight at the next instance.

Gottman and his colleague Robert Levenson also found two patterns that indicate unhappy marriages: first, when the husband's negative feelings get a strong counterresponse by the wife, and, second, when a wife's negative feelings get a weak counterresponse from the husband. Perhaps men want to vent their negative feelings and then to be left alone. In contrast, women need to have their negative feelings responded to.

This suggests that couples need some way of breaking the cycle of angry escalation—some soothing or affectionate gesture that will change the mood.

Touchstone: Playfulness

My own research has been directed toward finding a common ground, an area of agreement, that transcends troublesome gender-typical responses. I found this motif in play.

Most people have a sense of humor; most people enjoy

something comic. I realized that if we can glimpse even momentarily a funny or absurd aspect about our arguments, we will be better able to manage those conflicts. Along with that, playful teasing, even parody, can "touch the truth lightly" to carry the message that one person objects to the other's action or stance without a fierce confrontation.

I remember Jean and John, a couple in their late twenties whose bone of contention was Jean's bossiness, a trait she had picked up from her father, Harold. She recognized it but was defensive about it.

One day, while John was doing the cooking, Jean began to tell him that he was doing it all wrong, and he replied, "Why, yes, Harold."

It was exactly the right touch. Instead of getting angry, Jean answered him in her father's accent, pretending to peer over her eyeglasses as Harold always did. They both laughed, and the spat was over.

Since then, the joking "Yes, Harold" has taken the curse off the unspoken warning "Watch it. You're beginning to sound bossy again." As John commented to me, "The joking reminds us that we are together and that we have something better than we had in our original families."

Another wife told me, "It's the one clear sign of our feeling of closeness and trust in each other that we feel free to be oilly together. It . . . would be hard to express in any other way—it makes me aware of how relaxed I feel with him and him with me."

A third couple observed, "We never joke about a problem while one of us is really angry, but play is a probing to see if it still hurts and [whether we can] bring it back slowly without its being a crisis issue."

Touchstone: Negotiation
Another nearly level playing field without enormous gender differences is negotiation. The general negotiation strategies

cited in Chapter Four apply well to marital troubles: separate the people from the problem; focus on interests, not positions; invent ways that both sides can profit by coming to an agreement; and insist on some objective standard for the settlement terms.

This process, in trying to segregate affect and the irrational, is austere and "masculine"—a complexion few marital disputes will ever take on. It is, nevertheless, something worth trying for, and an appeal to people's sense of fairness is usually a strong one.

Touchstone: The Good Word

Sheer friendliness and warmth, commonplace rewards and gratifications—these can be quite as disarming as humor or negotiation. Over the years, married couples tend to forget how to praise, express affection or concern, show sensitivity in small things, or even use good manners. They have replaced these positive things with negative tactics such as criticism, withholding, or emotional blackmail.

The result is that both he and she feel that they have lost value as people. There must be something wrong with me, the subconscious suggests, if I'm no longer solicited, respected, or even listened to—unless I raise my voice in anger. I'm a nonperson unless I try to punish you in return.

Touchstone: Knowing the Tactics

The content of a quarrel is what we are arguing about—sex, money, power, etc.—but the tactics are how we conduct the fight. The substantive terms may outline a perfectly fair difference of opinion, while the tactics may be manipulative and dishonest. Some of the tactics to watch out for and identify are these:

* *One person always uses dominating tactics: raised voice, frequent interruptions and contradictions; a bullying manner.*

- *One person will resort to sarcasm because that always makes the other feel hurt and go silent.*
- *One or both people may turn from the substance to an argument over how badly he/she is being treated, that is, shifting the grounds to protest the other's tactics.*
- *One person will concentrate on* ad hominem *tactics—that is, a purely personal attack.*
- *One person may be arguing about substance while the other is arguing about tactics or personalities.*

The basic quarrel is always prolonged and embittered by the use of destructive tactics or by arguing nonequivalent cases along with the main argument. The point is that one should assess very clearly how the argument is taking place as well as why.

Touchstone: Curiosity
In Chapter Eight, I noted the thesis that people must keep up an active curiosity—although with no unwelcome intrusion —about each other. A marriage is headed toward living death when people can no longer surprise each other, listen to each other, or unexpectedly captivate each other.

After years of rubbing along together, a couple may have to make a fresh effort, but the rewards are wonderful. When one person delights the other in this way, two of the best talents of love are still at work—the capacity to astonish and the capacity to be astonished. Without curiosity, though, there can be nothing to amaze us.

CONCLUSION
I am invited into the most private and personal world of marriage. As a couples therapist, I can—figuratively—see into family bedrooms, living rooms, kitchens, and hear the voices raised there. I know the troubles of the security guard

and those of his wife, who is the mother of five children. I have heard the strident debates of two bright, competitive yuppie lawyers married to each other. I have caught the undertone of rancor in the exchanges of the cultured Beacon Hill couple. Over and over again, I am face to face with basic quarrels, and more than most people, I know how devastating they are.

I also know how surprisingly resourceful and resilient people can be. If there was something true and good that brought two people together in the first place, it has probably been misplaced rather than lost. I know, too, how much most people want their marriages to work and are themselves willing to work to preserve them.

Even though my job is to look at the somber side of marriage, I have learned to recognize hopes and promises in the most pessimistic climates. One reason for hope is that unhappiness is a powerful motivator for most people. Conflict —as I hope I've conveyed in this book—is not necessarily the portent of a breaking marriage. It can be a healthy outburst, a warning signal, or, at its worst, the evidence of a basic quarrel. It is the argument postponed or the repeated clash people won't work to understand that is the seed of the basic quarrel.

I also hope that we have conveyed what a diverse, complex thing marriage is—or rather, the series of stages and succession of changes we call by that all-inclusive name. If there is any such thing as an ideal marriage, it is one that a couple has been able to define and redefine over the years. In order to survive triumphantly, a marriage must have a large but firm tolerance. Disappointments and disillusionments great and small can be absorbed, but real transgression is fatal. The basic quarrel, if not checked, is perhaps the greatest of all the transgressions. And the basic pact is the greatest expression of a firm and fair tolerance.

BIBLIOGRAPHY

Abelin, Ernest L. "The role of the father in the separation-individuation process." In *Separation-Individuation: Essays in Honor of Margaret S. Mahler*, ed. J. McDevitt and C. Settlage, pp. 229–52. Madison, CT: International Universities Press, 1971.

Altman, Irwin. "Privacy regulation: culturally universal or culturally specific?" *Journal of Social Issues*, Vol 33, pp. 66–84, 1977.

Archea, John. "The place of architectural factors in behavioral theories of privacy," *Journal of Social Issues*, Vol 33, pp. 116–37, 1977.

Ardrey, Robert. *The Territorial Imperative*. New York: Dell, 1966.

Ariès, Philippe. *Centuries of Childhood: A Social History of the Family*, Translated by Robert Baldwick. New York: Knopf, 1962.

Astrachan, Anthony. *How Men Feel*. New York: Anchor, Doubleday, 1988.

Bailyn, Lotte. "Career and family orientations of husbands and wives in relation to marital happiness," *Human Relations*, Vol 23, pp. 97–113, 1970.

Baldassare, Mark. "Human spatial behavior," *Annual Review of Sociology*, Vol 4, pp. 29–56, 1978.

Barnett, Joseph. "Narcissism and dependency in the obsessional-hysteric marriage," *Family Process*, Vol 10, pp. 75–83, 1971.

Baruch, Grace K., and Barnett, Rosalind C. "Consequences of fathers' participation in family work: parents' role strain and well-being," *Journal of Personality and Social Psychology*, Vol 51, pp. 983–92, 1986.

Belsky, Jay. "Stability and change in marriage across the transition to parenthood," *Journal of Marriage and the Family*, Vol 70, pp. 567–77, 1983.

Benedek, Therese. "Parenthood as a developmental phase," *Journal of the American Psychoanalytic Association*, Vol 7, pp. 389–417, 1959.

Berg, Adriane G. *How to Stop Fighting About Money and Make Some: A Couple's Guide to Financial Success.* Scranton: Newmarket Press, 1988.

Bernardez, Teresa. "The female therapist in relation to male roles." In *Men in Transition*, ed. Kenneth Solomon and Norman B. Levy, New York: Plenum, 1982.

Berger, Peter, and Kellner, Hansfried. "Marriage and the construction of reality," *Diogenes*, Vol 46, pp. 1–23, 1964.

Betcher, William. *Intimate Play.* New York: Viking, 1987.

Betcher, William. "Intimate play and marital adaptation," *Psychiatry*, Vol 44, pp. 13–33, 1981.

Blood, Robert O., and Wolfe, Donald M. *Husbands and Wives: The Dynamics of Married Living.* New York: Free Press, 1960.

Blumstein, Philip, and Schwartz, Pepper. *American Couples.* New York: William Morrow, 1983.

Bolton, Charles D. "Mate selection as the development of a relationship," *Marriage and Family Living*, pp. 234–40, 1961.

Boszormenyi-Nagy, Ivan, and Spark, Geraldine M. *Invisible Loyalties.* New York: Brunner-Mazel, 1965.

Brody, Leslie R. "Gender differences in emotional development: a review of theories and research," *Journal of Personality*, Vol 53, pp. 102–49, 1985.

Broverman, Inge K., Broverman, Donald M., Clarkson, Frank E., Rosenkrantz, Paul S., and Vogel, Susan R. "Sex-role stereotypes and clinical judgments of mental health," *Journal of Consulting and Clinical Psychology*, Vol 34, pp. 1–7, 1970.

Burgess, Ernest W., and Wallin, Paul. *Engagement and Marriage.* Chicago: Lippincott, 1953.

Burr, Wesley, Ahern, Louis, and Knowles, Elmer. "An empirical test of Rodman's theory of resources in cultural context," *Journal of Marriage and the Family*, Vol 39, pp. 505–14, 1977.

Burton, Sir Richard, and Arbuthnot, F. F. (trans.). *The Kama Sutra of Vatsyayana.* New York: Capricorn Books, 1963.

Chodorow, Nancy. *The Reproduction of Mothering.* Berkeley: University of California Press, 1978.

Coen, Stanley J. "Sexual interviewing, evaluation, and therapy: psychoanalytic emphasis on the use of sexual fantasy," *Archives of Sexual Behavior*, Vol 7, pp. 229–41, 1978.

Cole, Martin. "Sex therapy—a critical appraisal," *British Journal of Psychiatry*, Vol 147, pp. 337–51, 1985.

Comfort, Alex, *The Joy of Sex*. New York: Crown, 1972.

Davis, Katharine B. *Factors in the Sex Life of Twenty-two Hundred Women*. New York: Ayer Co. 1929.

de Beauvoir, Simone. *The Second Sex*. Translated by H. M. Parshley. New York: Knopf, 1953.

Defoe, Daniel, *The Use and Abuse of the Marriage Bed*. London: T. Warner, 1727.

Dicks, Henry V. "Object relations theory and marital studies," *British Journal of Medical Psychology*, Vol 36, pp. 125–29, 1963.

Easterbrooks, M. Ann, and Goldberg, Wendy A. "Effects of early maternal employment on toddlers, mothers, and fathers," *Developmental Psychology*, Vol 21, pp. 774–83, 1985.

Erikson, Erik. "Identity and the life cycle." In *Psychological Issues*, Vol 1, New York: International Universities Press, 1959.

Fairbairn, W. Ronald D. *Psychoanalytic Studies of the Personality*. London: Routledge & Kegan Paul, 1952.

Felton, Judith R. "A psychoanalytic perspective on sexually open relations," *Psychoanalytic Review*, Vol 71, pp. 279–95, 1984.

Fenichel, Otto. "The drive to amass wealth," *Psychoanalytic Quarterly*, Vol 7, pp. 69–95, 1938.

Fields, Nina S. "Satisfaction in long-term marriages," *Social Work*, Vol 28, pp. 37–41, 1983.

Fisher, Roger, and Ury, William. *Getting to Yes*. Boston: Houghton Mifflin, 1981.

Fishman, Barbara. "The economic behavior of stepfamilies," *Family Relations*, Vol 32, pp. 359–66, 1983.

Fowers, Blaine J., and Olson, David H. "Predicting marital success with PREPARE: a predictive validity study," *Journal of Marital and Family Therapy*, Vol 12, pp. 403–13, 1986.

Fowers, Blaine J., and Olson, David H. "ENRICH marital inventory: a discriminant validity and cross-validation assessment," *Journal of Marital and Family Therapy*, Vol 15, pp. 65–79, 1989.

Freud, Sigmund. "Dreams in folklore." In *The Standard Edition of the Complete Psychological Works of Sigmund Freud*, Vol XII, London: Hogarth Press, 1958.

Freud, Sigmund. "On beginning the treatment." In *The Standard Edition*, Vol I, London: Hogarth Press, 1913.

Geiss, Susan K., and O'Leary, K. Daniel. "Therapist ratings of frequency and severity of marital problems: implications for research," *Journal of Marital and Family Therapy*, Vol 7, pp. 515–20, 1981.

Gilbert, Lucia, and Rachlin, Vicki. "The husband-wife relationship." In *Men in Dual-Career Families*, ed. Lucia Gilbert. Hillsdale, N.J.: Lawrence Erlbaum Assocs., Inc., 1985.

Gillespie, Dair L. "Who has the power? The marital struggle," *Journal of Marriage and the Family*, Vol 33, pp. 445–58, 1971.

Gilligan, Carol. *In a Different Voice*. Cambridge: Harvard University Press, 1982.

Goffman, Erving. *The Presentation of Self in Everyday Life*. New York: Doubleday, 1959.

Goffman, Erving. *Asylums*. New York: Doubleday, 1961.

Gottman, John M., and Levenson, Robert W. "Assessing the role of emotion in marriage," *Behavioral Assessment*, Vol 8, pp. 31–48, 1986.

Gray-Little, Bernadette, and Burks, Nancy. "Power and satisfaction in marriage: a review and critique," *Psychological Bulletin*, Vol 93, pp. 513–38, 1983.

Grossman, Frances K., Pollack, William S., and Golding, Ellen. "Fathers and children: predicting the quality and quantity of fathering," *Developmental Psychology*, Vol 24, pp. 82–91, 1988.

Grunebaum, Henry. "Thoughts on love, sex, and commitment," *Journal of Sex and Marital Therapy*, Vol 2, pp. 277–83, 1976.

Haley, Jay. "Marriage therapy," *Archives of General Psychiatry*, Vol 8, pp. 25–46, 1963.

Haley, Jay. *Problem Solving Therapy*. San Francisco: Jossey-Bass, 1976.

Hall, Edward T. "The anthropology of space: an organizing model." In *Environmental Psychology* (2nd ed.), ed. Harold M. Proshansky, William H. Ittelson, and Leanne G. Rivlin, New York: Holt, Rinehart & Winston, 1970.

Hall, Edward T. *The Dance of Life*. New York: Doubleday, 1984.

Hallowell, Edward M., and Grace, William J. *What Are You Worth?* Weidenfeld, 1989.

Harriman, Lynda Cooper. "Personal and marital changes accompanying parenthood," *Family Relations Journal of Applied Family and Child Studies*, Vol 32, pp. 387–94, 1983.

Hawton, Keith. "The behavioural treatment of sexual dysfunction," *British Journal of Psychiatry*, Vol 140, pp. 94–101, 1982.

Hawton, Keith, Catalan, Jose, Martin, Pauline, and Fagg, Joan. "Long-term outcome of sex therapy," *Behavioural Research and Therapy*, Vol 24, pp. 665–75, 1986.

Heiman, Julia R., and LoPiccolo, Joseph. "Clinical outcome of sex therapy," *Archives of General Psychiatry*, Vol 40, pp. 443–49, 1983.

Hertz, Rosanna. *More Equal Than Others, Women and Men in Dual-Career Marriages*. Los Angeles: Univ. of California Press, 1986.

Hiller, Dana V., and Philliber, William W. "Predicting marital and career success among dual-worker couples," *Journal of Marriage and the Family*, Vol 44, pp. 53–62, 1982.

Hiller, Dana V., and Philliber, William W. "The division of labor in contemporary marriage: expectations, perceptions and performance," *Social Problems*, Vol 33, pp. 191–201, 1986.

Hirsch, Irwin. "Sexual disorders: a perspective," *The American Journal of Psychoanalysis*, Vol 46, pp. 239–48, 1986.

Hochschild, Arlie, and Machung, Anne. *The Second Shift*. New York: Penguin, 1989.

Holtzworth-Munroe, Amy, and Jacobson, Neil S. "Causal attributions of married couples: when do they search for causes? What do they conclude when they do?" *Journal of Personality and Social Psychology*, Vol 48, pp. 1398–1412, 1985.

Homans, George C. *Social Behavior: Its Elementary Forms*. New York: Harcourt Brace, 1961.

Horner, Matina S. "Toward an understanding of achievement-related conflicts in women," *Journal of Social Issues*, Vol 28, pp. 157–75, 1972.

Horney, Karen. "On the genesis of the castration complex in women," *International Journal of Psycho-analysis*, Vol 5, pp. 50–65, 1924.

Howard, Judith A., Blumstein, Philip, and Schwartz, Pepper. "Sex, power, and influence tactics in intimate relationships," *Journal of Personality and Social Psychology*, Vol 51, pp. 102–109, 1986.

Huber, Joan, and Spitze, Glenna. *Sex, Stratification, Children, Housework, and Jobs*. New York: Academic Press, 1983.

Hunt, Jennifer, and Rudden, Marie. "Gender differences in the psychology of parenting," *Journal of the American Academy of Psychoanalysis*, Vol 14, pp. 213–25, 1986.

Hyde, Lewis. *The Gift*. New York: Random House, 1983.

Jones, Ernest. "Early female sexuality." In *Papers on Psychoanalysis*. Boston: Beacon Press, 1935.

Jordan, Judith. "Clarity in connection; empathic knowing, desire, and sexuality," Work in progress, The Stone Center for Developmental Services and Studies, 1987.

Jordan, Judith. "The meaning of mutuality," Work in progress, The Stone Center for Developmental Services and Studies, 1986.

Jung, Carl G. *Psychological Reflections: An Anthology* (Jolande Jacobi, ed.). New York: Pantheon, 1953.

Kaplan, Helen Singer. *Disorders of Sexual Desire and Other New Concepts and Techniques in Sex Therapy*. New York: Brunner-Mazel, 1979.

Kaplan, Helen Singer. *The New Sex Therapy*. New York: Brunner-Mazel, 1974.

Kelvin, Peter. "A social-psychological examination of privacy," *British Journal of Social and Clinical Psychology*, Vol 12, pp. 248–61, 1973.

Kerckhoff, Richard K. "Marriage and middle age," *The Family Co-ordinator*, Vol 25, pp. 5–11, 1976.

Kernberg, Otto. "Boundaries and structure in love relations," *Journal of the American Psychoanalytic Association*, Vol 25, pp. 81–114, 1977.

Kernberg, Otto. "Mature love: prerequisites and characteristics," *Journal of the American Psychoanalytic Association*, Vol 22, pp. 743–68, 1974.

Kernberg, Otto. "Barriers to falling and remaining in love," *Journal of the American Psychoanalytic Association*, Vol 22, pp. 486–511, 1974.

Kinsey, Alfred, et al. *Sexual Behavior in the Human Female*. Philadelphia: Saunders, 1953.

Kinsey, Alfred, et al. *Sexual Behavior in the Human Male*. Philadelphia: Saunders, 1948.

Klagsbrun, Francine. *Married People*. New York: Bantam, 1985.

Klein, George S. *Psychoanalytic Theory*. New York: International Universities Press, 1976.

Kottler, Tamara. "A balanced distance: aspects of marital quality," *Human Relations*, Vol 38, pp. 391–407, 1985.

Kramer, Peter D. *Moments of Engagement*. New York: Norton, 1989.

Krueger, David W. *The Last Taboo: Money as Symbol and Reality in Psychotherapy and Psychoanalysis*. New York: Brunner-Mazel, 1986.

Lamb, Michael E., Pleck, Joseph H., Charnov, Eric L., and Levine, James A. "A biosocial perspective on paternal behavior and involvement." In *Parenting Across the Life Span: Biosocial Dimensions*, ed. Jane B. Lancaster, Jeanne Altmann, Alice S. Rossi, and Connie R. Sherrod, Hawthorne, NY: Aldine de Gruyter, 1987.

LaRossa, Ralph. "The transition to parenthood and the social reality of time," *Journal of Marriage and the Family*, Vol 45, pp. 579–89, 1983.

Laslett, Barbara. "The family as a public and private institution: an historical perspective," *Journal of Marriage and the Family*, Vol 35, pp. 480–92, 1973.

Laufer, Robert S., and Wolfe, Maxine. "Privacy as a concept and a social issue: a multidimensional developmental theory," *Journal of Social Issues*, Vol 33, pp. 22–42, 1977.

Lederer, William J., and Jackson, Don D. *The Mirages of Marriage*. New York: Norton, 1968.

Levay, Alexander N. "Long-term psychodynamic treatment needs in sex therapy," *The American Journal of Psychoanalysis*, Vol 43, pp. 139–47, 1983.

Levay, Alexander N. "Personality change in sex therapy," *Journal of the American Academy of Psychoanalysis*, Vol 11, pp. 425–33, 1983.

Levay, Alexander N., and Kagle, Arlene. "A study of treatment needs following sex therapy," *American Journal of Psychiatry*, Vol 134, pp. 970–73, 1977.

Levenson, Robert W., and Gottman, John M. "Marital interaction: physiological linkage and affective exchange," *Journal of Personality and Social Psychology*, Vol 45, pp. 587–97, 1983.

Levenson, Robert W., and Gottman, John M. "Physiological and affective predictors of change in relationship satisfaction," *Journal of Personality and Social Psychology*, Vol 49, pp. 85 94, 1985.

Levinson, Daniel J. *The Seasons of a Man's Life*. New York: Knopf, 1978.

Locke, Harvey J. *Predicting Adjustment in Marriage: A Comparison of a Divorced and a Happily Married Group*. New York: Holt, 1951.

LoPiccolo, Joseph, and Miller, Vinnie H. "A program for enhancing the sexual relationship of normal couples," *The Counseling Psychologist*, Vol 5, pp. 41–45, 1975.

Low, Natalie S. "Projective identification and gender." Talk presented at the annual meeting of Division 39 of the American Psychological Association, Boston, April, 1989.

Maltas, Carolynn. "The dynamics of narcissism in marriage," *Psychoanalytic Review*. In press.

Markman, Howard J. "The prediction and prevention of marital distress: summary of results." Annual report submitted to the National Institute of Mental Health, November, 1987.

Markman, Howard J., and Kraft, Shelley A. "Men and women in marriage: implications for treatment and prevention of marital distress." *The Behavior Therapist*. In press.

Masters, William H., and Johnson, Virginia E. *Human Sexual Inadequacy*. Boston: Little, Brown, 1970.

Masters, William H., and Johnson, Virginia E. "Principles of the new sex therapy," *American Journal of Psychiatry*, Vol 133, pp. 540–54, 1976.

McClelland, David C. *Power the Inner Experience*. New York: John Wiley, 1975.

Mead, Margaret. *Male and Female: A Study of the Sexes in a Changing World*. New York: Morrow, 1977.

Messinger, Lillian. "Remarriage between divorced people with children from previous marriages: a proposal for preparation for remarriage," *Journal of Marriage and Family Counseling*, Vol 2, pp. 193–200, 1976.

Miller, Brent C., and Sollie, Donna L. "Normal stresses during the transition to parenthood," *Family Relations*, Vol 29, pp. 459–65, 1980.

Miller, Jean Baker. *Toward a New Psychology of Women*, 2nd ed. New York: Beacon Press, 1986.

Miller, Jean Baker. "What do we mean by relationships?" Work in progress, The Stone Center for Developmental Services and Studies, 1986.

Miller, Jean Baker. "Women and power." Work in progress, The Stone Center for Developmental Services and Studies, 1982.

Money, John. *Man and Woman, Boy and Girl: The Differentiation and Dimorphism of Gender Identity from Conception to Maturity.* Baltimore: Johns Hopkins Press, 1972.

Mosher, Clelia Duel. *The Mosher Survey: Sexual Attitudes of Forty-Five Victorian Women,* ed. James Mahood and Kristine Wenburg. New York: Arno Press, 1980.

Murphy, Robert F. "Social distance and the veil," *American Anthropologist,* Vol 66, pp. 1257–74, 1964.

Murstein, Bernard I., ed. *Theories of Attraction and Love.* New York: Springer, 1971.

Nadelson, Carol, and Marcotte, D. *Treatment Interventions in Human Sexuality.* New York: Plenum, 1983.

Osherson, Samuel. *Finding Our Fathers.* New York: Ballantine, 1986.

Paddock, John R., and Schwartz, Karen M. "Rituals for dual-career couples." *Psychotherapy,* Vol 23, pp. 453–59, 1986.

Pahl, Jan. "The allocation of money and the structuring of inequality within marriage," *Sociological Review,* pp. 237–62, 1983.

Paz, Octavio. *Teatro de Signos/Tranparencias.* Julian Rios, ed. Madrid: Espiral/Fundamentos, 1974.

Person, Ethel S. "The influence of values in psychoanalysis: the case of female psychology," *Psychoanalytic Inquiry,* Vol 3, pp. 623–46, 1983.

Person, Ethel S. "Male sexuality and power," *Psychoanalytic Inquiry,* Vol 6, pp. 3–25, 1986.

Person, Ethel S., and Ovesey, Lionel. "Psychoanalytic theories of gender identity," *Journal of the American Academy of Psychoanalysis,* Vol 11, pp. 203–26, 1983.

Pollak, Susan, and Gilligan, Carol. "Images of violence in thematic apperception test stories," *Journal of Personality and Social Psychology,* Vol 42, pp. 159–67, 1982.

Quinn, Naomi. " 'Commitment' in American marriage: a cultural analysis," *American Ethnologist,* Vol 9, pp. 775–98, 1982.

Rapoport, Rhona. "The transition from engagement to marriage," *Acta Sociologica,* Vol 8, pp. 36–55, 1964.

Rexroat, Cynthia, and Shehan, Constance. "The family life cycle and spouses' time in housework," *Journal of Marriage and the Family,* Vol 49, pp. 737–50, 1987.

Robson, B., and Mandel, D. "Marital adjustment and fatherhood," *Canadian Journal of Psychiatry,* Vol 30, pp. 169–72, 1985.

Rolfe, David J. "The financial priorities inventory," *The Family Co-ordinator*, Vol 23, pp. 139–44, 1974.

Rollins, Boyd C., and Bahr, Stephen J. "A theory of power relationships in marriage," *Journal of Marriage and the Family*, Vol 38, pp. 619–27, 1976.

Rose, Phyllis. *Parallel Lives*. New York: Vintage, 1984.

Rosenbaum, Maj-Britt. "Sex therapy today," *Bulletin of the Menninger Clinic*, Vol 49, pp. 270–79, 1985.

Rossi, Alice S. "Gender and parenthood," *American Sociological Review*, Vol 49, pp. 1–19, 1984.

Rossi, Alice S. "Transition to parenthood," *Journal of Marriage and the Family*, Vol 30, pp. 26–39, 1968.

Rusbult, Caryl E., Johnson, Dennis J., and Morrow, Gregory D. "Impact of couple patterns of problem solving on distress and nondistress in dating relationships," *Journal of Personality and Social Psychology*, Vol 50, pp. 744–53, 1986.

Russell, Candyce Smith. "Transition to parenthood: problems and gratifications," *Journal of Marriage and the Family*, Vol 36, pp. 294–301, 1974.

Sager, Clifford, Walker, Elizabeth, Brown, Hollis Steer, Crohn, Helen M., and Rodstein, Evelyn. "Improving functioning of the remarried family system," *Journal of Marriage and Family Therapy*, Vol 7, pp. 3–13, 1981.

Sauer, Raymond. "Emotional mortgage," *American Journal of Family Therapy*, Vol 7, pp. 49–51, 1979.

Schaninger, Charles M., and Buss, W. Christian. "A longitudinal comparison of consumption and finance handling between happily married and divorced couples," *Journal of Marriage and the Family*, Vol 48, pp. 129–36, 1986.

Scharff, David E. *The Sexual Relationship*. Boston: Routledge, Chapman & Hall, 1982.

Schwartz, Barry. "The social psychology of privacy," *American Journal of Sociology*, Vol 73, pp. 741–52, 1968.

Schwartz, Richard S., Olds, Jacqueline, Eisen, Susan, Betcher, William, and Van Niel, Anthony. "A study of the effects of differing parental work and childcare responsibilities on marital satisfaction and stability." Paper delivered at annual meeting of the American Psychiatric Association, Montreal, 1988.

Seiden, Anne M. "Overview: research on the psychology of women. I. Gender differences and sexual and reproductive life," *American Journal of Psychiatry*, Vol 133, pp. 995–1007, 1976.

Seiden, Anne M. "Overview: research on the psychology of women: II. Women in families, work, and psychotherapy," *American Journal of Psychiatry*, Vol 133, pp. 1111–23, 1976.

Shapiro, David. *Neurotic Styles*. New York: Basic Books, 1965.

Shapiro, Edward R. "On curiosity: intrapsychic and interpersonal boundary formation in family life," *International Journal of Family Psychiatry*, Vol 3, pp. 69–89, 1982.

Simmel, Arnold. "Privacy is not an isolated freedom." In *Privacy*, ed. J. Roland Pennock and John W. Chapman, New York: Atherton, 1971.

Simmel, Georg. *The Sociology of Georg Simmel*, Kurt H. Wolff, ed. New York: Free Press, 1950.

Slater, Philip. *The Pursuit of Loneliness: American Culture at the Breaking Point*. Boston: Beacon Press, 1976.

Snyder, Douglas K., and Berg, Phyllis. "Determinants of sexual dissatisfaction in sexually distressed couples," *Archives of Sexual Behavior*, Vol 12, pp. 237–46, 1983.

Sternberg, Daniel P., and Beier, Ernst G. "Changing patterns of conflict," *Journal of Communication*, Vol 27, pp. 97–100, 1977.

Stiver, Irene P. "The meanings of 'dependency' in female-male relationships," Work in progress, The Stone Center for Developmental Services and Studies, 1985.

Stockham, Alice B. *Karezza*. Chicago: Leonidas Publishing Company, 1896.

Stoller, Robert J. "Overview: the impact of new advances in sex research on psychoanalytic theory," *American Journal of Psychiatry*, Vol 130, pp. 241–51, 1973.

Stoller, Robert J. "Sexual excitement," *Archives of General Psychiatry*, Vol 33, pp. 899–909, 1976.

Stoller, Robert J. "Symbiosis anxiety and the development of masculinity," *Archives of General Psychiatry*, Vol 30, pp. 164–72, 1974.

Stoller, Robert J. *Perversion*. New York: Pantheon, 1975.

Stone, Michael H. "Traditional psychoanalytic characterology reexamined in the light of constitutional and cognitive differences between the sexes," *Journal of the American Academy of Psychoanalysis*, Vol 8, pp. 381–401, 1980.

Storr, Anthony. *Solitude*. New York: Free Press, 1988.

Sullivan, Harry Stack. *The Interpersonal Theory of Psychiatry*. New York: W. W. Norton, 1953.

Thies, Jill Matthews. "Beyond divorce: the impact of remarriage on children," *Journal of Clinical Child Psychology*, Vol 6, pp. 59–61, 1977.

Toulmin, Stephen. "Divided loyalties and ambiguous relationships," *Social Science and Medicine*, Vol 23, pp. 783–87, 1986.

Travis, Robert P., and Travis, Patricia Y. "Intimacy based sex therapy," *Journal of Sex Education and Therapy*, Vol 12, pp. 21–27, 1986.

Turkel, Ann Ruth. "Money as a Mirror of Marriage," *Journal of the American Academy of Psychoanalysis*, Vol 16, pp. 525–35, 1988.

Vaillant, George E. *Adaptation to Life*. Boston: Little, Brown, 1977.

Vuchinich, Samuel. "Starting and stopping spontaneous family conflicts," *Journal of Marriage and the Family*, Vol 49, pp. 591–601, 1987.

Warner, Rebecca L., Lee, Gary R., and Lee, Janet. "Social organization, spousal resources, and marital power: a cross-cultural study," *Journal of Marriage and the Family*, Vol 48, pp. 121–28, 1986.

Westin, Alan F. *Privacy and Freedom*. New York: Atheneum, 1967.

Wexler, Joan, and Steidl, John. "Marriage and the capacity to be alone," *Psychiatry*, Vol 41, pp. 72–82, 1978.

Whitehouse, Jeane. "The role of the initial attracting quality in marriage: virtues and vices," *Journal of Marital and Family Therapy*, Vol 7, pp. 60–67, 1981.

Winnicott, Donald W. *The Maturational Processes and the Facilitating Environment*. Madison, CT: International Universities Press, 1965.

Yogev, Sara, and Brett, Jeanne. "Patterns of work and family involvement among single- and dual-earner couples," *Journal of Applied Psychology*, Vol 70, pp. 754–68, 1985.

Zilbergeld, Bernie, and Evans, Michael. "The inadequacy of Masters and Johnson," *Psychology Today*, pp. 29–43, 1980.

Zilbergeld, Bernie, and Kilmann, Peter R. "The scope and effectiveness of sex therapy," *Psychotherapy*, Vol 21, pp. 319–26, 1984.

Zinner, John, and Shapiro, Roger. "The family group as a single psychic entity: implications for acting out in adolescence," *International Review of Psycho-analysis*, Vol 1, pp. 179–86, 1974.

ABOUT THE AUTHORS

DR. WILLIAM BETCHER is a clinical fellow in psychiatry at Harvard Medical School and a psychotherapist in private practice, specializing in work with couples and the family. He and his family live in Newton, Massachusetts.

ROBIE MACAULEY is a novelist, critic, and a former executive editor at Houghton Mifflin. He lives in Boston.